WHEN WIL

SOICHIRO YAMAMOTO

EDITORIAL ASSISTANCE FROM
MADOKA KITAO / NEKOMADO

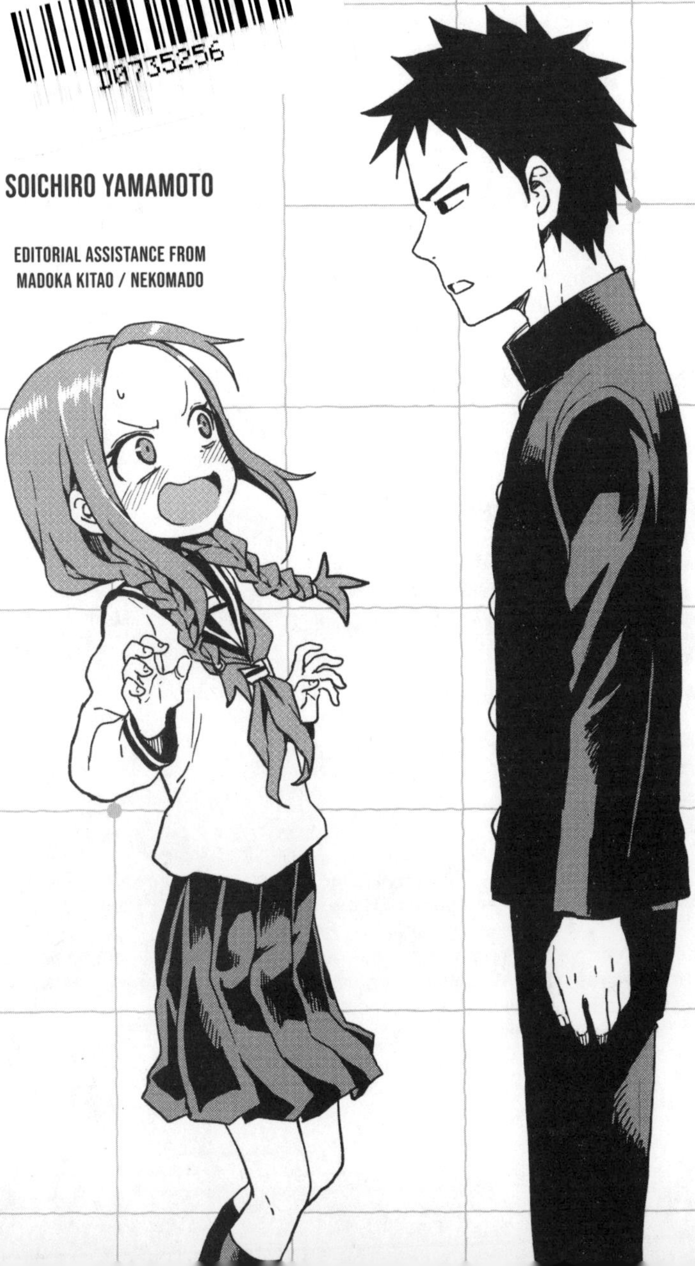

ABOUT SHOGI

This manga is a nearly-rom-com set in a high school shogi club. This game isn't well known outside Japan, but if you're familiar with chess, it's easy to grasp! Check out this explainer before reading, or jump right in and come back if you want to learn more!

Shogi is a two-player board game in the same family as chess. It's ancestor arrived in Japan over a thousand years ago and evolved into roughly its current form around the sixteenth century. Two players face off across a board with nine ranks (rows) and nine files (columns). Each player has a small army of pieces that start on their side of the board, and players can move one of these pieces per turn. The goal, like in chess, is to "checkmate" the other player's king piece by putting it into a situation where it cannot avoid being captured.

The two players are called *sente* and *gote* ("moves first" and "moves next"). These are sometimes called "black" and "white" in English; however, all pieces in shogi are the same color. They are differentiated by orientation, with the pointed end facing the opposing player.

PIECES AND MOVES

There are many different types of pieces, each with its own set of legal moves. Some of these will be familiar to chess players: For example, pawns move one square forward, while bishops move any number of squares diagonally. See the following pages for a detailed list of pieces and their moves.

When a piece legally moves into a square already occupied by an enemy piece, the enemy piece is "captured"—meaning that it is removed from the board and held "in hand" by the capturing player. (Pieces cannot move into squares occupied by friendly pieces.)

DROPPING

One big difference between shogi and chess is that, instead of moving a piece, players can use their turn to place a piece they have in hand back on the board under their control. This is called "dropping" a piece.

A piece can be dropped almost anywhere on the board, although there are some restrictions. A player can never have two unpromoted pawns on the same file, and a piece cannot be dropped onto a square from which it has no legal move.

PROMOTION

If a piece reaches the three ranks at the far end of the board (the "enemy camp"), it can be "promoted." The piece is flipped over to reveal its other side, and gains a new set of moves. For example, a promoted pawn becomes a *tokin*, which moves like a gold general. (Note that kings and gold generals cannot be promoted.)

Promotion is not compulsory unless the piece would have no legal move otherwise. If a piece is left unpromoted, it can be promoted at the end of any subsequent move that begins within the enemy camp.

CHECK AND CHECKMATE

Moving a piece into a position that would let the enemy king be captured on the next move is called an *ote* ("king move"). This corresponds to "check" in chess. The "checked" player must protect their king, either by moving it, capturing the checking piece, or placing (or dropping) another piece in between the two. If the checked player has no way to save the king, they lose the game. This corresponds to "checkmate" in chess. As in chess, it is also against the rules for a player to make a move that puts their own king in check.

CASTLES

A key concept in shogi strategy is the castle (in Japanese, *kakoi*, "enclosure"). A castle is a formation of pieces that protects your king. Over the centuries, shogi players have come up with many types of castles, and also ways to undermine and attack them.

Note that building a castle involves arranging pieces using standard legal moves. This makes it different from the special move of "castling" in chess, although the objective (protect the king) is similar.

SHOGI PIECES

 FUHYO

English name: Pawn (P)
Move: One square directly forward
Comments: Unlike in chess, pawns do not capture diagonally

 TOKIN

English name: Tokin (+P)
Move: Replaced by gold general rules
Comments: Most English-speaking players use the Japanese name for this piece instead of "promoted pawn"

 KYOSHA

English name: Lance (L)
Move: Any number of squares directly forward

 NARIKYO

English name: Promoted lance (+L)
Move: Replaced by gold general rules

 KEIMA

English name: Knight (N)
Move: L-shaped "jump" two squares forward and one square to left or right
Comments: Knights can "jump" over pieces that are in their way. Unlike in chess, they cannot jump in any direction.

 NARIKEI

English name: Promoted knight (+N)
Move: Replaced by gold general rules

 GINSHO

English name: Promoted knight (S)
Move: One square in any direction except left, right, or directly back

NARIGIN

English name: Promoted silver (+S)
Move: Replaced by gold general rules

 KINSHO

English name: Gold general (or just "Gold") (G)
Move: One square in any direction except diagonally backward (left or right)
Comments: Gold generals cannot be promoted.

 KAKUGYO

English name: Bishop (B)
Move: Any number of squares diagonally

 RYUMA

English name: Promoted bishop (or "Dragon horse") (+B)
Move: Any number of squares diagonally OR one square in any direction

 HISHA

English name: Rook (R)
Move: Any number of squares forward, back, left, or right

 RYUO

English name: Promoted rook (or "Dragon king") (+R)
Move: Any number of squares forward, back, left, or right, OR one square
in any direction

 OSHO

English name: King (K)
Move: One square in any direction
Comments: Kings cannot be promoted. This tile is used by the higher-
ranking player, while the lower-ranking player traditionally uses the
gyokusho tile (below) for their king.

 GYOKUSHO

English name: King (or "Jewel") (K)
Move: One square in any direction
Comments: This tile is used as the king of the lower-ranking player, but
the rules are the same as for the *osho* tile.

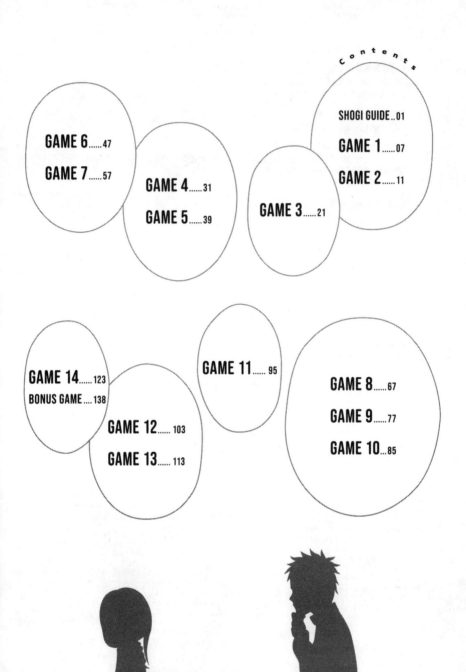

Contents

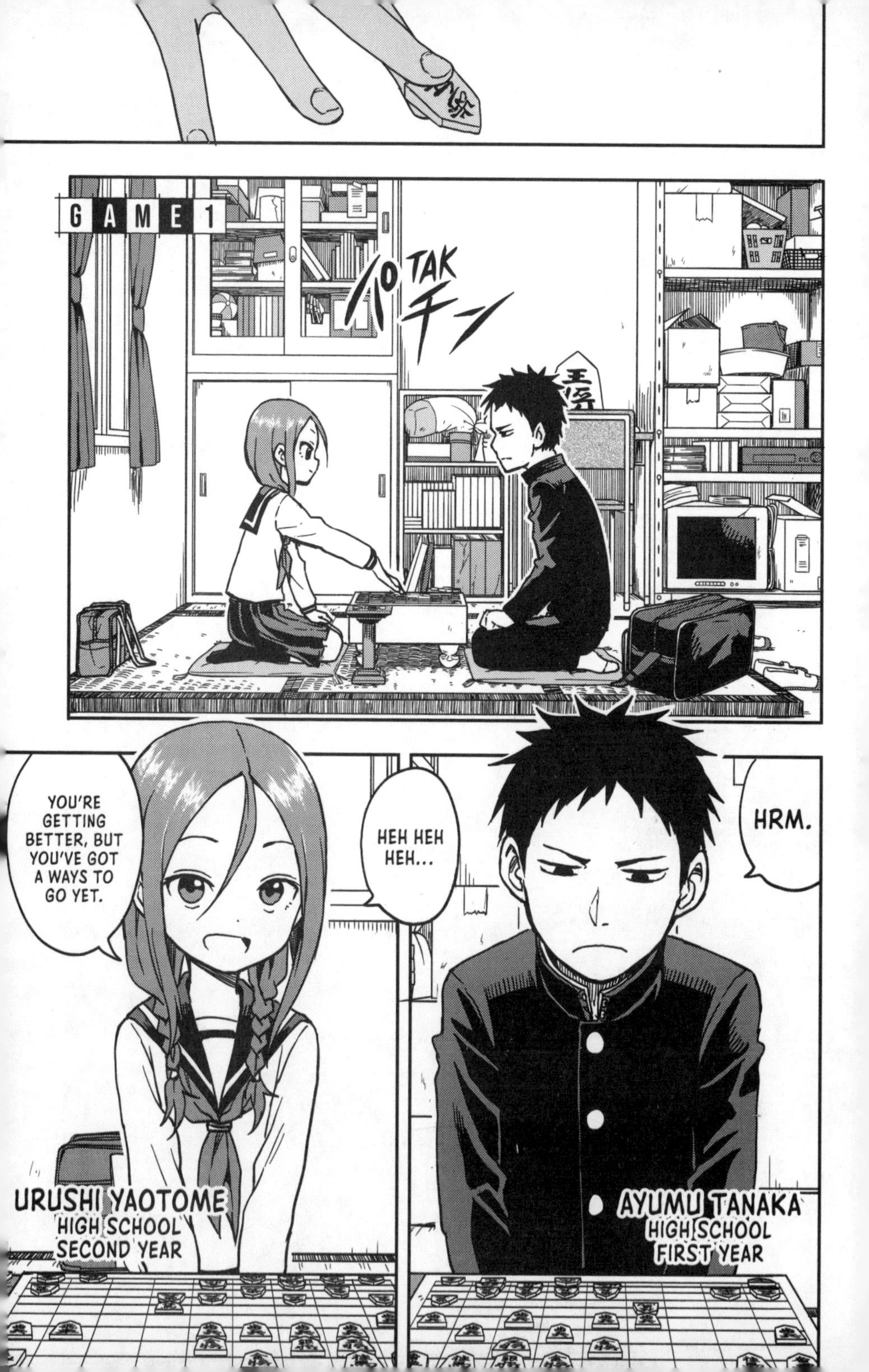
GAME 1
TAK
HRM.
AYUMU TANAKA
HIGH SCHOOL FIRST YEAR
YOU'RE GETTING BETTER, BUT YOU'VE GOT A WAYS TO GO YET.
HEH HEH HEH...
URUSHI YAOTOME
HIGH SCHOOL SECOND YEAR

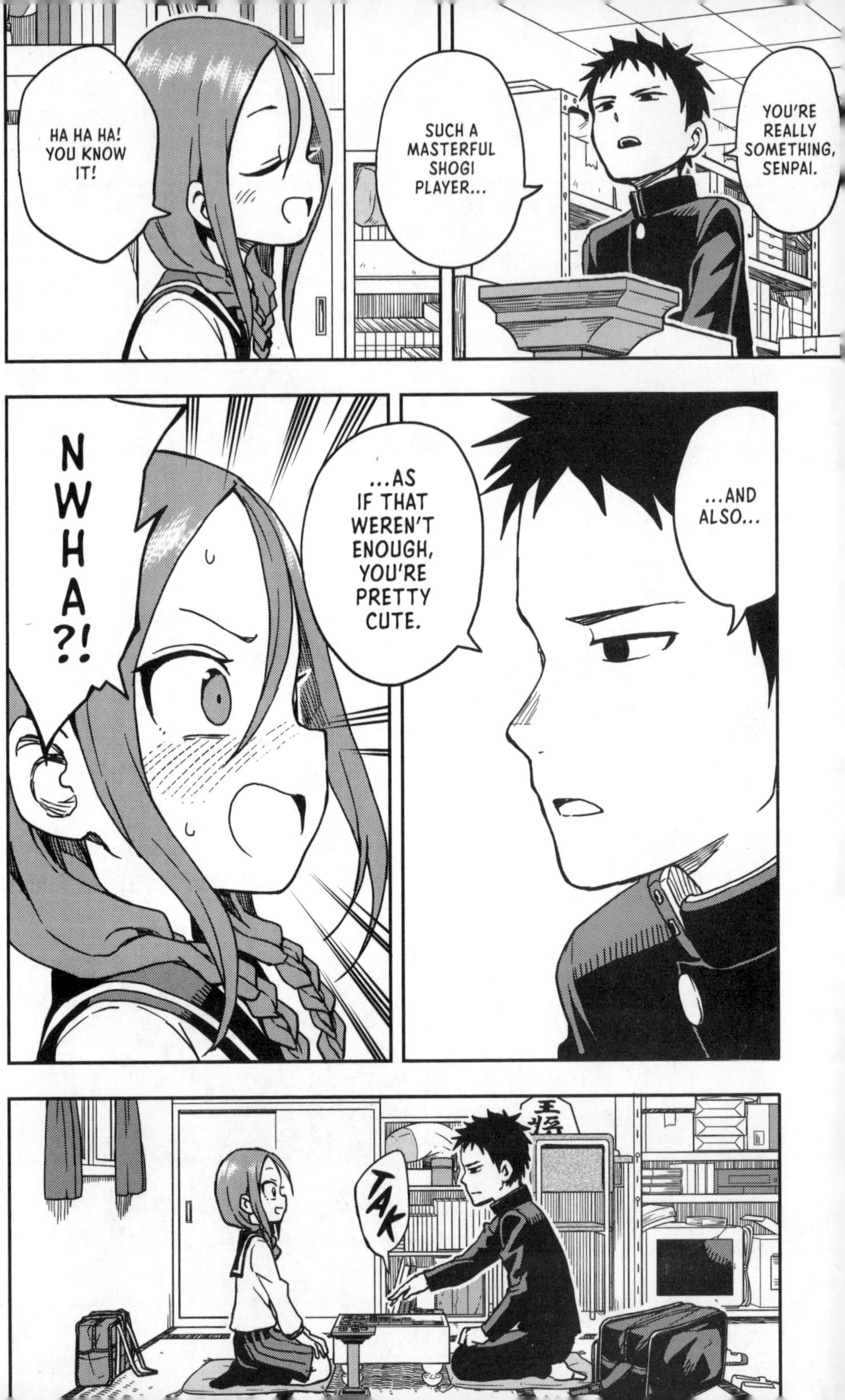
YOU'RE REALLY SOMETHING, SENPAI.
SUCH A MASTERFUL SHOGI PLAYER...
HA HA HA! YOU KNOW IT!
...AND ALSO...
...AS IF THAT WEREN'T ENOUGH, YOU'RE PRETTY CUTE.
NWHA?!
王将
TAK

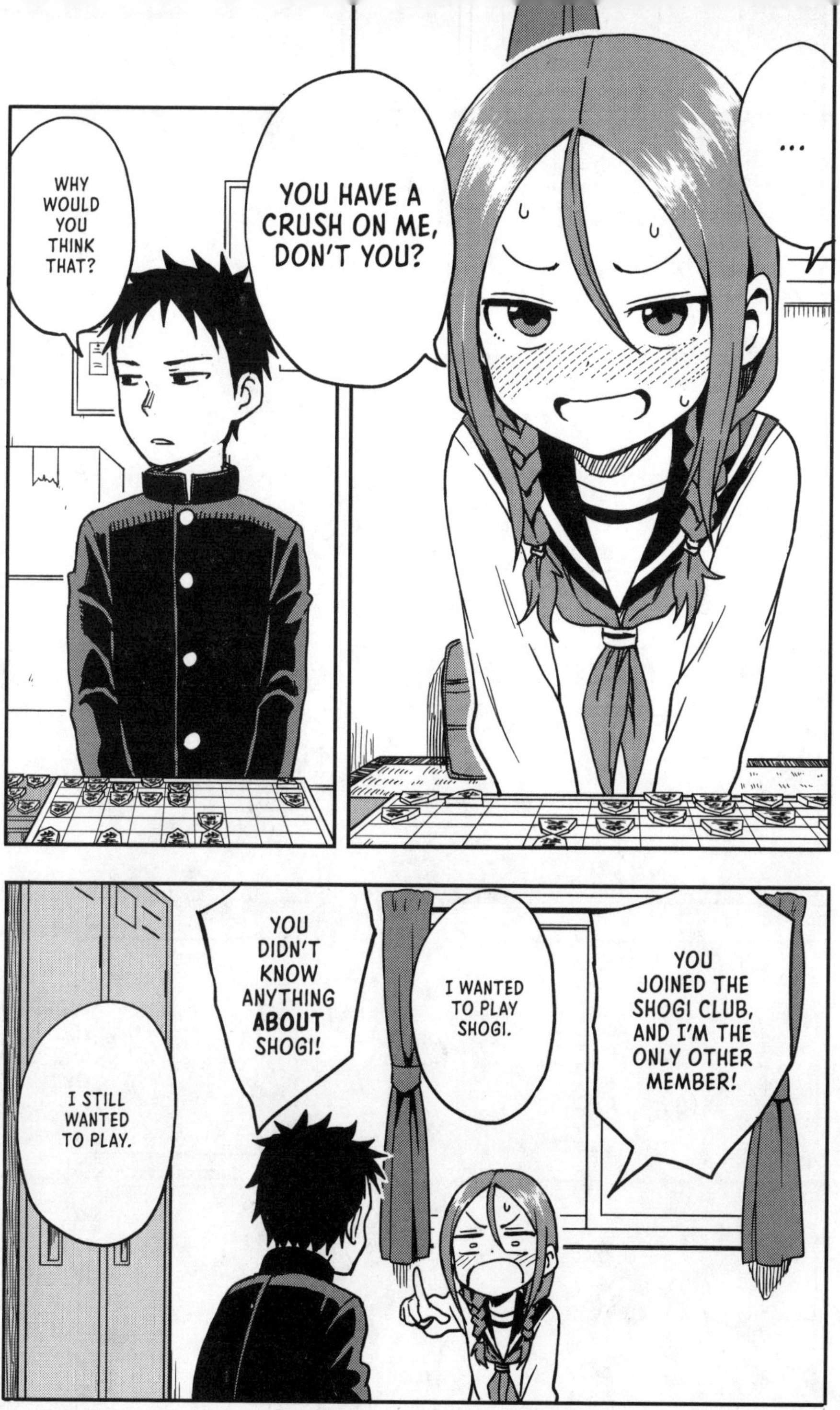
...
YOU HAVE A CRUSH ON ME, DON'T YOU?
WHY WOULD YOU THINK THAT?
YOU JOINED THE SHOGI CLUB, AND I'M THE ONLY OTHER MEMBER!
I WANTED TO PLAY SHOGI.
YOU DIDN'T KNOW ANYTHING ABOUT SHOGI!
I STILL WANTED TO PLAY.

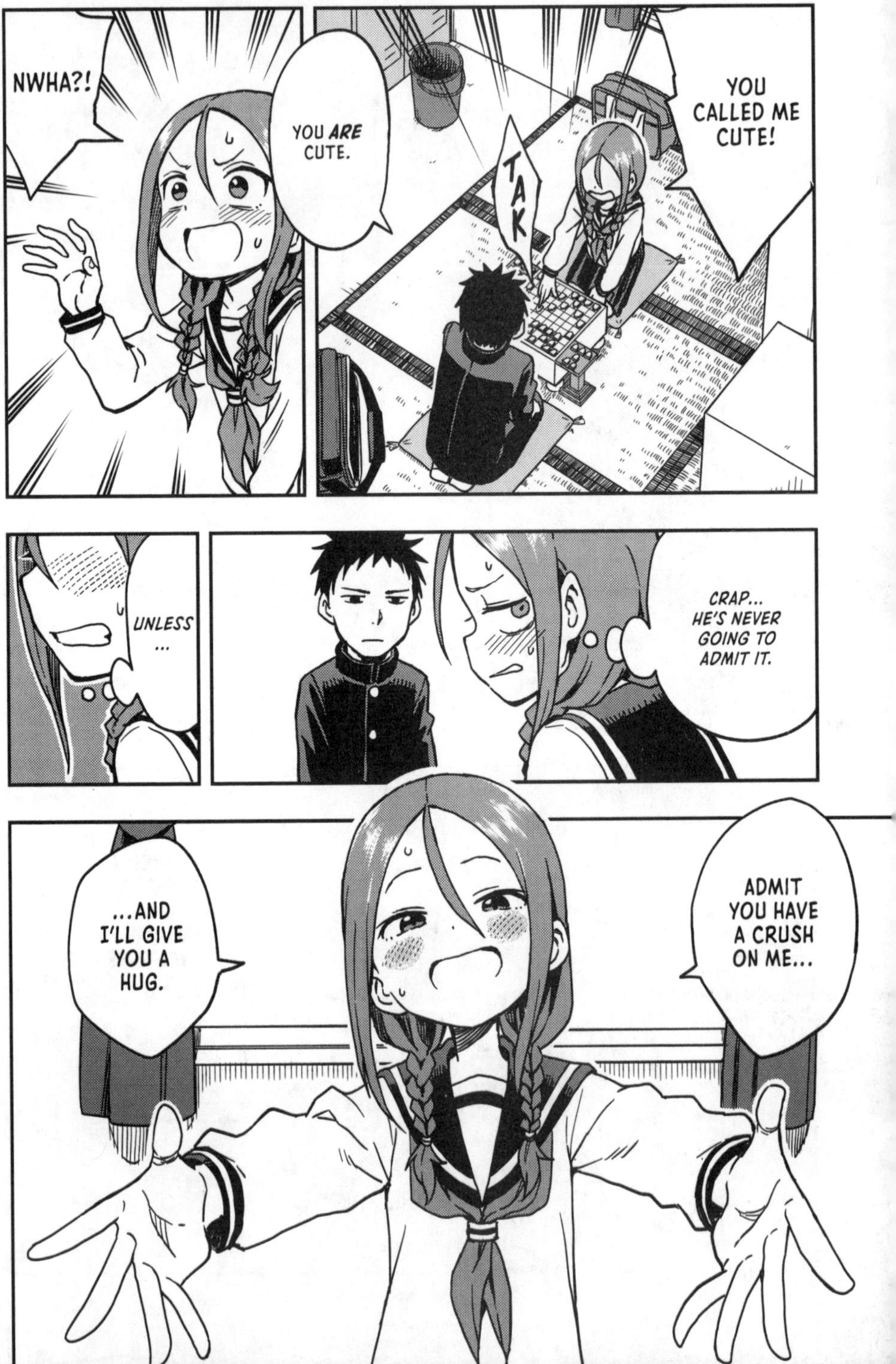
YOU CALLED ME CUTE!
TAK
YOU ***ARE*** CUTE.
NWHA?!
CRAP... HE'S NEVER GOING TO ADMIT IT.
UNLESS ...
ADMIT YOU HAVE A CRUSH ON ME...
...AND I'LL GIVE YOU A HUG.

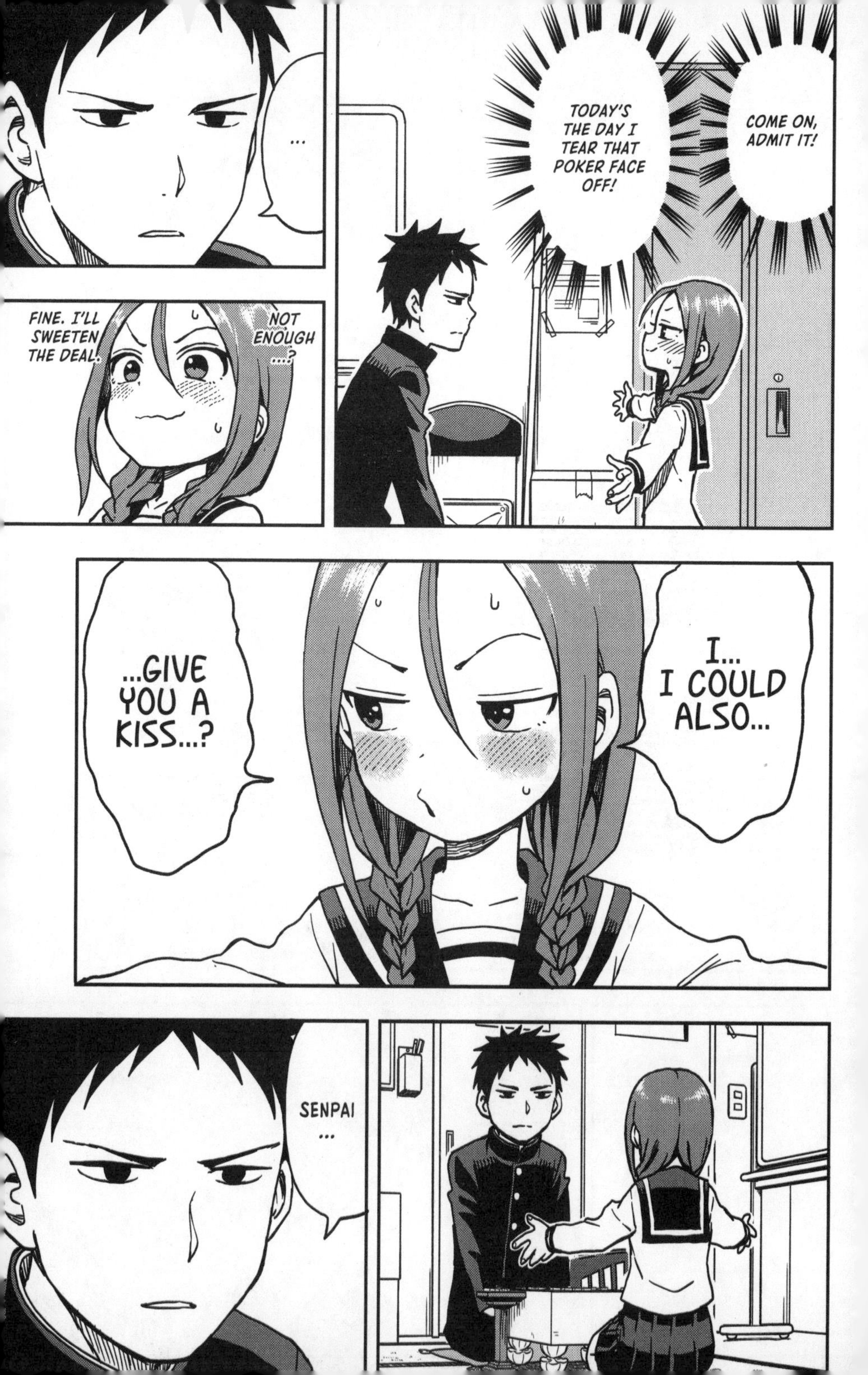
COME ON, ADMIT IT!
TODAY'S THE DAY I TEAR THAT POKER FACE OFF!
...
NOT ENOUGH ...?
FINE. I'LL SWEETEN THE DEAL.
I... I COULD ALSO...
...GIVE YOU A KISS...?
SENPAI ...

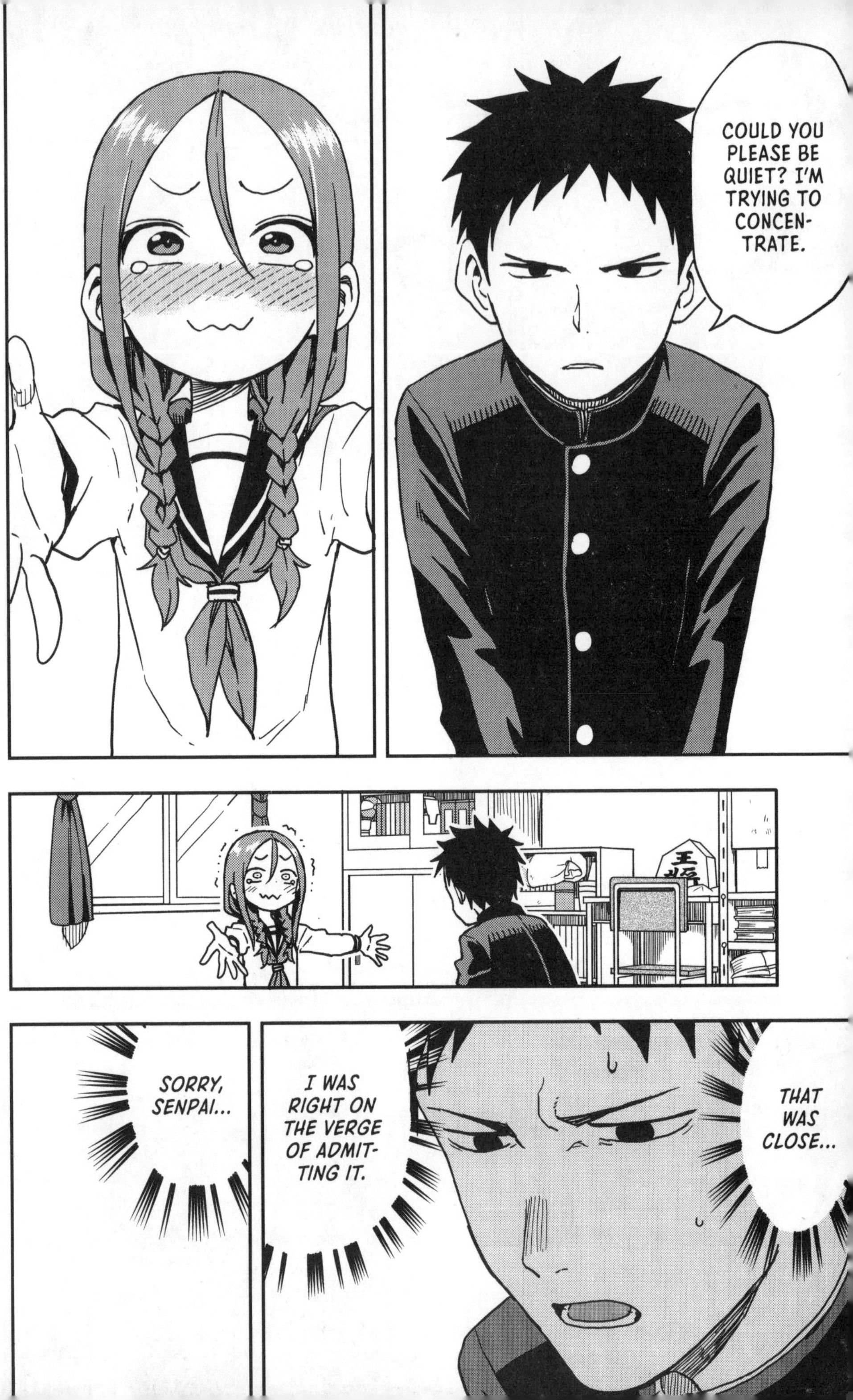
COULD YOU PLEASE BE QUIET? I'M TRYING TO CONCEN-TRATE.
THAT WAS CLOSE...
I WAS RIGHT ON THE VERGE OF ADMIT-TING IT.
SORRY, SENPAI...

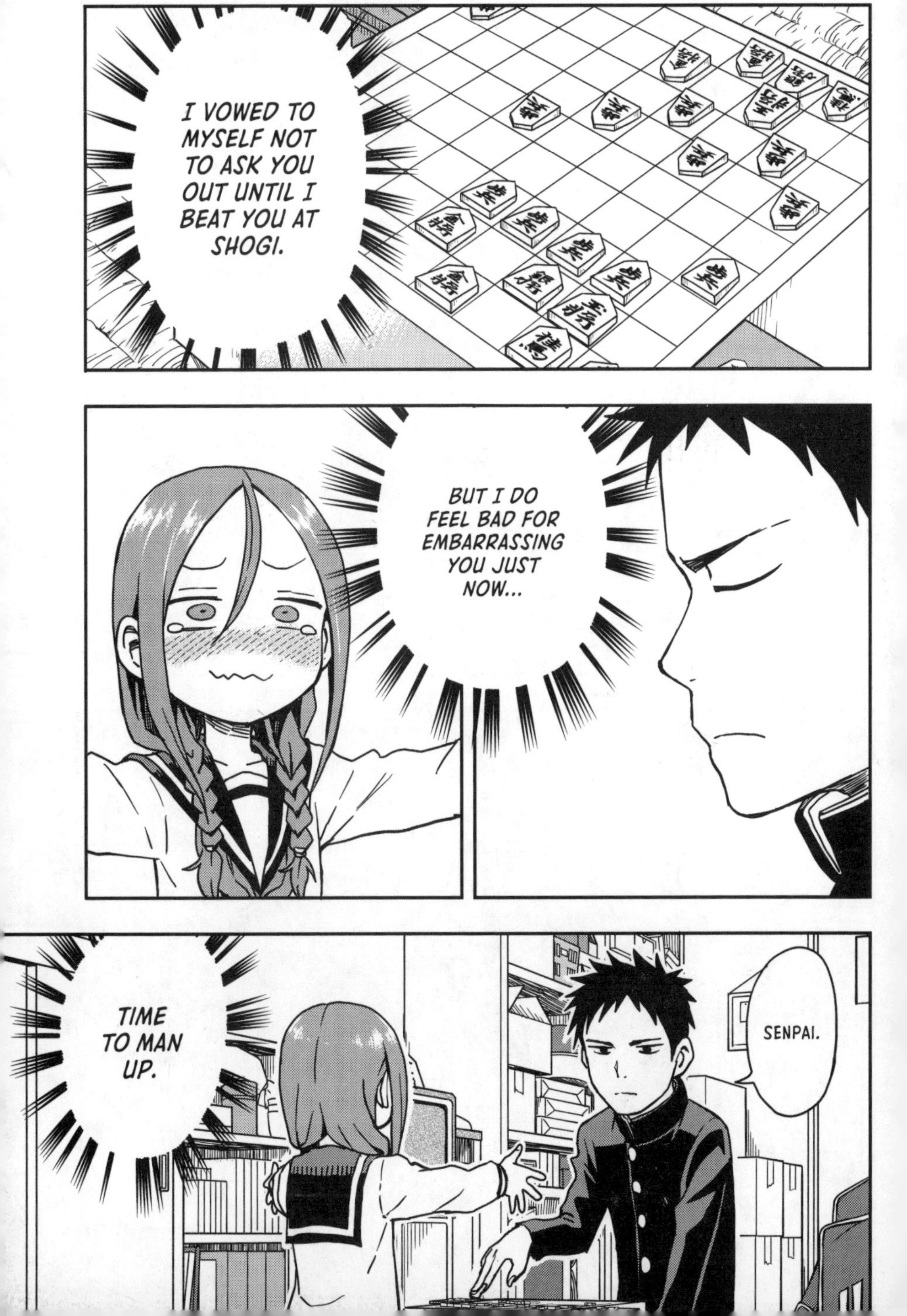
I VOWED TO MYSELF NOT TO ASK YOU OUT UNTIL I BEAT YOU AT SHOGI.
BUT I DO FEEL BAD FOR EMBARRASSING YOU JUST NOW...
SENPAI.
TIME TO MAN UP.

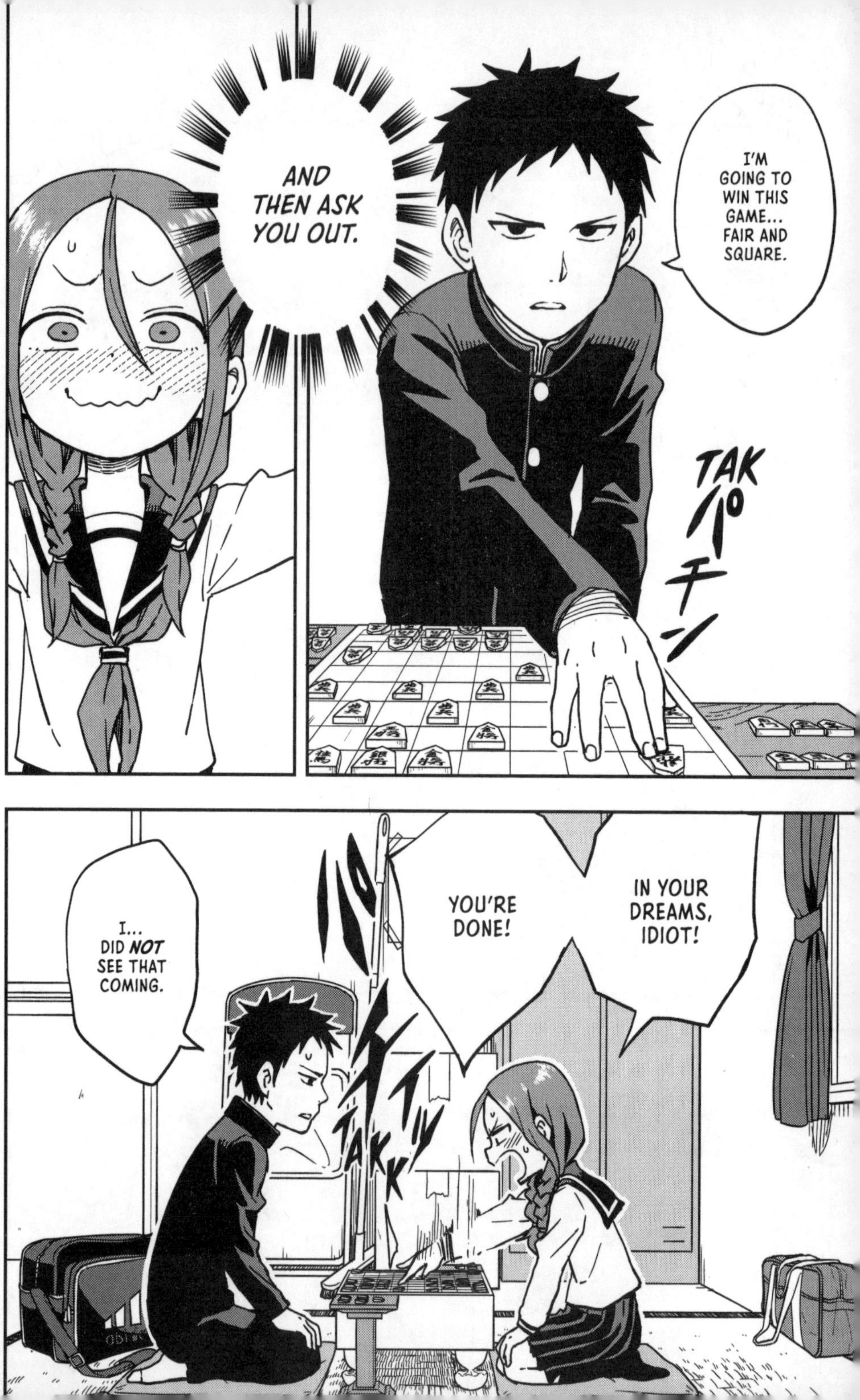
I'M GOING TO WIN THIS GAME... FAIR AND SQUARE.
AND THEN ASK YOU OUT.
TAK
IN YOUR DREAMS, IDIOT!
YOU'RE DONE!
TAKK
I... DID **NOT** SEE THAT COMING.

GAME 1 RECORD

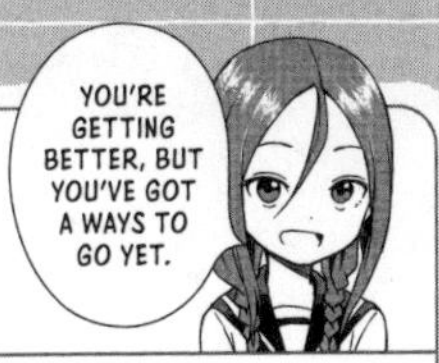
YOU'RE GETTING BETTER, BUT YOU'VE GOT A WAYS TO GO YET.

▲ BLACK (SENTE): URUSHI YAOTOME △ WHITE (GOTE): AYUMU TANAKA

(TO MOVE 51, ▲ B×5E)

◁AYUMU: B, S, N, L, P×3

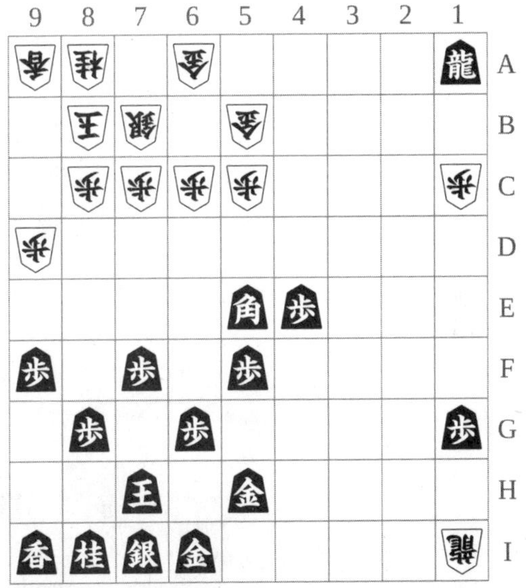
9
8
7
6
5
4
3
2
1
A
B
C
D
E
F
G
H
I

▲URUSHI: S, N, L, P×2

▲ P-2F	△ P-3D	▲ S×3E	△ P-4E
▲ P-2E	△ B-3C	▲ B×3C+	△ N×3C
▲ P-7F	△ P-4D	▲ P-2D	△ P×2D
▲ S-4H	△ R-4B	▲ S×2D	△ S-3B
▲ K-6H	△ K-6B	▲ S-2C+	△ S×2C
▲ K-7H	△ K-7B	▲ R×2C+	△ P-4F
▲ G4I-5H	△ K-8B	▲ P×4F	△ R×4F
▲ P-5F	△ S-7B	▲ P×4G	△ R-4C
▲ S-5G	△ P-9D	▲ +R-2A	△ N-4E
▲ P-9F	△ G4A-5B	▲ +R×1A	△ R-2C
▲ S-4F	△ S-3B	▲ P-4F	△ R×2I+
▲ P-3F	△ S-4C	▲ P×4E	△ +R×1I
▲ P-3E	△ P×3E	▲ B×5E	

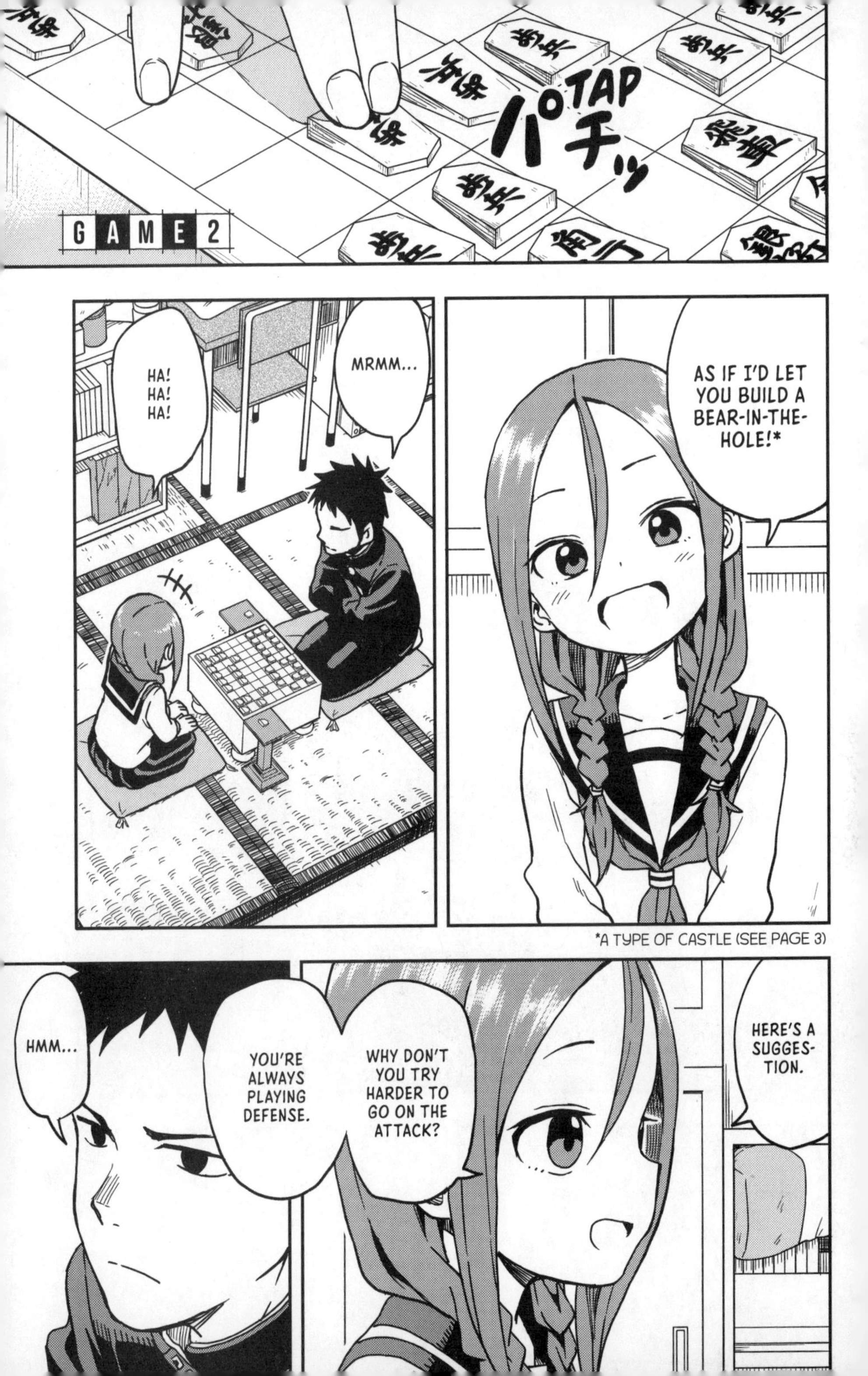
GAME 2
パチッ
TAP
AS IF I'D LET YOU BUILD A BEAR-IN-THE-HOLE!*
MRMM...
HA! HA! HA!
*A TYPE OF CASTLE (SEE PAGE 3)
HERE'S A SUGGES-TION.
WHY DON'T YOU TRY HARDER TO GO ON THE ATTACK?
YOU'RE ALWAYS PLAYING DEFENSE.
HMM...

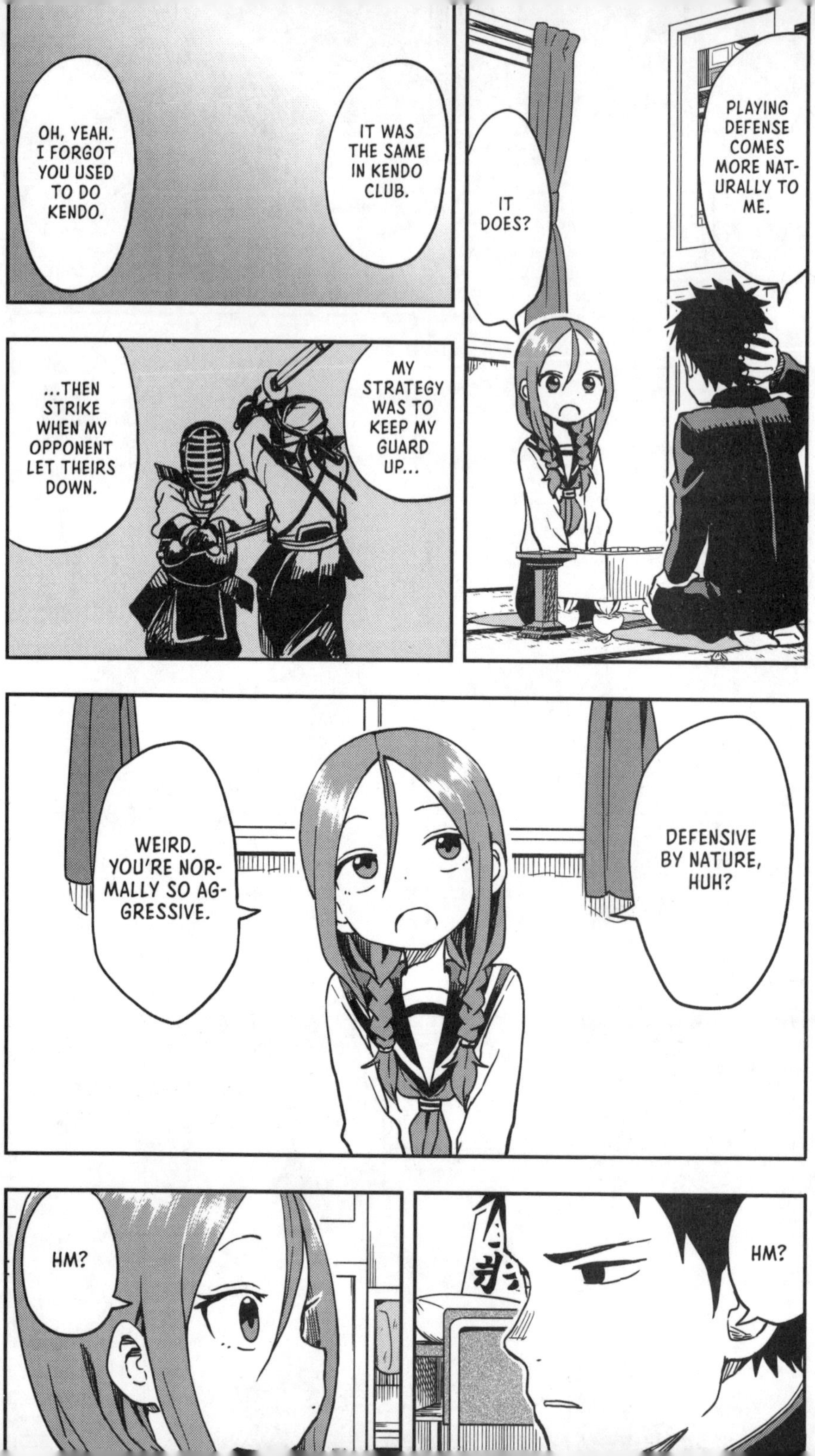
PLAYING DEFENSE COMES MORE NATURALLY TO ME.
IT DOES?
IT WAS THE SAME IN KENDO CLUB.
OH, YEAH. I FORGOT YOU USED TO DO KENDO.
MY STRATEGY WAS TO KEEP MY GUARD UP...
...THEN STRIKE WHEN MY OPPONENT LET THEIRS DOWN.
DEFENSIVE BY NATURE, HUH?
WEIRD. YOU'RE NORMALLY SO AGGRESSIVE.
HM?
HM?

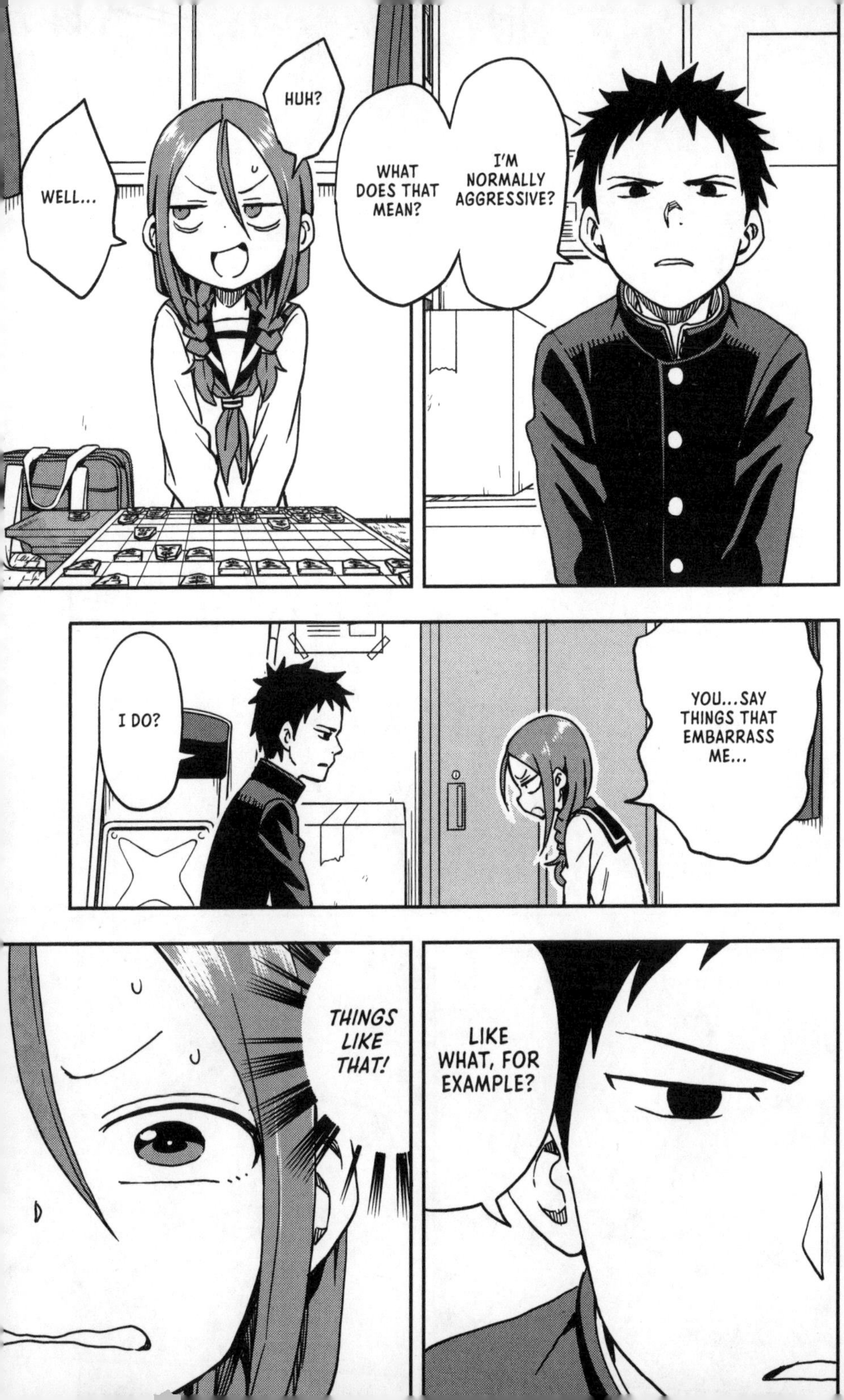
I'M NORMALLY AGGRESSIVE?
WHAT DOES THAT MEAN?
HUH?
WELL...
YOU...SAY THINGS THAT EMBARRASS ME...
I DO?
LIKE WHAT, FOR EXAMPLE?
THINGS LIKE THAT!

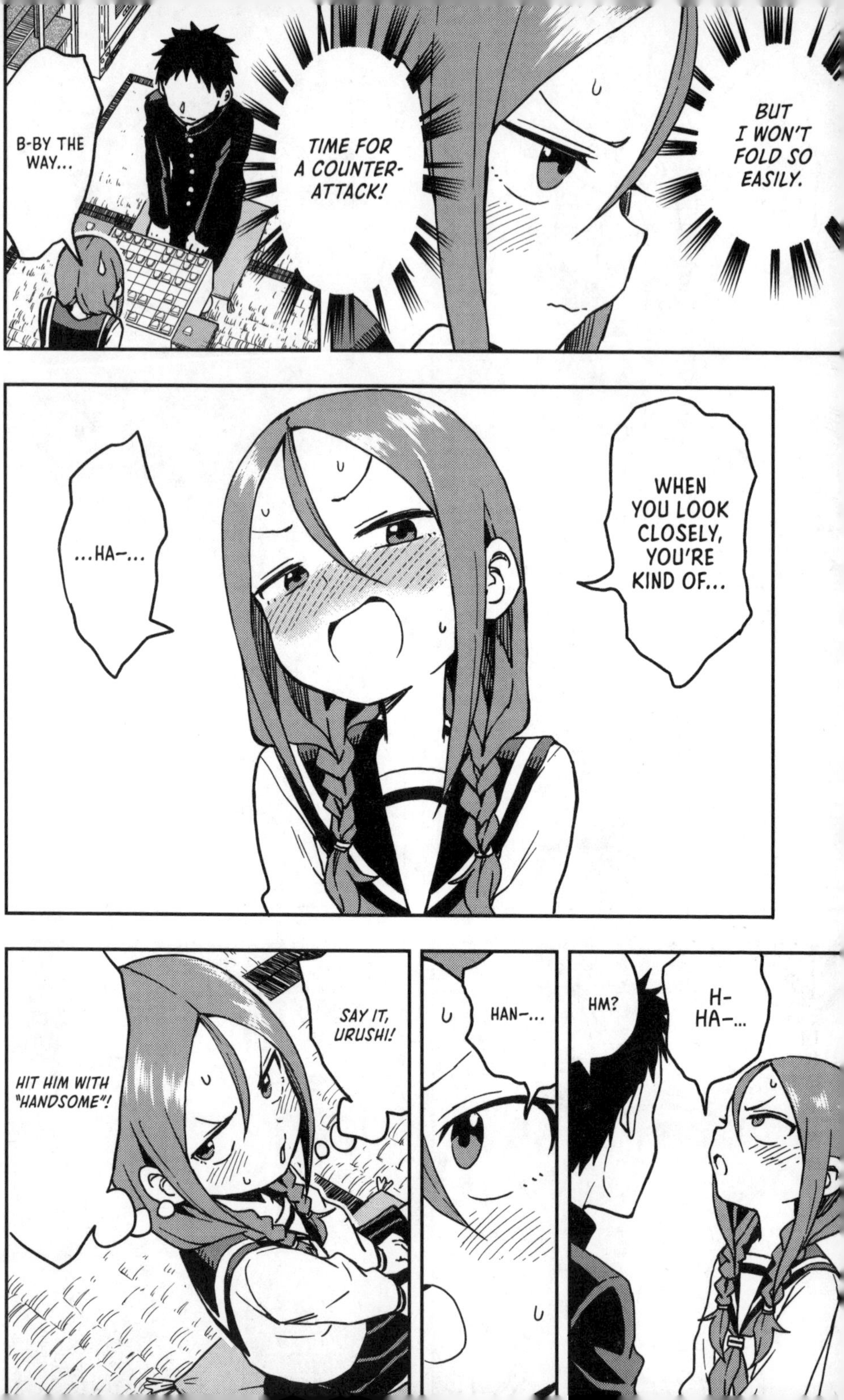
BUT I WON'T FOLD SO EASILY.
TIME FOR A COUNTER-ATTACK!
B-BY THE WAY...
WHEN YOU LOOK CLOSELY, YOU'RE KIND OF...
...HA-...
H-HA-...
HM?
HAN-...
SAY IT, URUSHI!
HIT HIM WITH "HANDSOME"!

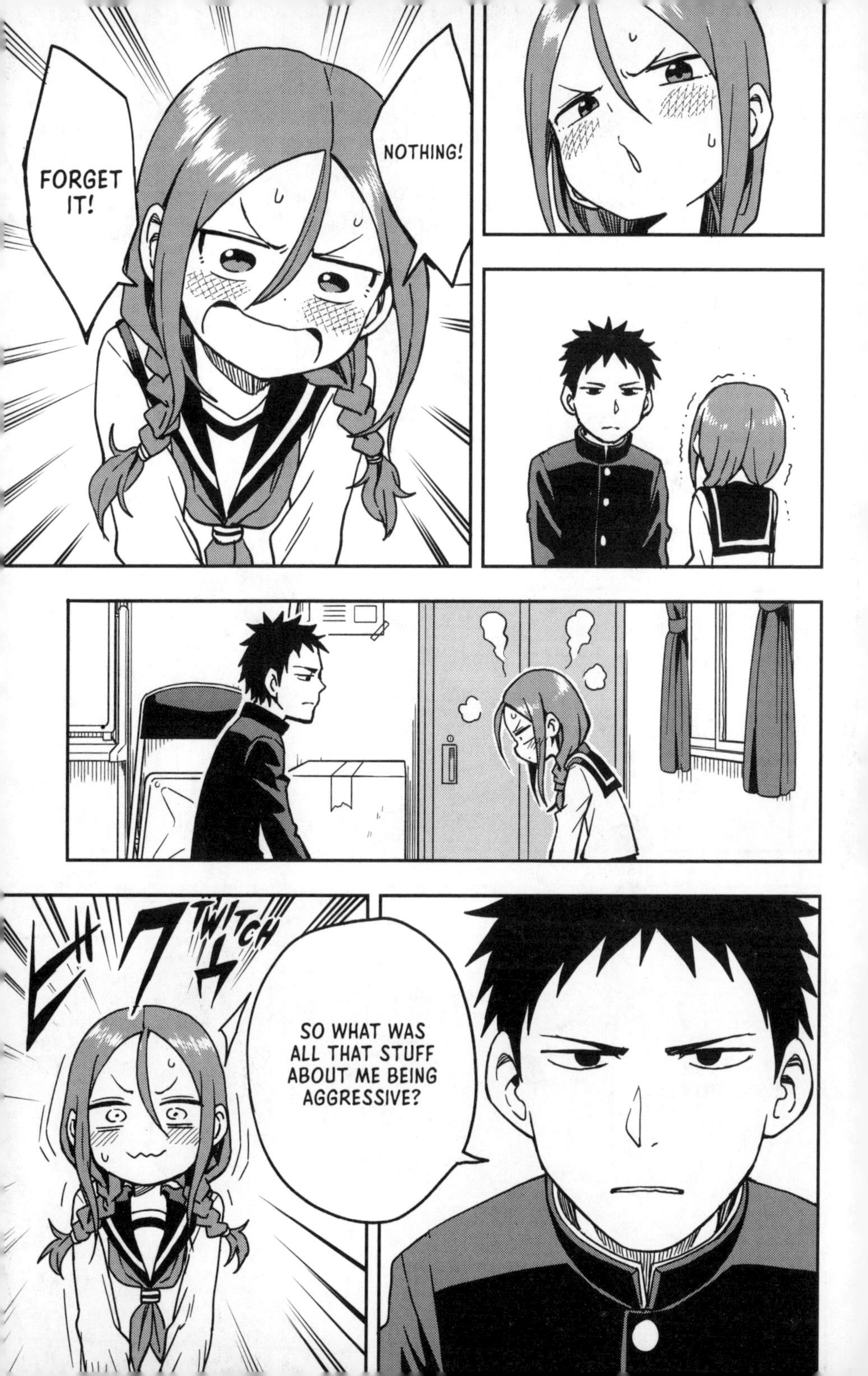
NOTHING!
FORGET IT!
SO WHAT WAS ALL THAT STUFF ABOUT ME BEING AGGRESSIVE?
TWITCH

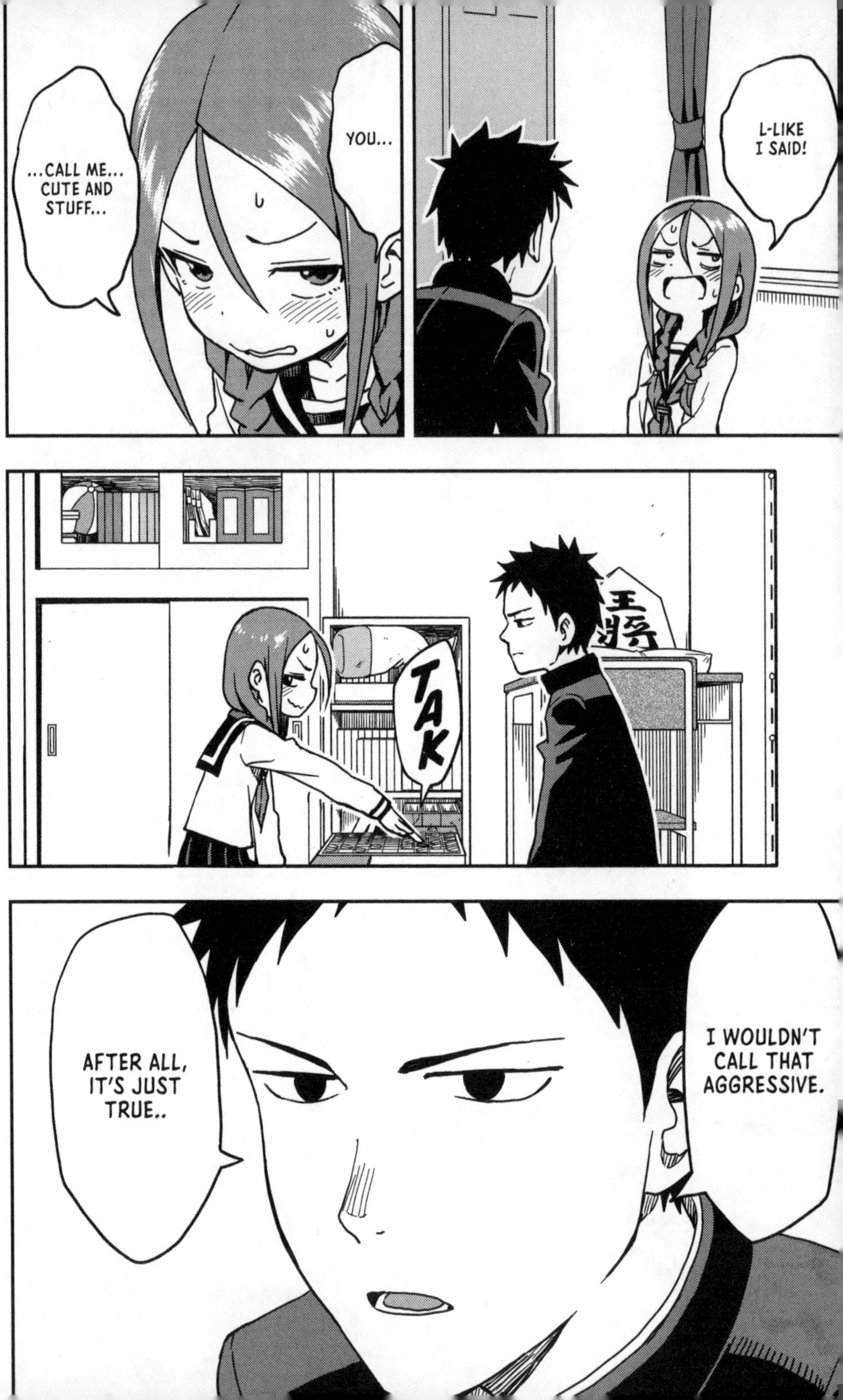
L-LIKE I SAID!
YOU...
...CALL ME... CUTE AND STUFF...
王将
TAK
I WOULDN'T CALL THAT AGGRESSIVE.
AFTER ALL, IT'S JUST TRUE..

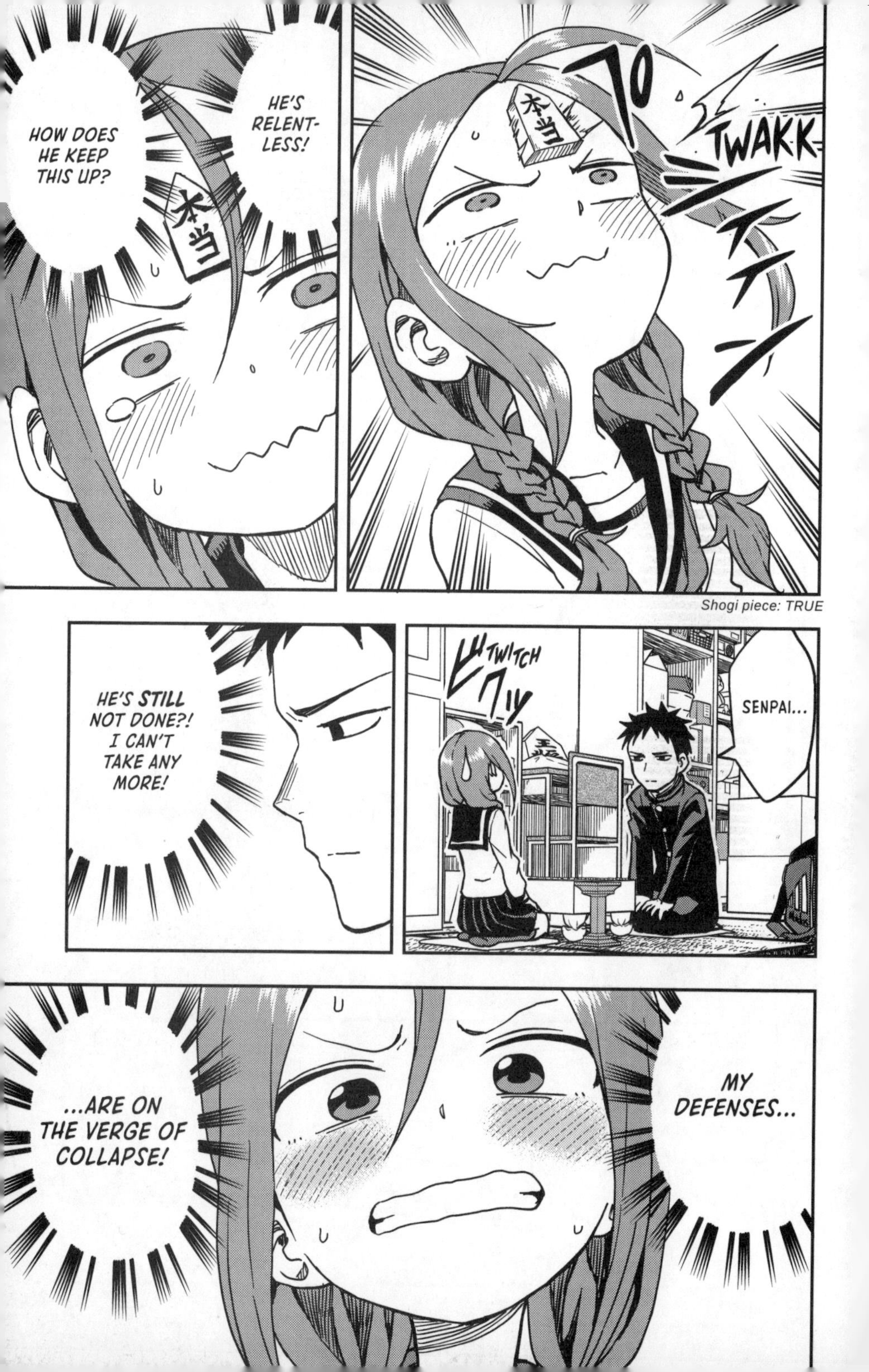
TWAKK
HE'S RELENT-LESS!
HOW DOES HE KEEP THIS UP?
Shogi piece: TRUE
TWITCH
SENPAI...
HE'S **STILL** NOT DONE?! I CAN'T TAKE ANY MORE!
MY DEFENSES...
...ARE ON THE VERGE OF COLLAPSE!

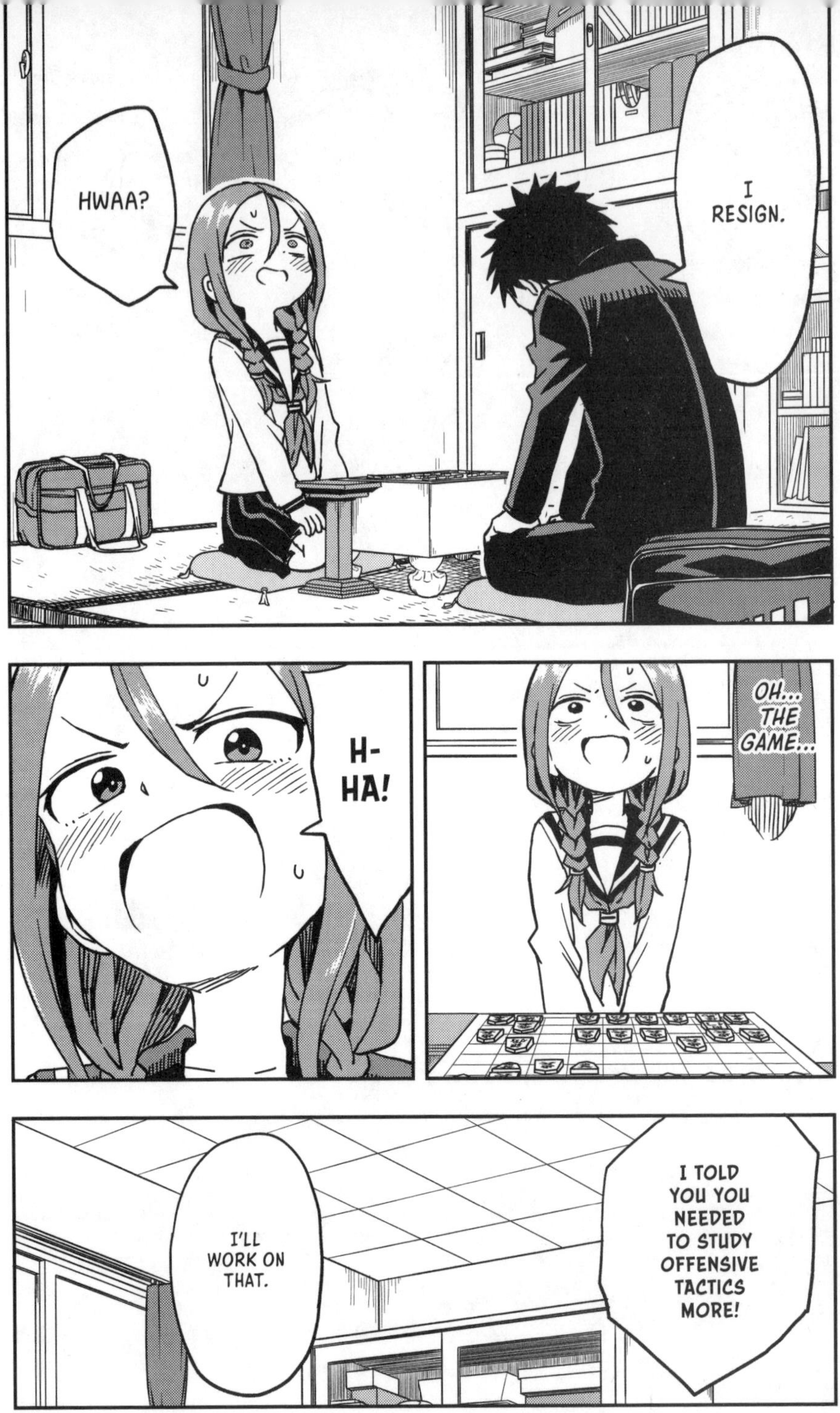
I RESIGN.
HWAA?
OH... THE GAME...
H- HA!
I TOLD YOU YOU NEEDED TO STUDY OFFENSIVE TACTICS MORE!
I'LL WORK ON THAT.

GAME 2 RECORD

▲ BLACK (SENTE): AYUMU TANAKA △ WHITE (GOTE): URUSHI YAOTOME

(WHITE WINS ON MOVE 22, △ P×8G)

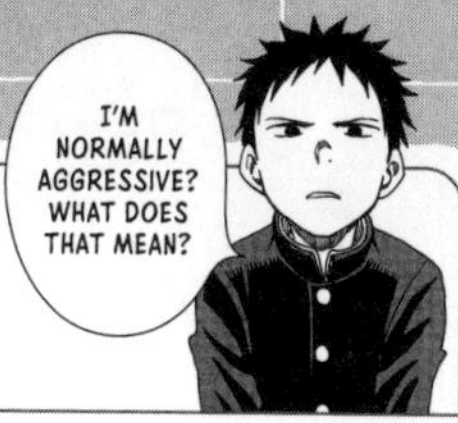
I'M NORMALLY AGGRESSIVE? WHAT DOES THAT MEAN?

◁URUSHI:

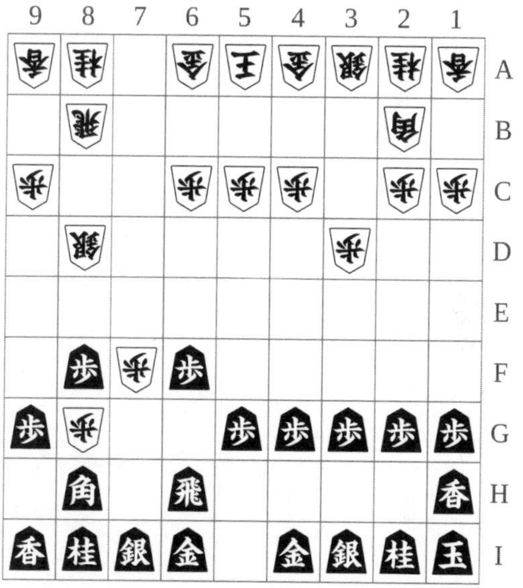
9
8
7
6
5
4
3
2
1
A
B
C
D
E
F
G
H
I

▲AYUMU: P

▲ P-7F	△ P-3D
▲ P-6F	△ P-8D
▲ R-6H	△ P-8E
▲ B-7G	△ S-7B
▲ K-4H	△ S-8C
▲ K-3H	△ S-8D
▲ K-2H	△ P-7D
▲ L-1H	△ P-7E
▲ K-1I	△ P×7F
▲ B-8H	△ P-8F
▲ P×8F	△ P×8G

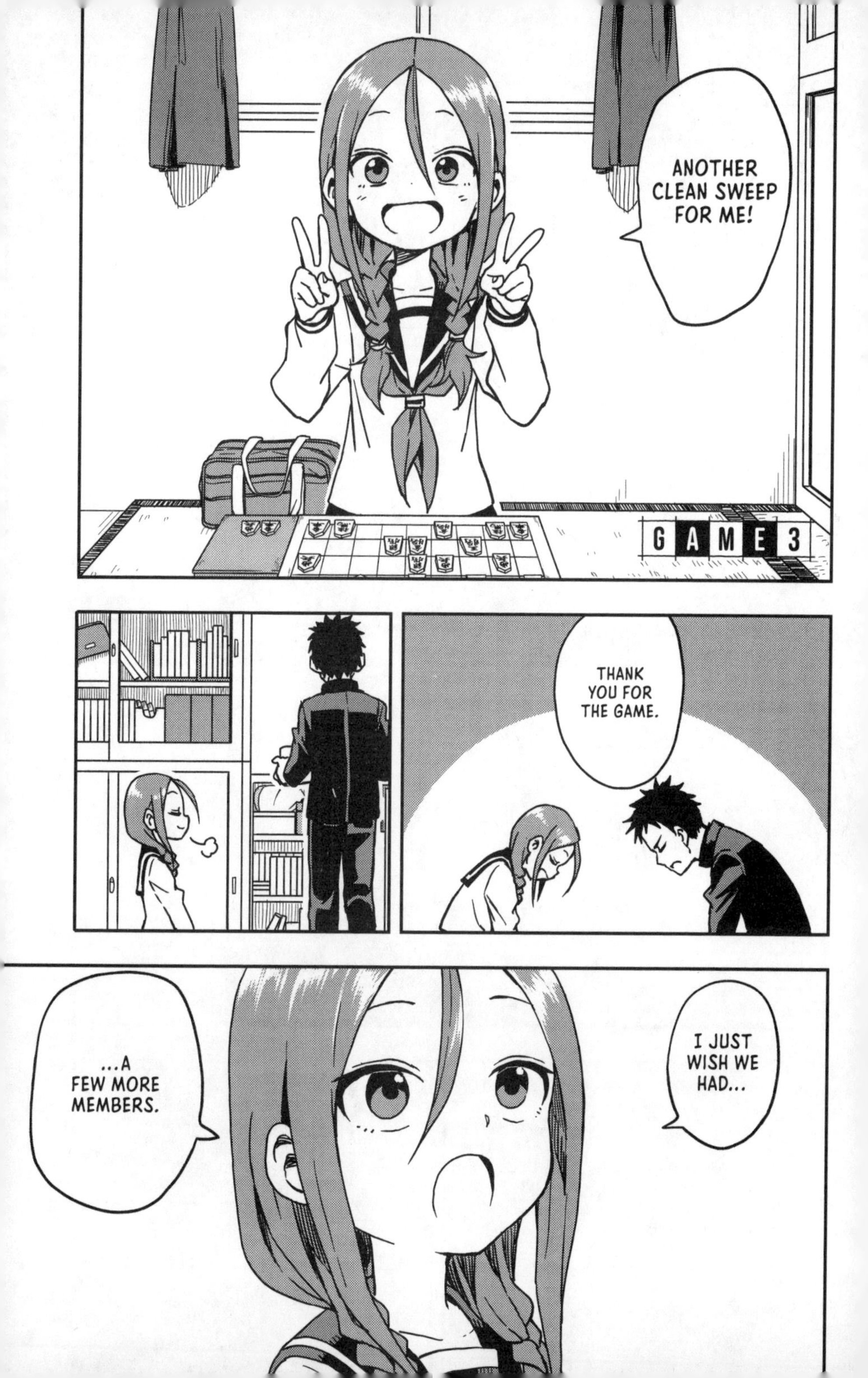
ANOTHER CLEAN SWEEP FOR ME!
GAME 3
THANK YOU FOR THE GAME.
I JUST WISH WE HAD...
...A FEW MORE MEMBERS.

VWIP

HM?

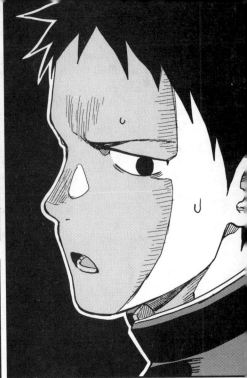

WELL, YEAH!

YOU... WANT MORE MEMBERS?

I WANT TO MAKE THIS A CLUB, FOR ONE THING.

WHY...?

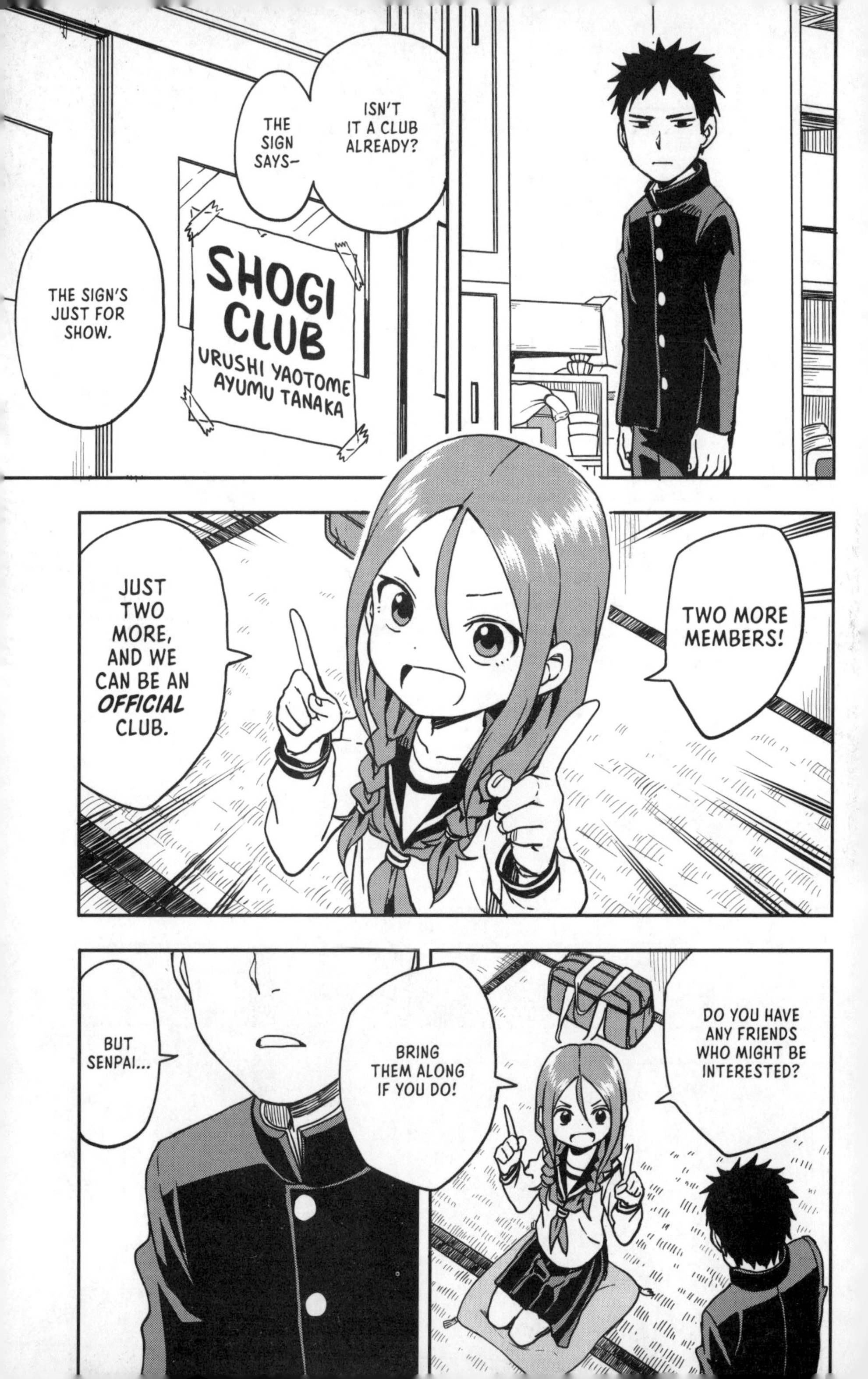
ISN'T IT A CLUB ALREADY?
THE SIGN SAYS–
SHOGI CLUB
URUSHI YAOTOME
AYUMU TANAKA
THE SIGN'S JUST FOR SHOW.
TWO MORE MEMBERS!
JUST TWO MORE, AND WE CAN BE AN *OFFICIAL* CLUB.
DO YOU HAVE ANY FRIENDS WHO MIGHT BE INTERESTED?
BRING THEM ALONG IF YOU DO!
BUT SENPAI...

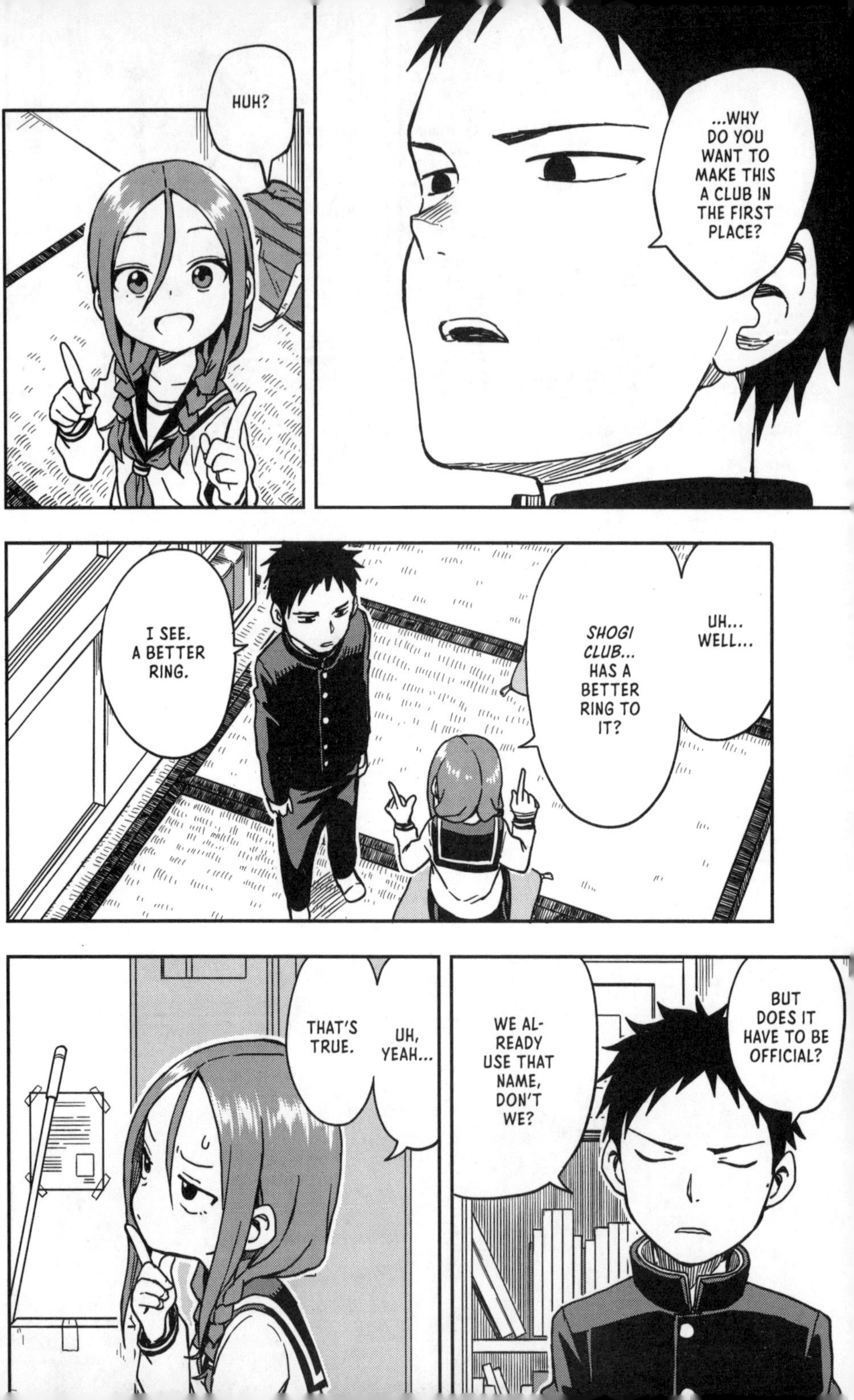
...WHY DO YOU WANT TO MAKE THIS A CLUB IN THE FIRST PLACE?
HUH?
UH... WELL...
SHOGI CLUB... HAS A BETTER RING TO IT?
I SEE. A BETTER RING.
BUT DOES IT HAVE TO BE OFFICIAL?
WE AL-READY USE THAT NAME, DON'T WE?
UH, YEAH...
THAT'S TRUE.

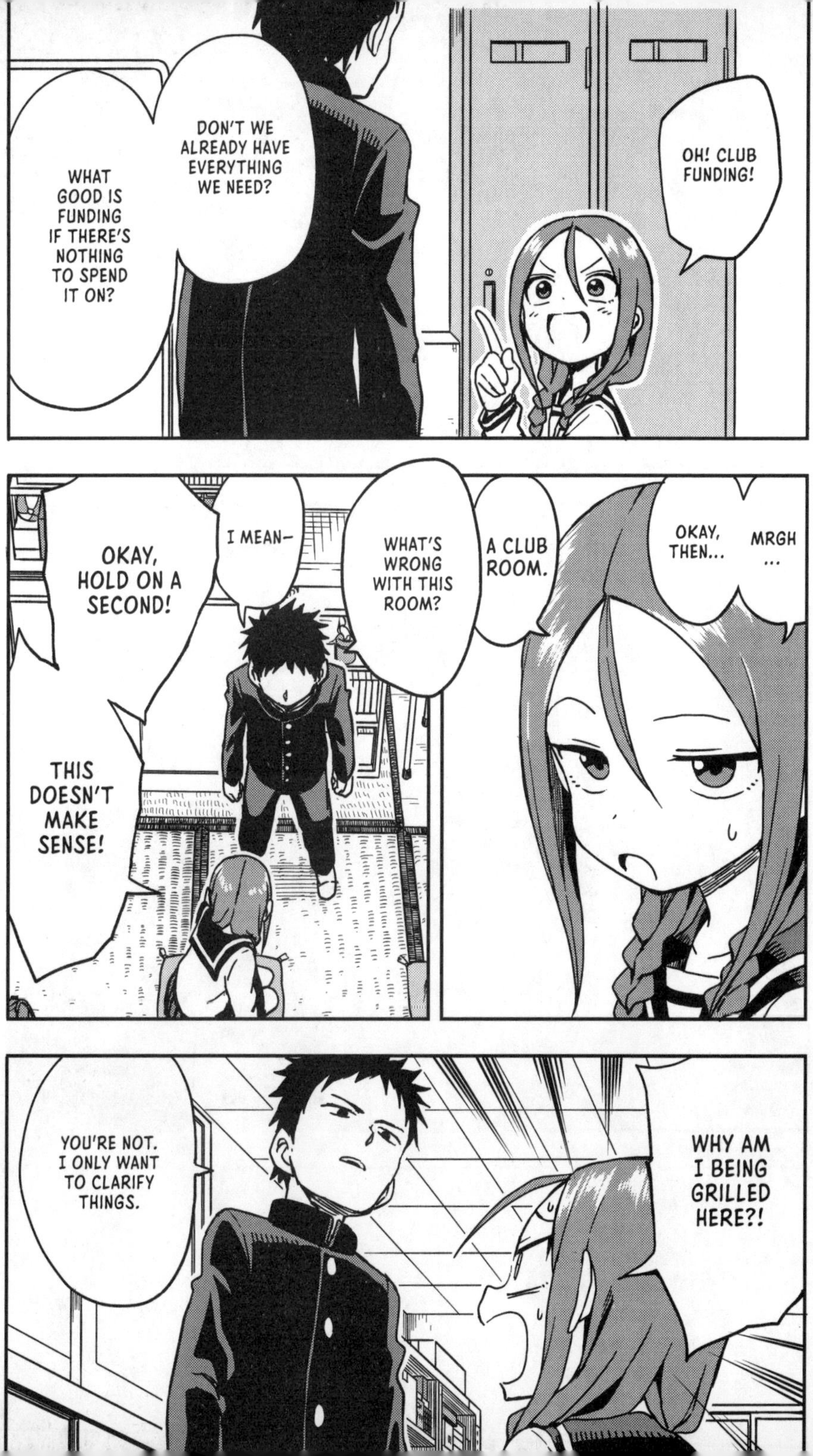
OH! CLUB FUNDING!
DON'T WE ALREADY HAVE EVERYTHING WE NEED?
WHAT GOOD IS FUNDING IF THERE'S NOTHING TO SPEND IT ON?
MRGH ...
OKAY, THEN...
A CLUB ROOM.
WHAT'S WRONG WITH THIS ROOM?
I MEAN—
OKAY, HOLD ON A SECOND!
THIS DOESN'T MAKE SENSE!
WHY AM I BEING GRILLED HERE?!
YOU'RE NOT. I ONLY WANT TO CLARIFY THINGS.

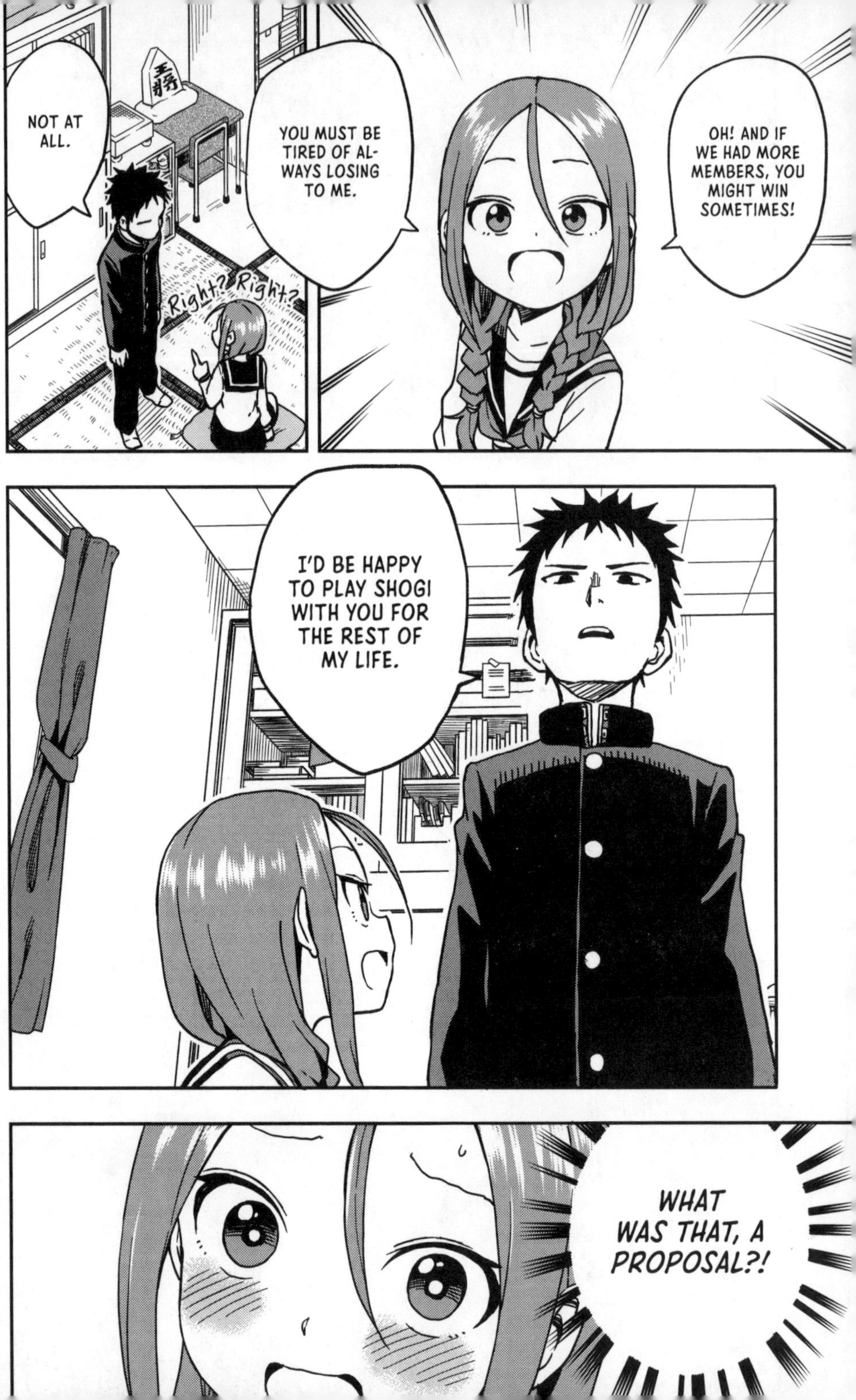
OH! AND IF WE HAD MORE MEMBERS, YOU MIGHT WIN SOMETIMES!
YOU MUST BE TIRED OF AL- WAYS LOSING TO ME.
Right? Right?
NOT AT ALL.
I'D BE HAPPY TO PLAY SHOGI WITH YOU FOR THE REST OF MY LIFE.
WHAT WAS THAT, A PROPOSAL?!

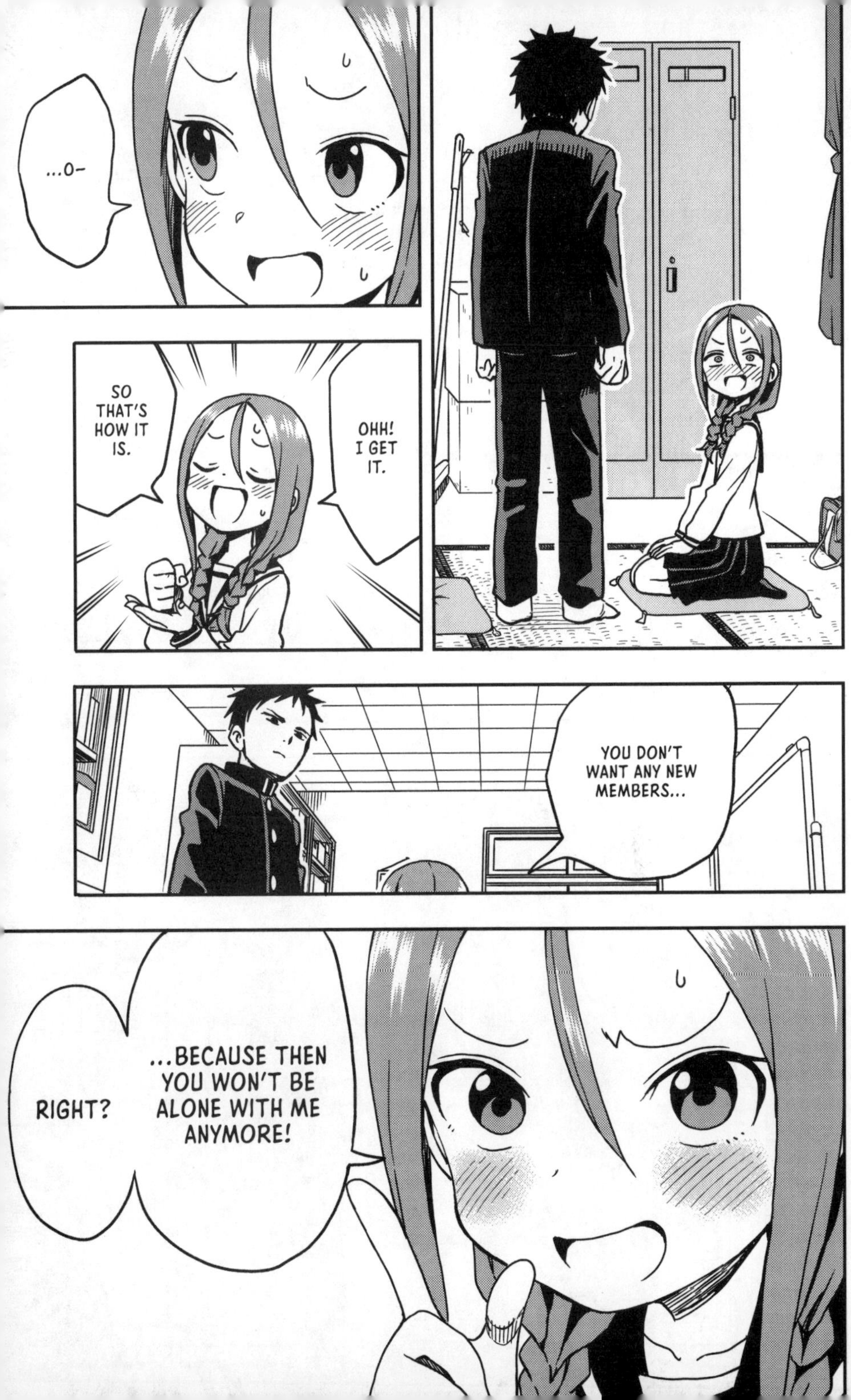
...O-
OHH! I GET IT.
SO THAT'S HOW IT IS.
YOU DON'T WANT ANY NEW MEMBERS...
...BECAUSE THEN YOU WON'T BE ALONE WITH ME ANYMORE!
RIGHT?

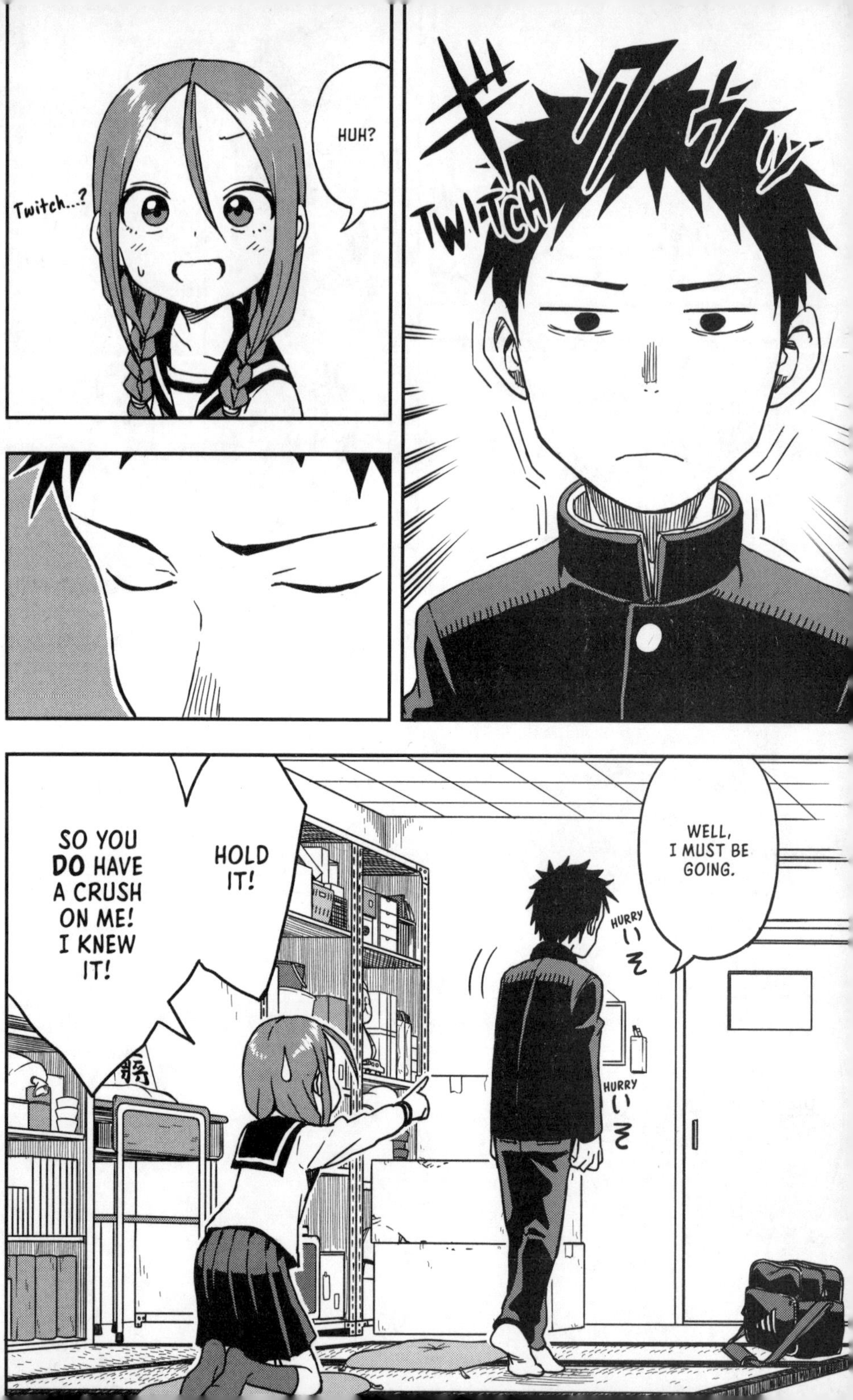
ギクゥッ
TWITCH
HUH?
Twitch...?
WELL, I MUST BE GOING.
HURRY いそ
HURRY いそ
HOLD IT!
SO YOU **DO** HAVE A CRUSH ON ME! I KNEW IT!

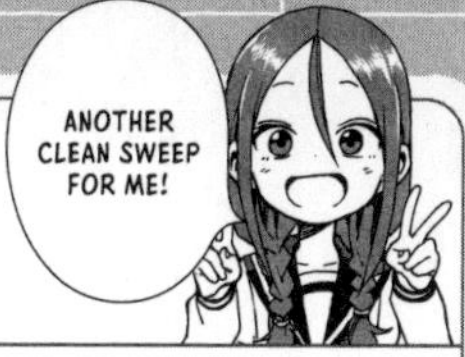
ANOTHER CLEAN SWEEP FOR ME!

GAME 3 RECORD

▲ BLACK (SENTE): AYUMU TANAKA △ WHITE (GOTE): URUSHI YAOTOME

(WHITE WINS ON MOVE 54, △ P×8G)

◁URUSHI: L, P

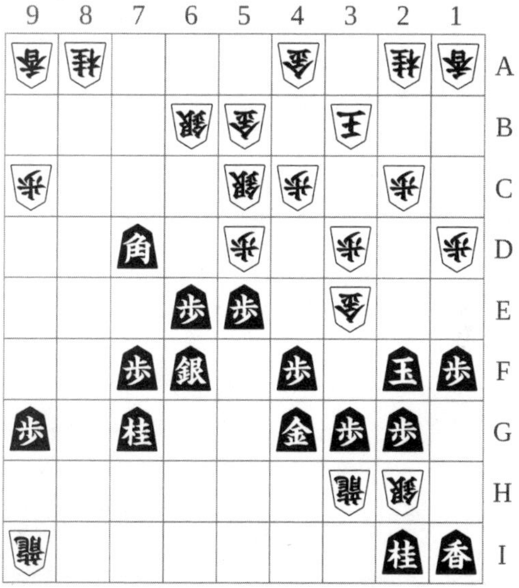

▲AYUMU: B, P×3

▲ P-7F	△ P-3D
▲ P-6F	△ P-8D
▲ R-6H	△ P-8E
▲ B-7G	△ S-6B
▲ K-4H	△ K-4B
▲ K-3H	△ K-3B
▲ K-2H	△ G6A-5B
▲ S-3H	△ P-5D
▲ S-7H	△ S-4B
▲ G6I-5H	△ S4B-5C
▲ P-1F	△ P-1D
▲ P-5F	△ P-7D
▲ S-6G	△ P-6D
▲ R-7H	△ P-6E
▲ P×6E	△ B×7G+
▲ R×7G	△ B×2B
▲ P-4F	△ P-8F
▲ P×8F	△ B×7G+
▲ N×7G	△ R×8F
▲ G-4G	△ R-8I+
▲ B×7H	△ +R×9I
▲ S-6F	△ R×7I
▲ B-9F	△ R×4I+
▲ B×7D	△ +R-3I
▲ K-1G	△ +R×3H
▲ P-5E	△ S×2H
▲ K-2F	△ G×3E

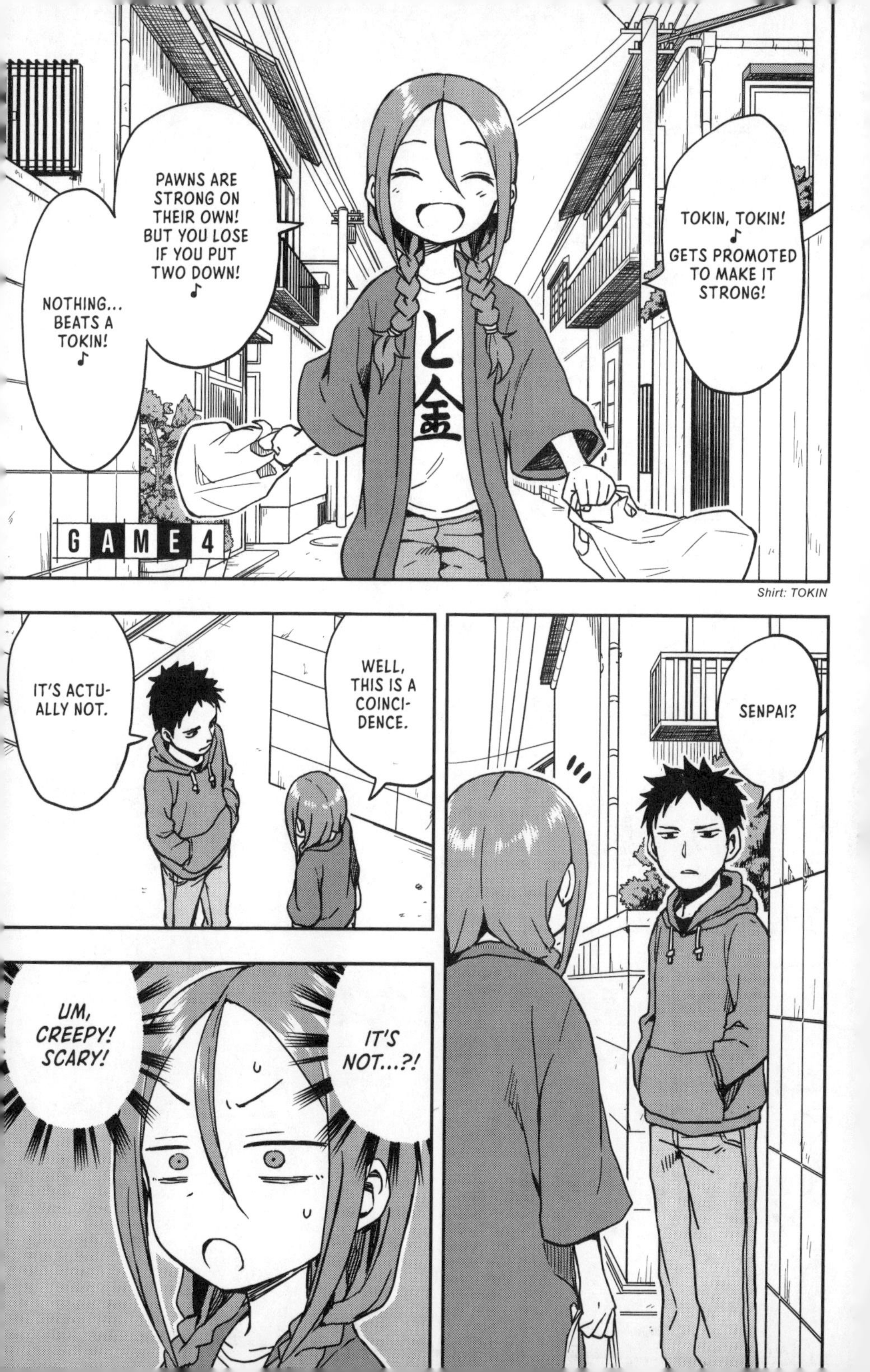
TOKIN, TOKIN! ♪ GETS PROMOTED TO MAKE IT STRONG!
PAWNS ARE STRONG ON THEIR OWN! BUT YOU LOSE IF YOU PUT TWO DOWN! ♪
NOTHING... BEATS A TOKIN! ♪
GAME 4
と金
SENPAI?
WELL, THIS IS A COINCIDENCE.
IT'S ACTUALLY NOT.
IT'S NOT...?!
UM, CREEPY! SCARY!
Shirt: TOKIN

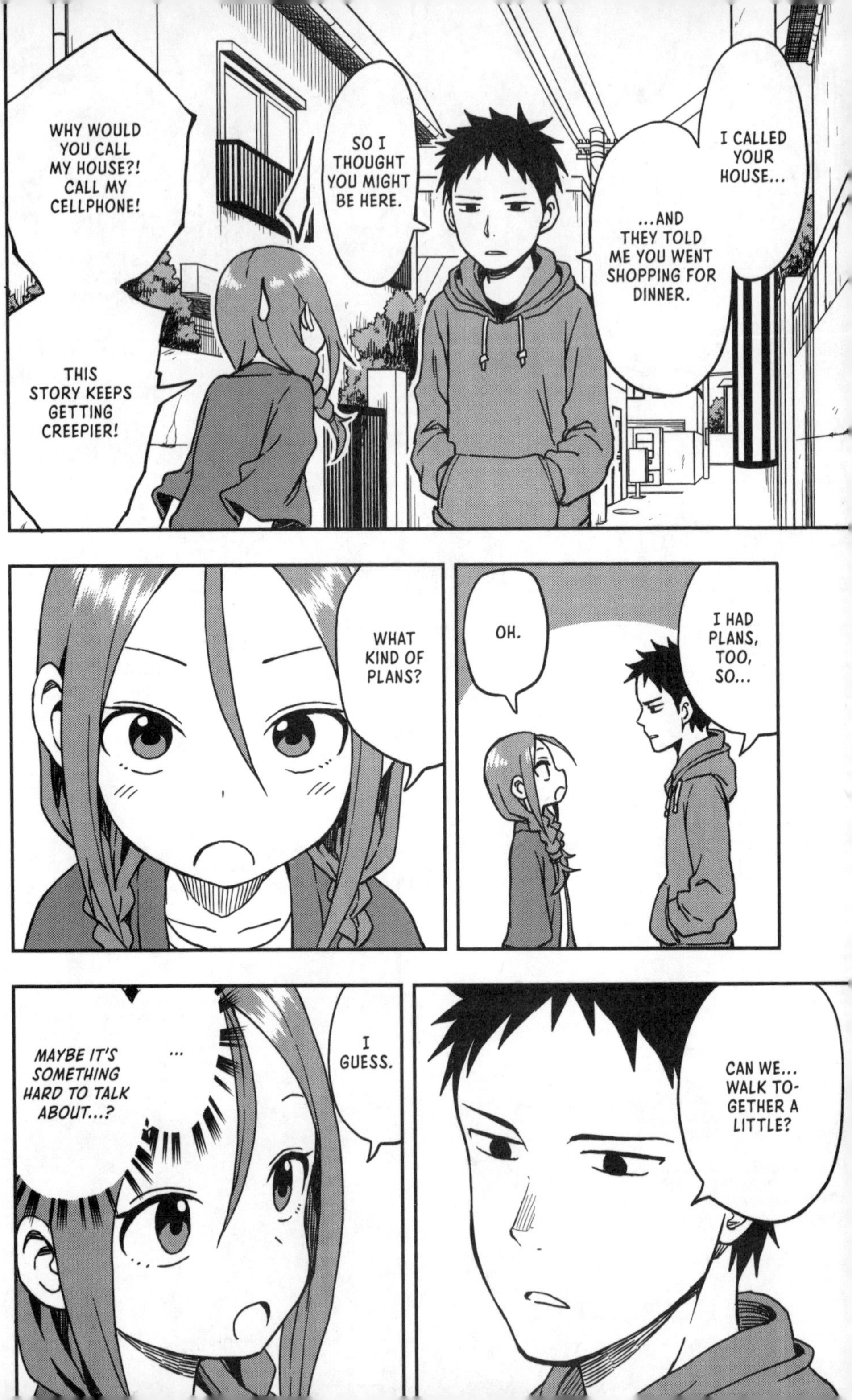
I CALLED YOUR HOUSE...
...AND THEY TOLD ME YOU WENT SHOPPING FOR DINNER.
SO I THOUGHT YOU MIGHT BE HERE.
WHY WOULD YOU CALL MY HOUSE?! CALL MY CELLPHONE!
THIS STORY KEEPS GETTING CREEPIER!
I HAD PLANS, TOO, SO...
OH.
WHAT KIND OF PLANS?
CAN WE... WALK TO-GETHER A LITTLE?
I GUESS.
...
MAYBE IT'S SOMETHING HARD TO TALK ABOUT...?

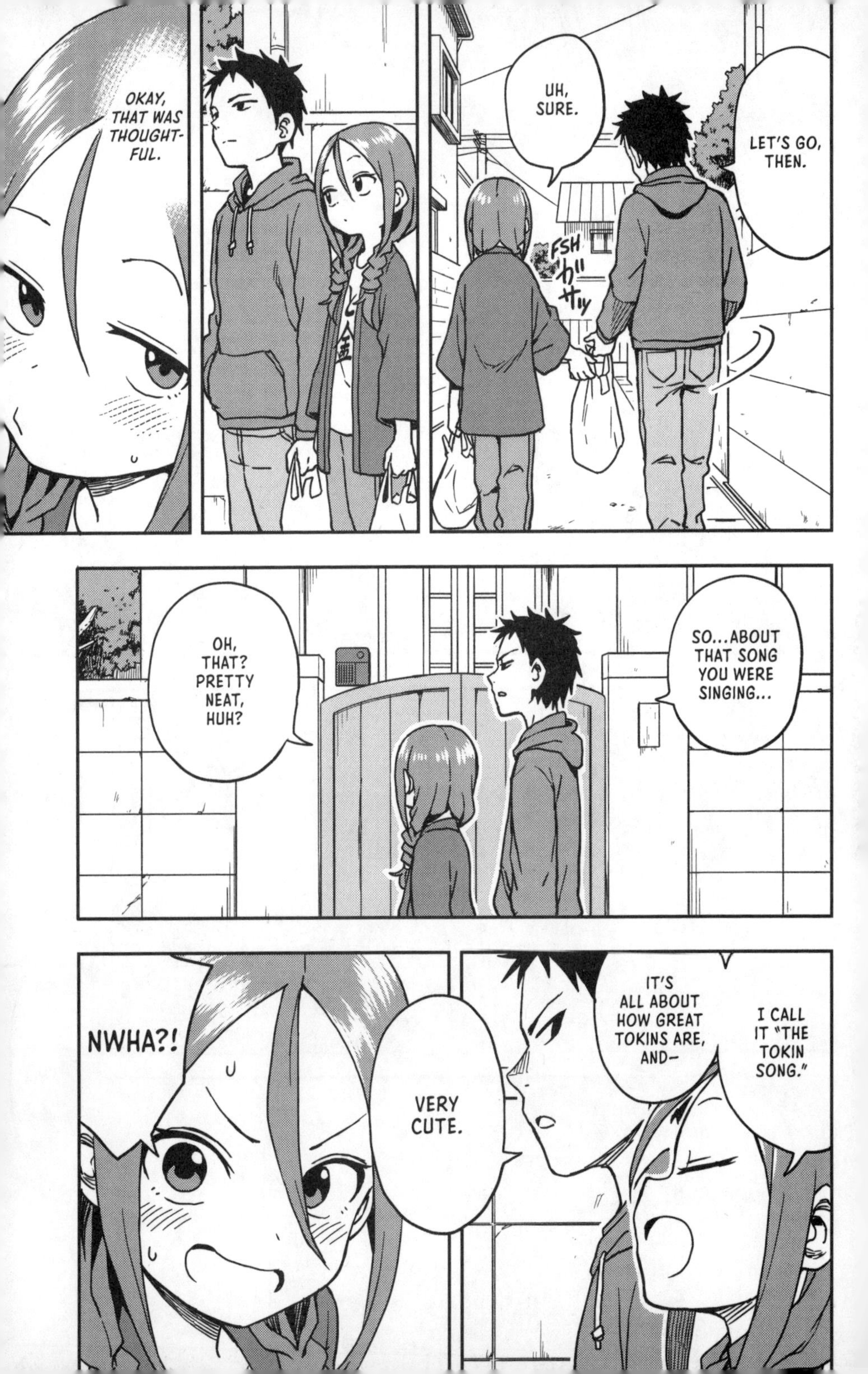
LET'S GO, THEN.
UH, SURE.
FSH
ガサッ
OKAY, THAT WAS THOUGHT-FUL.
SO...ABOUT THAT SONG YOU WERE SINGING...
OH, THAT? PRETTY NEAT, HUH?
I CALL IT "THE TOKIN SONG."
IT'S ALL ABOUT HOW GREAT TOKINS ARE, AND—
VERY CUTE.
NWHA?!

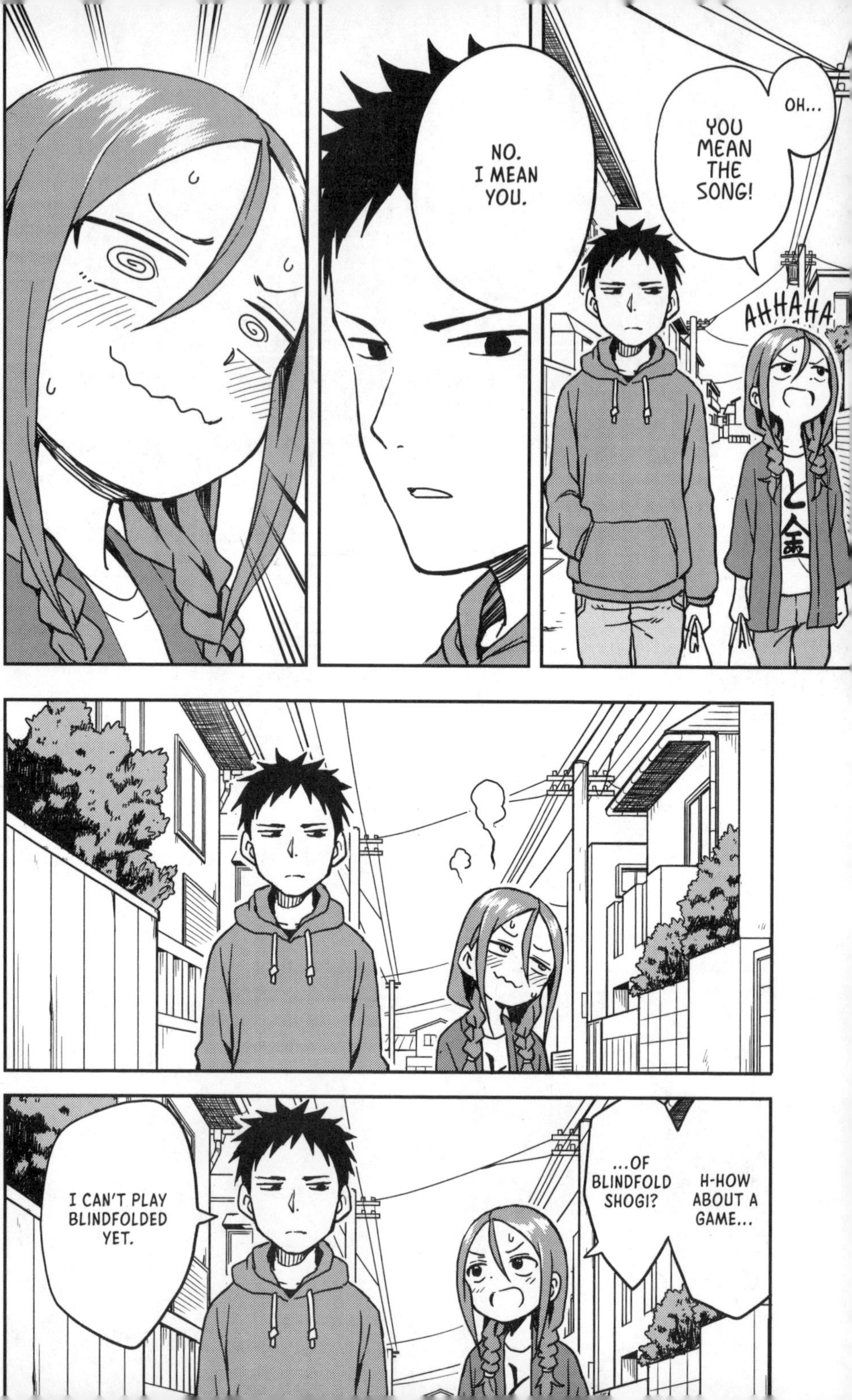
OH...
YOU MEAN THE SONG!
AHHAHA
NO. I MEAN YOU.
H-HOW ABOUT A GAME...
...OF BLINDFOLD SHOGI?
I CAN'T PLAY BLINDFOLDED YET.

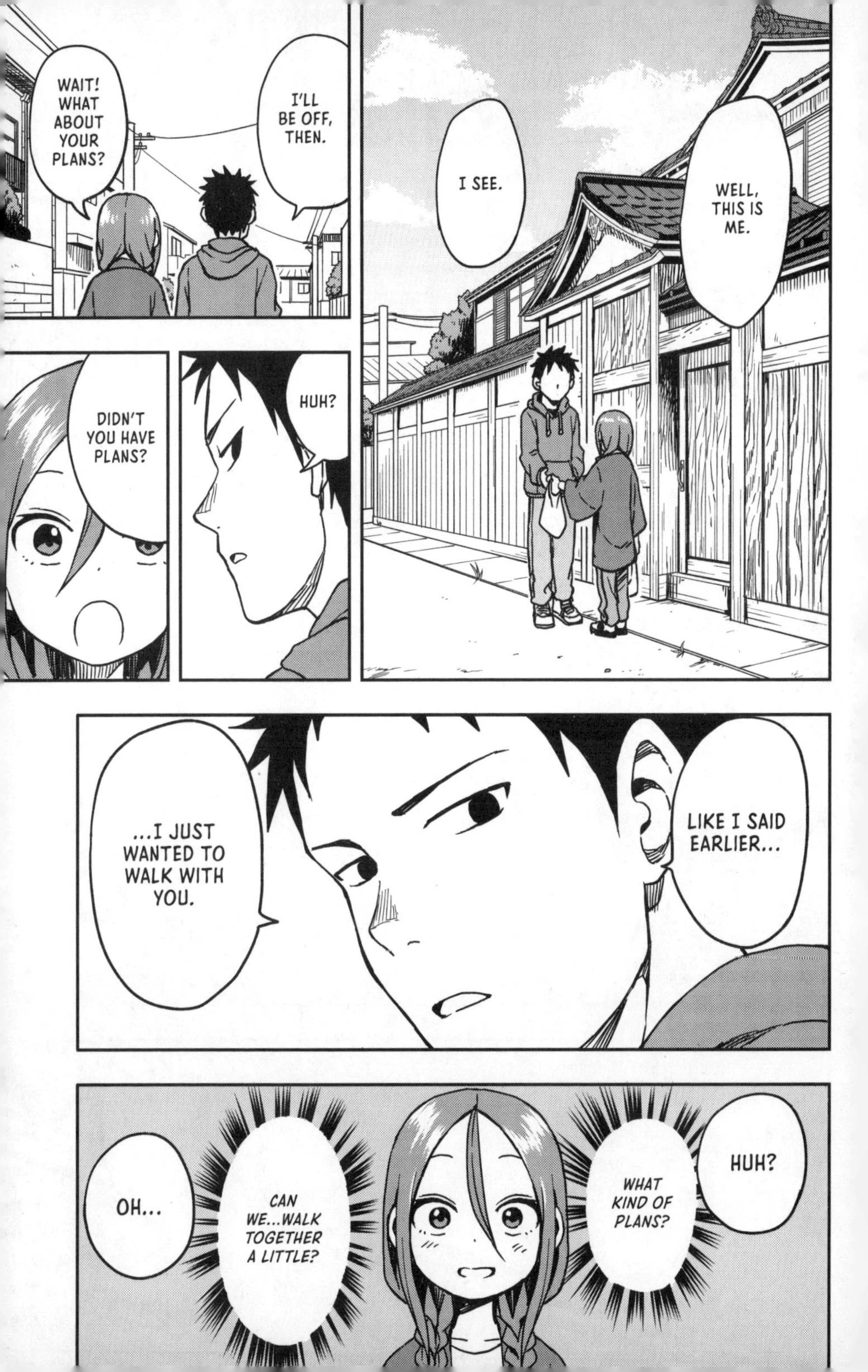
WELL, THIS IS ME.
I SEE.
I'LL BE OFF, THEN.
WAIT! WHAT ABOUT YOUR PLANS?
HUH?
DIDN'T YOU HAVE PLANS?
LIKE I SAID EARLIER...
...I JUST WANTED TO WALK WITH YOU.
HUH?
WHAT KIND OF PLANS?
CAN WE...WALK TOGETHER A LITTLE?
OH...

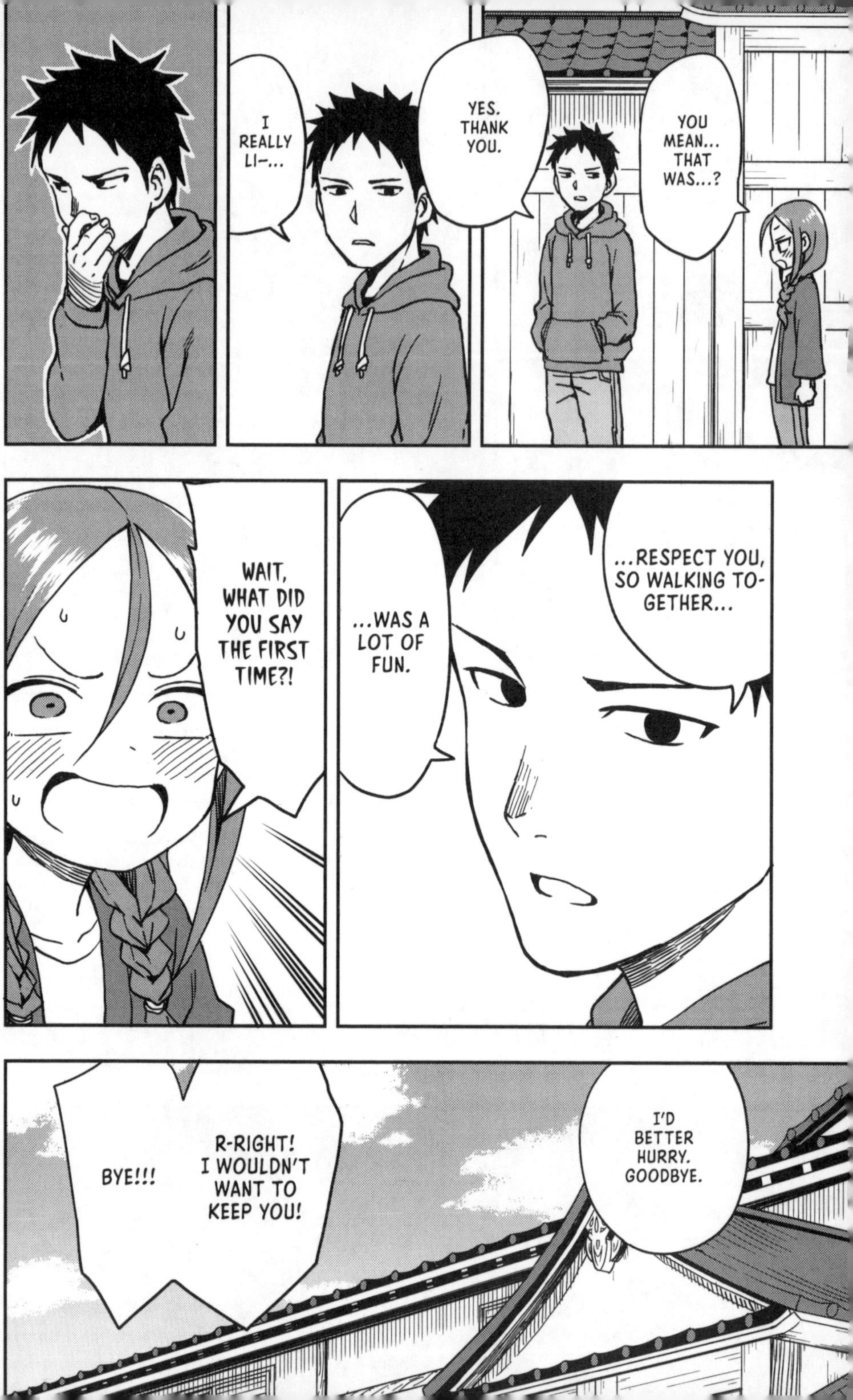
YOU MEAN... THAT WAS...?
YES. THANK YOU.
I REALLY LI–...
...RESPECT YOU, SO WALKING TO-GETHER...
...WAS A LOT OF FUN.
WAIT, WHAT DID YOU SAY THE FIRST TIME?!
I'D BETTER HURRY. GOODBYE.
R-RIGHT! I WOULDN'T WANT TO KEEP YOU!
BYE!!!

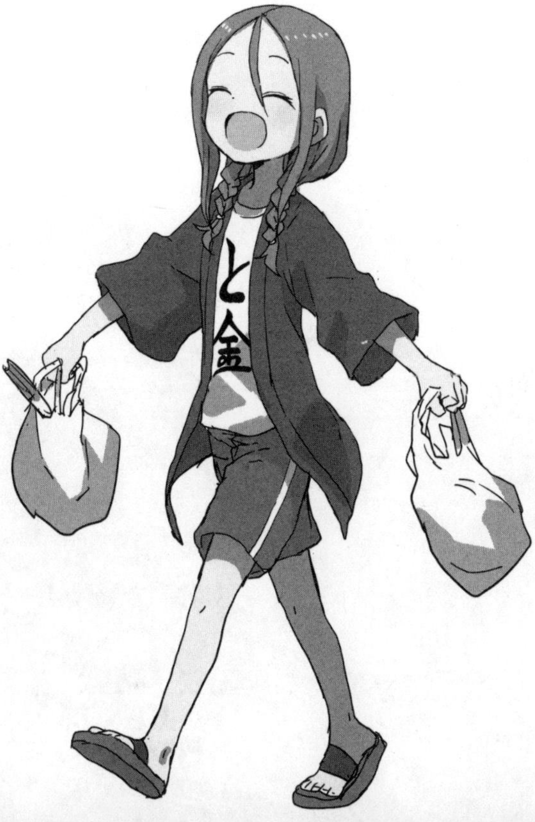
と金

WHEN WILL AYUMU MAKE HIS MOVE?

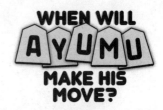

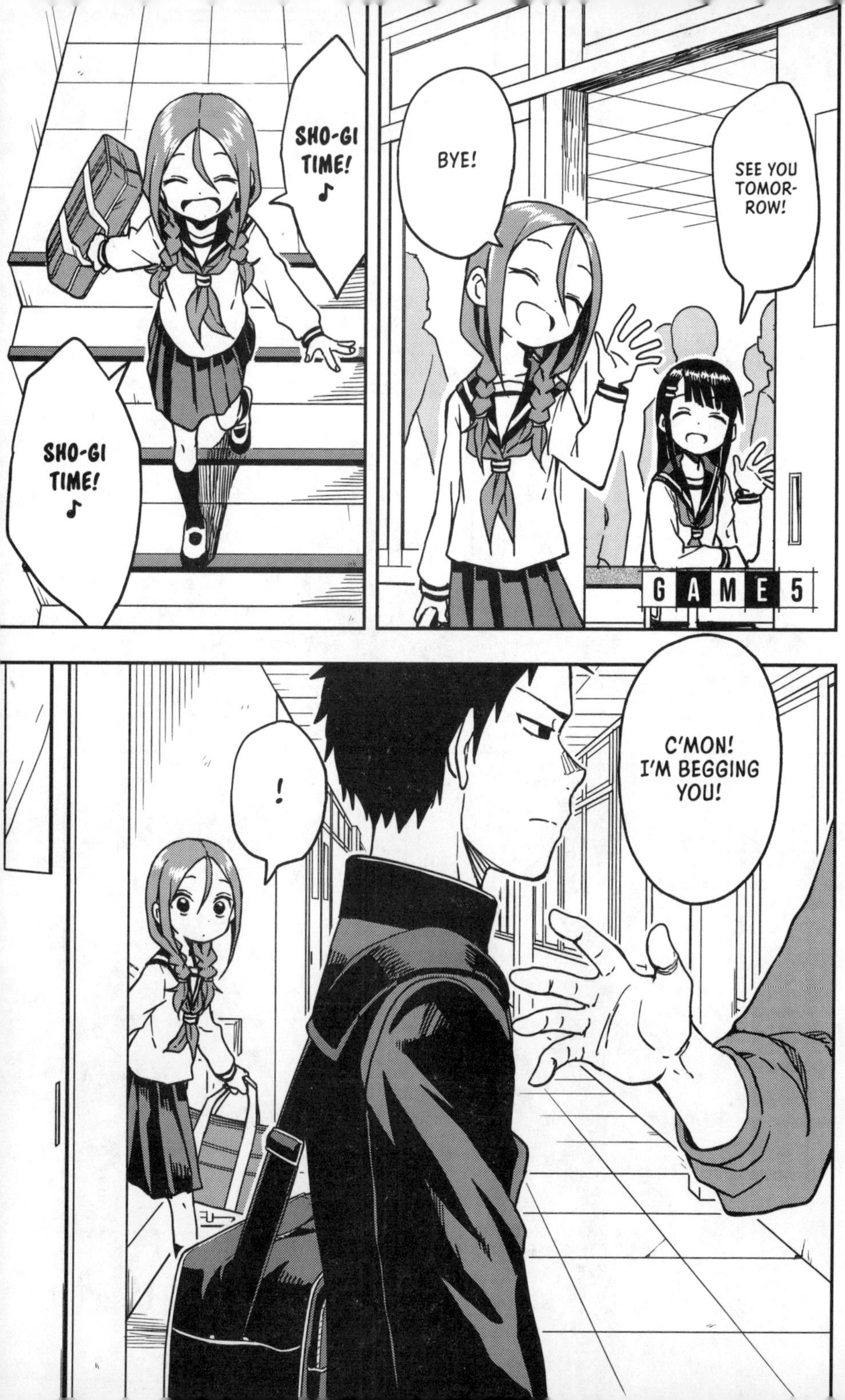
SEE YOU TOMOR-ROW!
BYE!
GAME 5
SHO-GI TIME! ♪
SHO-GI TIME! ♪
C'MON! I'M BEGGING YOU!
!

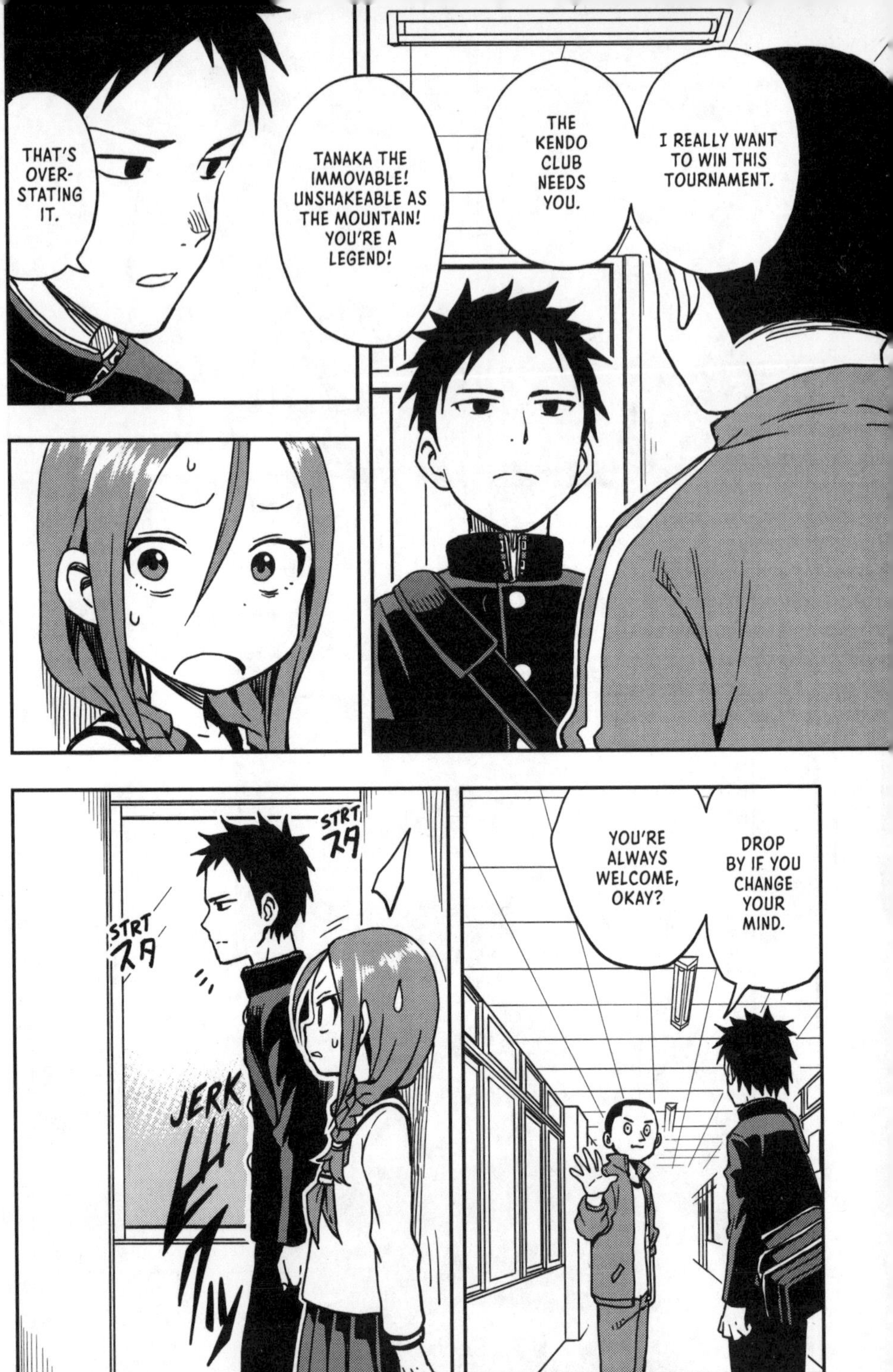
I REALLY WANT TO WIN THIS TOURNAMENT.
THE KENDO CLUB NEEDS YOU.
TANAKA THE IMMOVABLE! UNSHAKEABLE AS THE MOUNTAIN! YOU'RE A LEGEND!
THAT'S OVER-STATING IT.
DROP BY IF YOU CHANGE YOUR MIND.
YOU'RE ALWAYS WELCOME, OKAY?
STRT スタ
STRT スタ
JERK

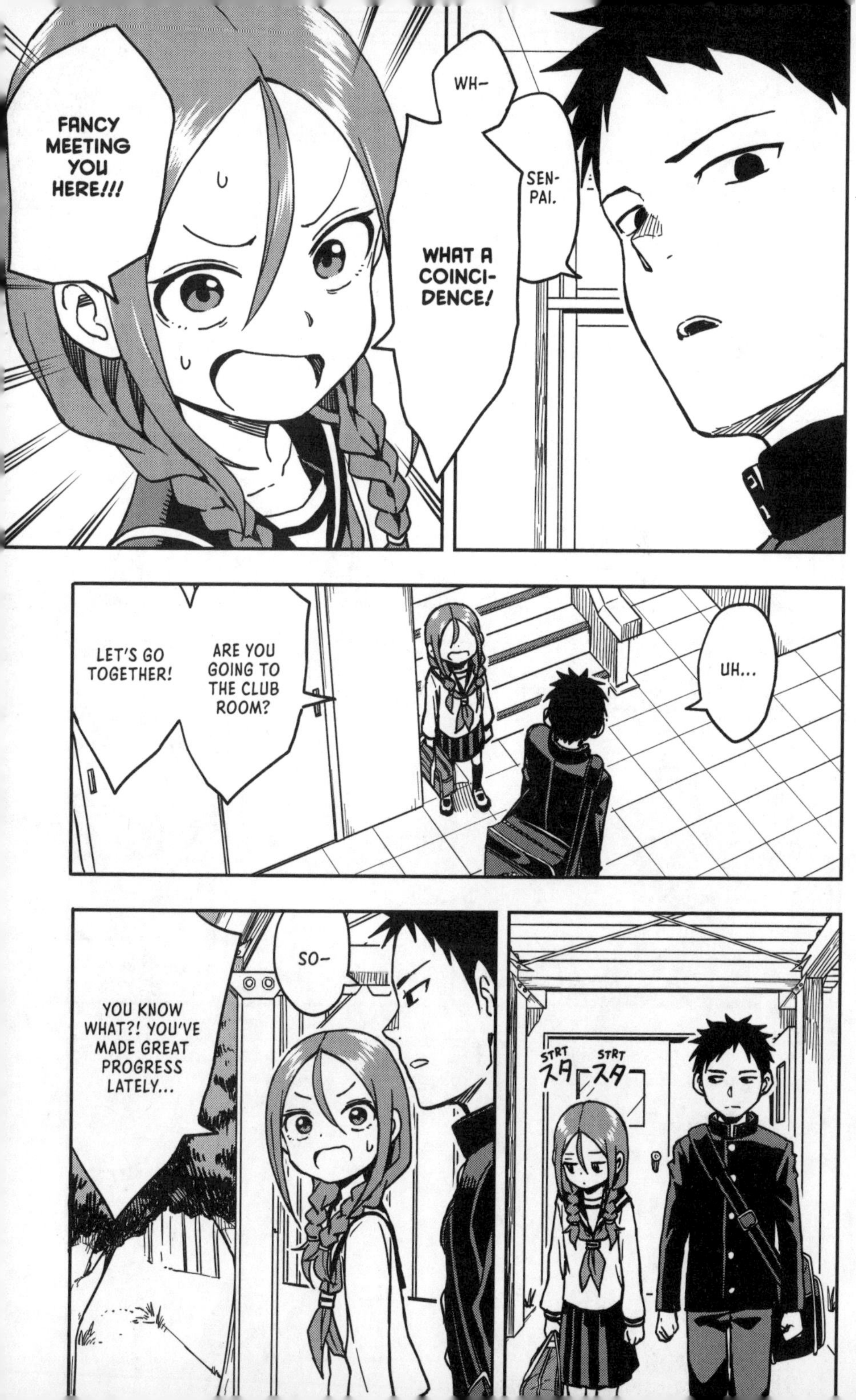
WH-
SEN-PAI.
WHAT A COINCIDENCE!
FANCY MEETING YOU HERE!!!
UH...
ARE YOU GOING TO THE CLUB ROOM?
LET'S GO TOGETHER!
STRT スタ STRT スタ
SO-
YOU KNOW WHAT?! YOU'VE MADE GREAT PROGRESS LATELY...

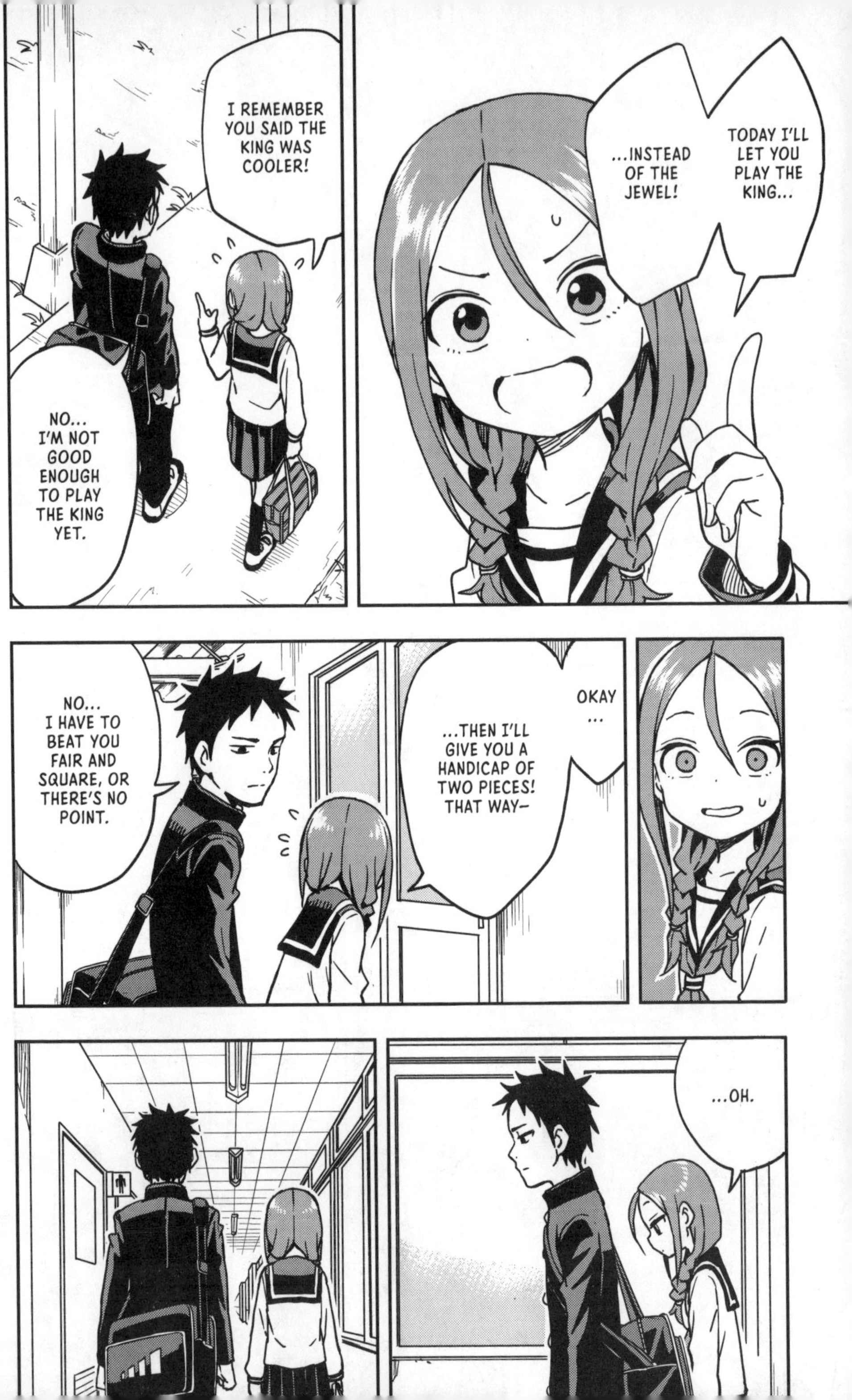
TODAY I'LL LET YOU PLAY THE KING...
...INSTEAD OF THE JEWEL!
I REMEMBER YOU SAID THE KING WAS COOLER!
NO... I'M NOT GOOD ENOUGH TO PLAY THE KING YET.
OKAY ...
...THEN I'LL GIVE YOU A HANDICAP OF TWO PIECES! THAT WAY–
NO... I HAVE TO BEAT YOU FAIR AND SQUARE, OR THERE'S NO POINT.
...OH.

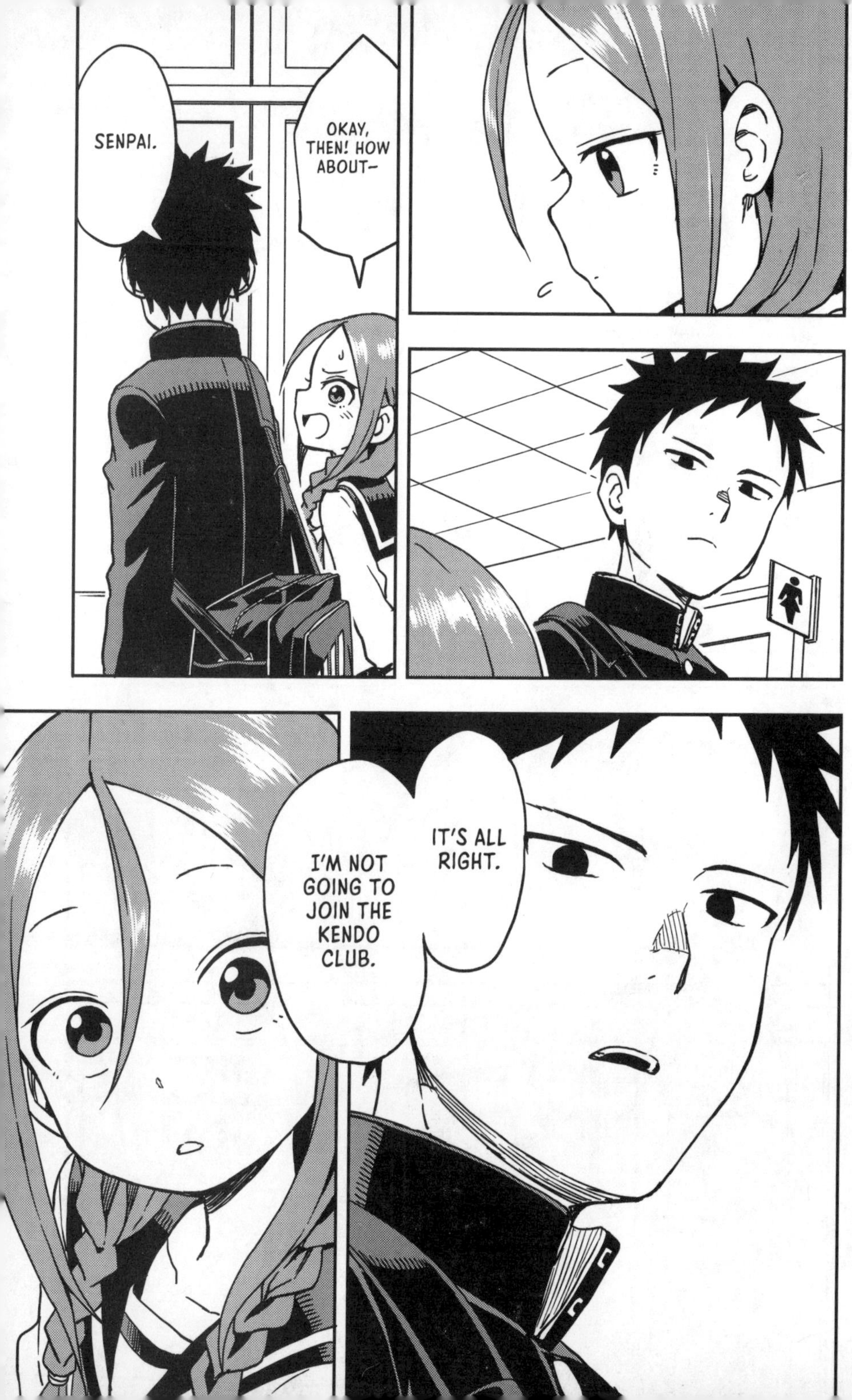
OKAY, THEN! HOW ABOUT–
SENPAI.
IT'S ALL RIGHT.
I'M NOT GOING TO JOIN THE KENDO CLUB.

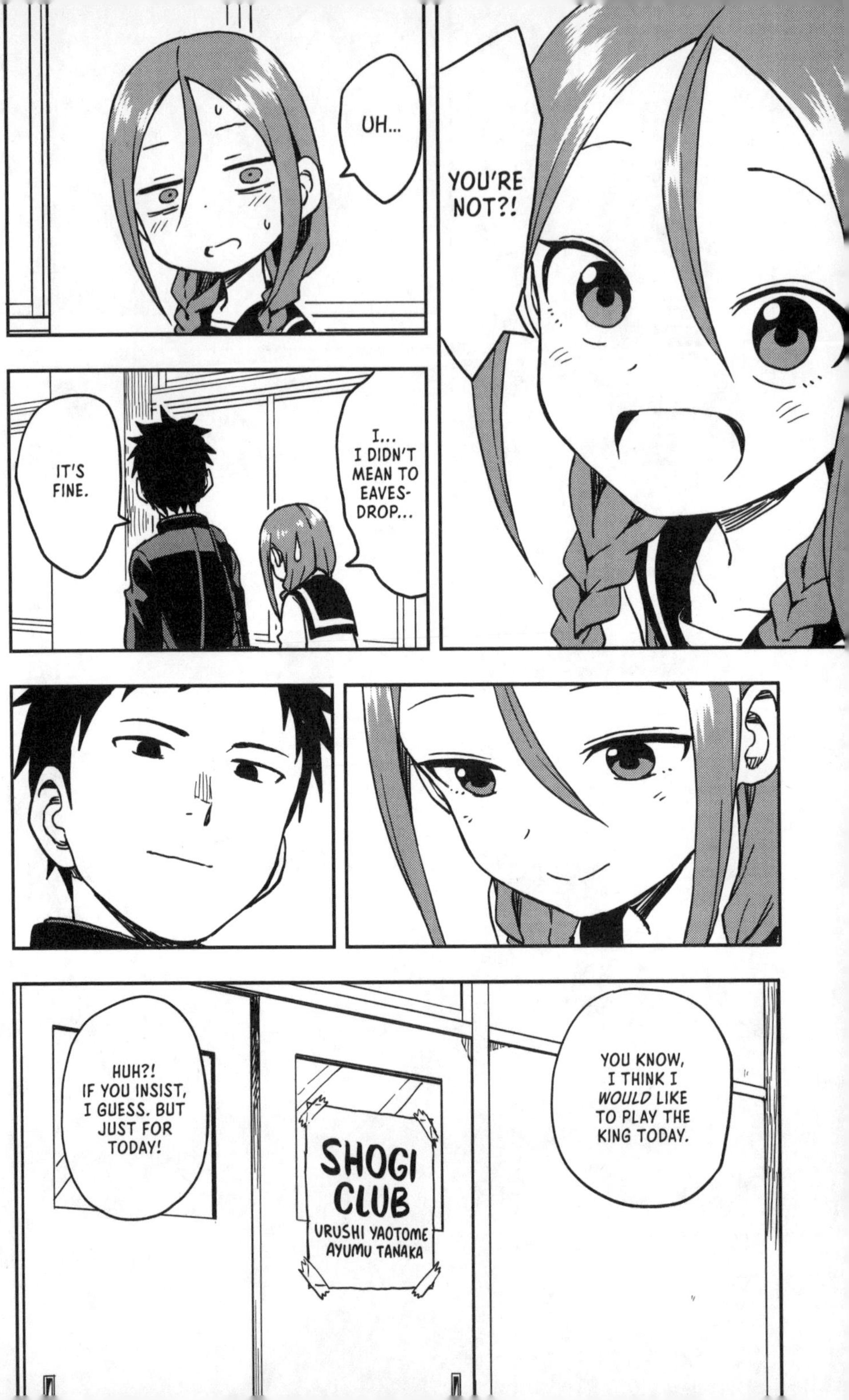

YOU'RE NOT?!
UH...
I... I DIDN'T MEAN TO EAVES-DROP...
IT'S FINE.
YOU KNOW, I THINK I *WOULD* LIKE TO PLAY THE KING TODAY.
SHOGI CLUB
URUSHI YAOTOME AYUMU TANAKA
HUH?! IF YOU INSIST, I GUESS. BUT JUST FOR TODAY!

WHEN WILL AYUMU MAKE HIS MOVE?

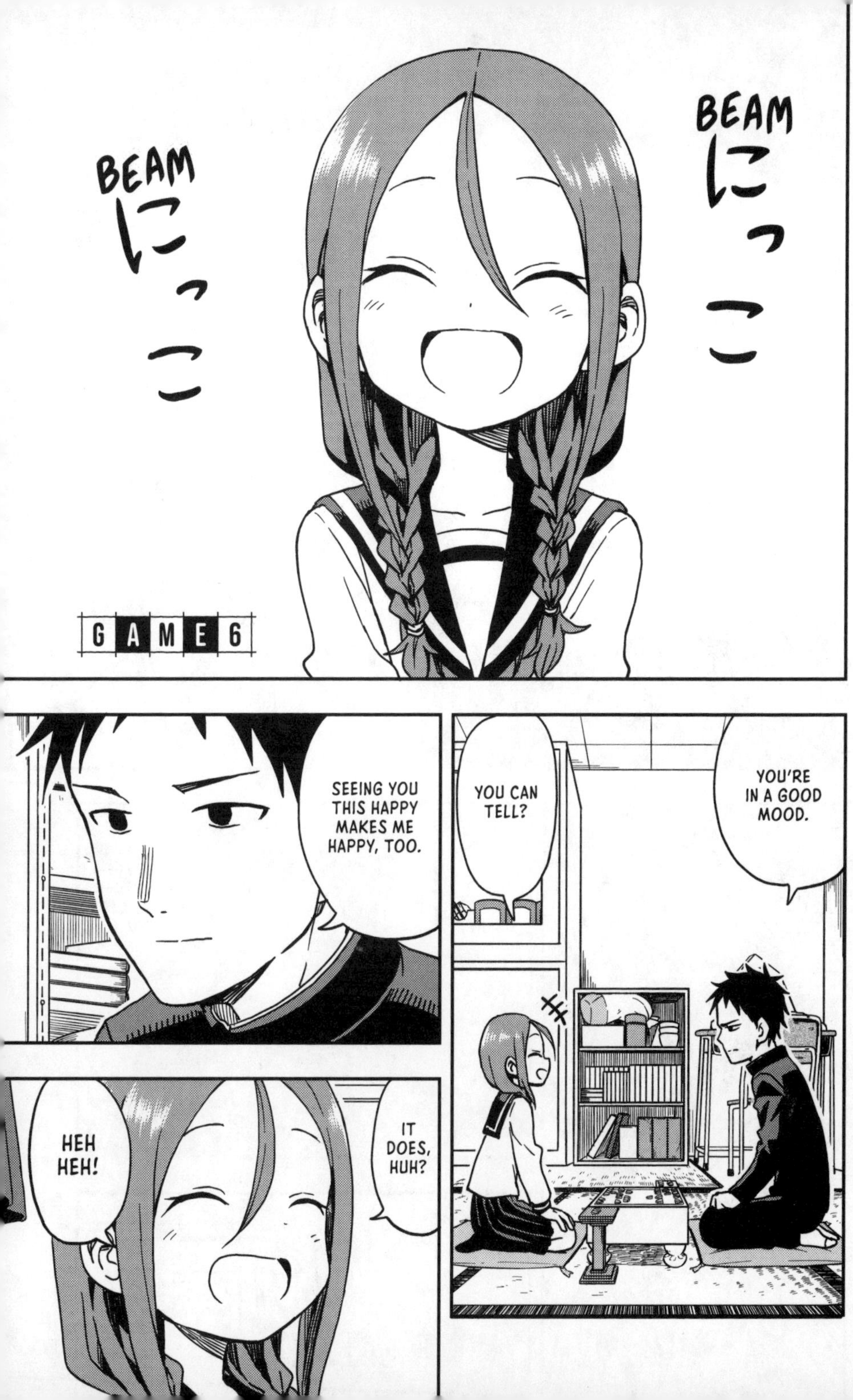
BEAM
にっこ
BEAM
にっこ
GAME 6
YOU'RE IN A GOOD MOOD.
YOU CAN TELL?
SEEING YOU THIS HAPPY MAKES ME HAPPY, TOO.
IT DOES, HUH?
HEH HEH!

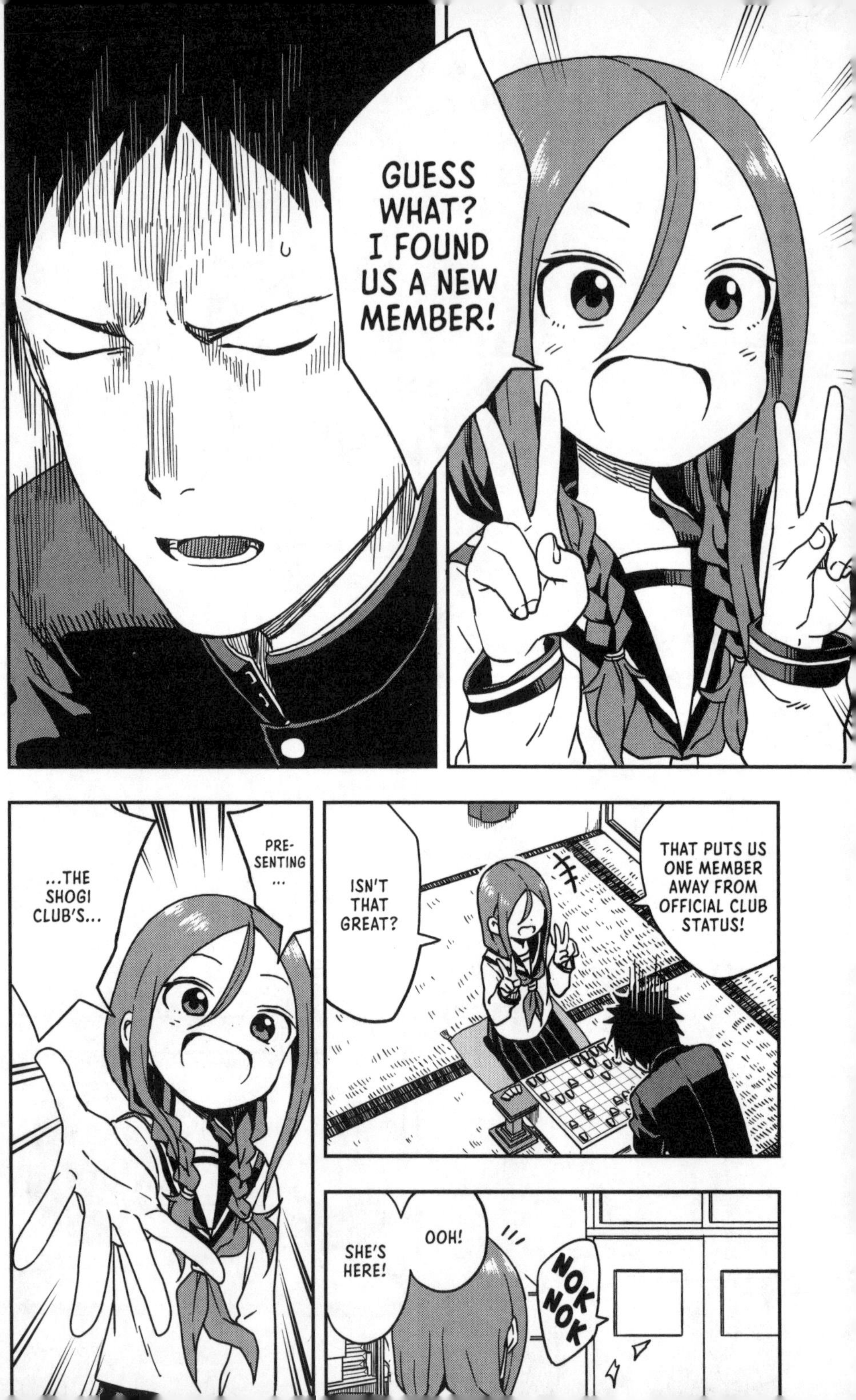
GUESS WHAT? I FOUND US A NEW MEMBER!
THAT PUTS US ONE MEMBER AWAY FROM OFFICIAL CLUB STATUS!
ISN'T THAT GREAT?
NOK NOK
OOH!
SHE'S HERE!
PRE-SENTING...
...THE SHOGI CLUB'S...

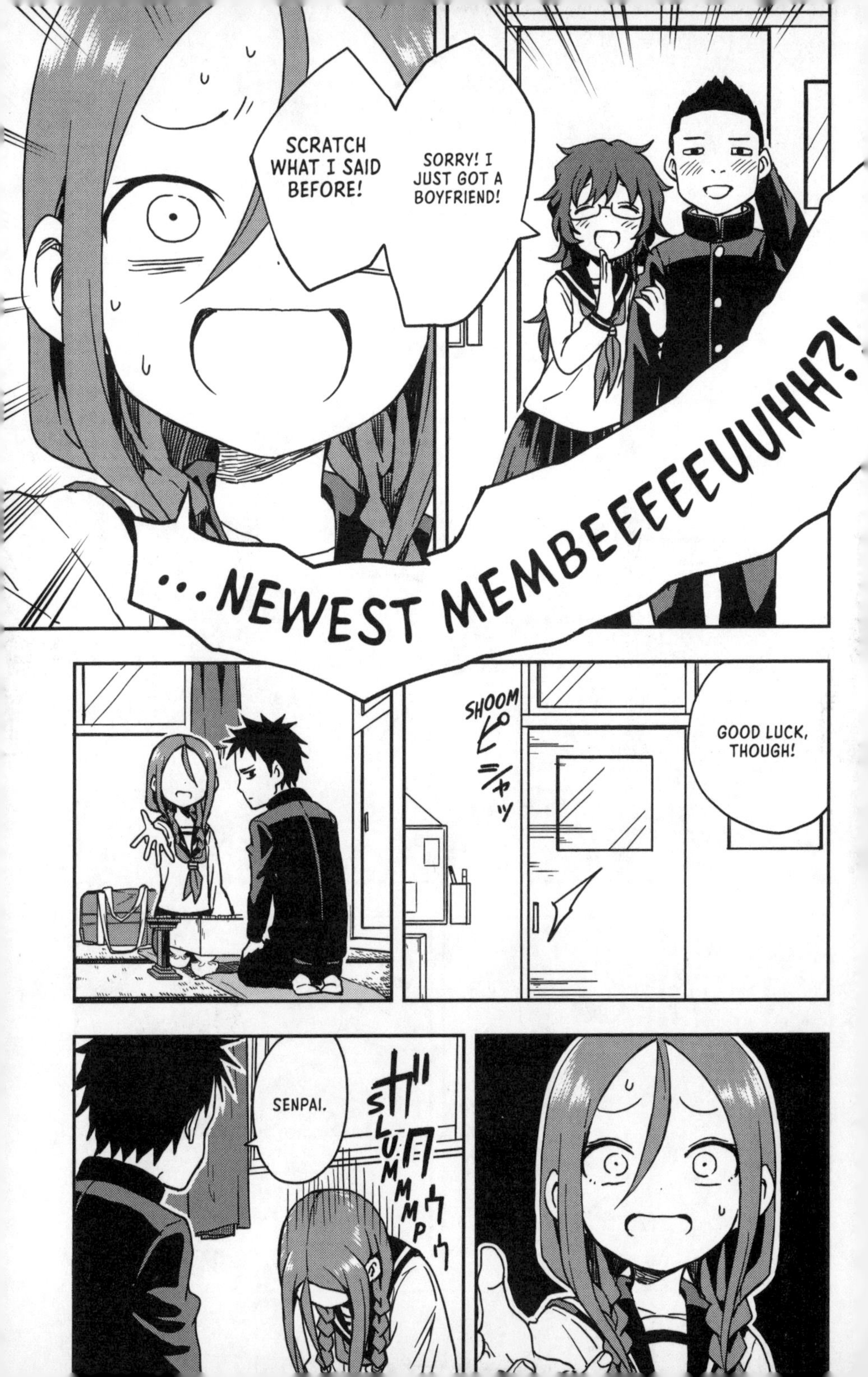
SORRY! I JUST GOT A BOYFRIEND!
SCRATCH WHAT I SAID BEFORE!
...NEWEST MEMBEEEEEEUUHH?!
GOOD LUCK, THOUGH!
SHOOM
ピシャッ
SENPAI.
SLUMMMP

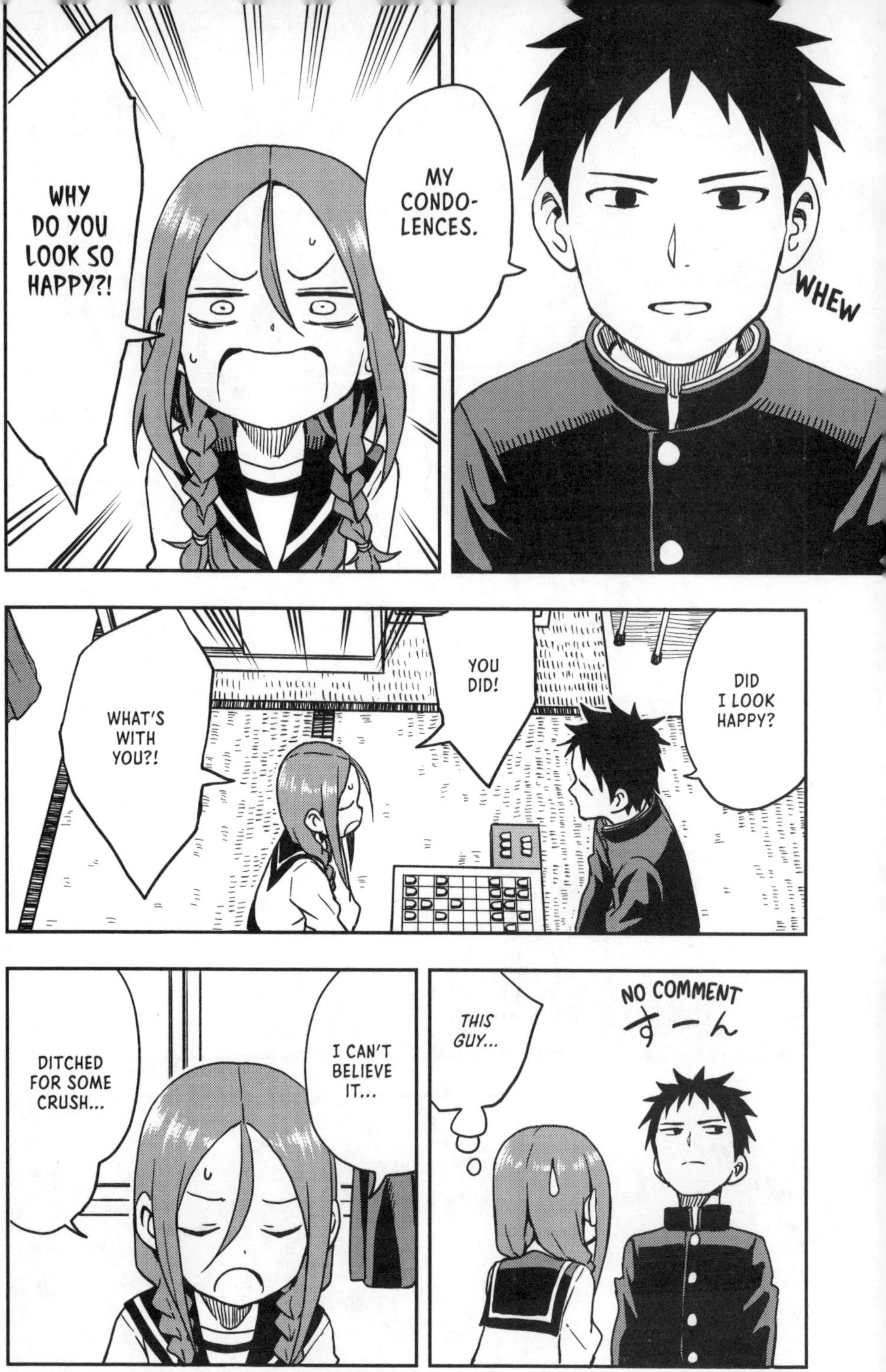
WHEW
MY CONDOLENCES.
WHY DO YOU LOOK SO HAPPY?!
DID I LOOK HAPPY?
YOU DID!
WHAT'S WITH YOU?!
NO COMMENT
すーん
THIS GUY...
I CAN'T BELIEVE IT...
DITCHED FOR SOME CRUSH...

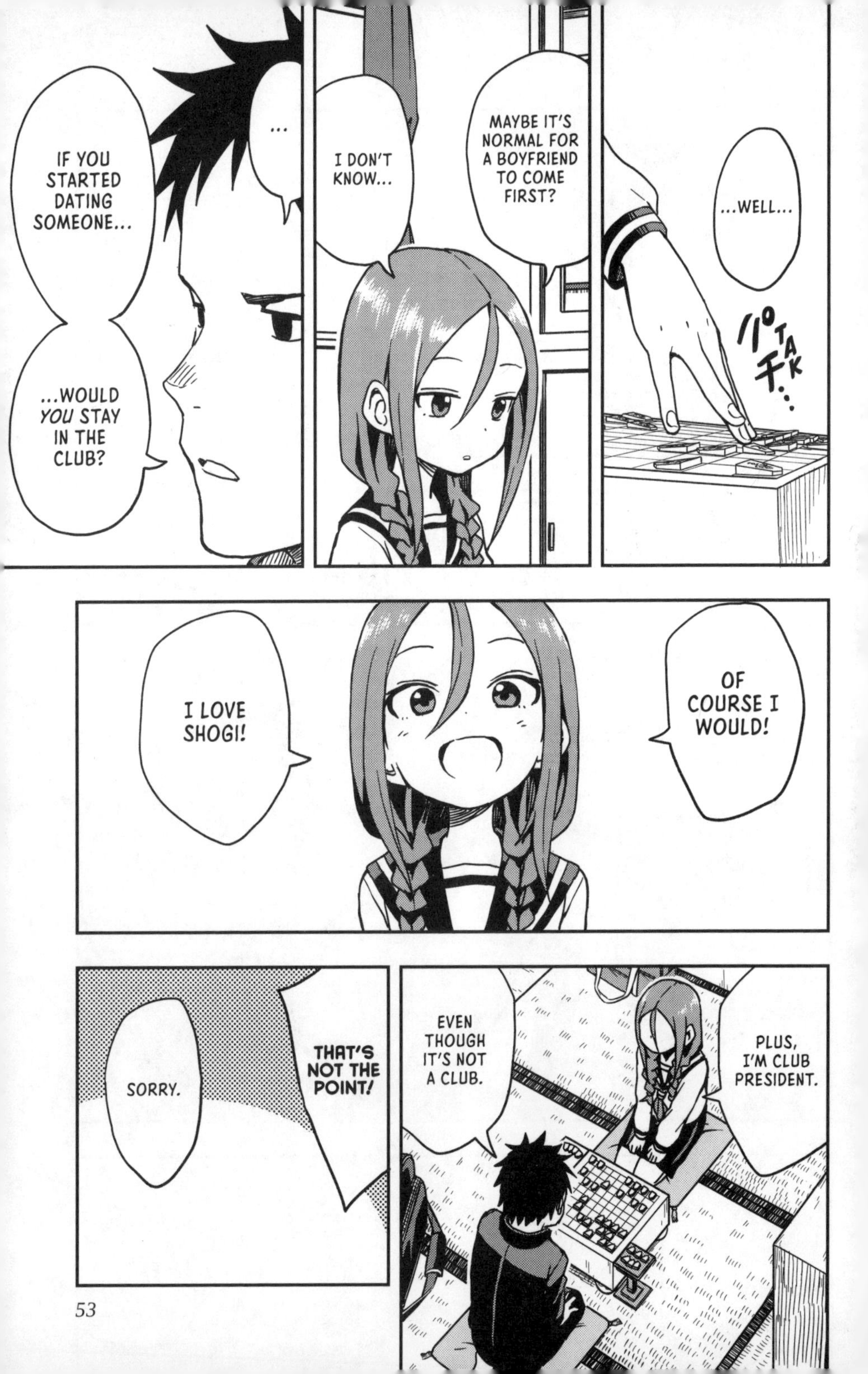
...WELL...
TAK...
MAYBE IT'S NORMAL FOR A BOYFRIEND TO COME FIRST?
I DON'T KNOW...
...
IF YOU STARTED DATING SOMEONE...
...WOULD *YOU* STAY IN THE CLUB?
OF COURSE I WOULD!
I LOVE SHOGI!
PLUS, I'M CLUB PRESIDENT.
EVEN THOUGH IT'S NOT A CLUB.
THAT'S NOT THE POINT!
SORRY.

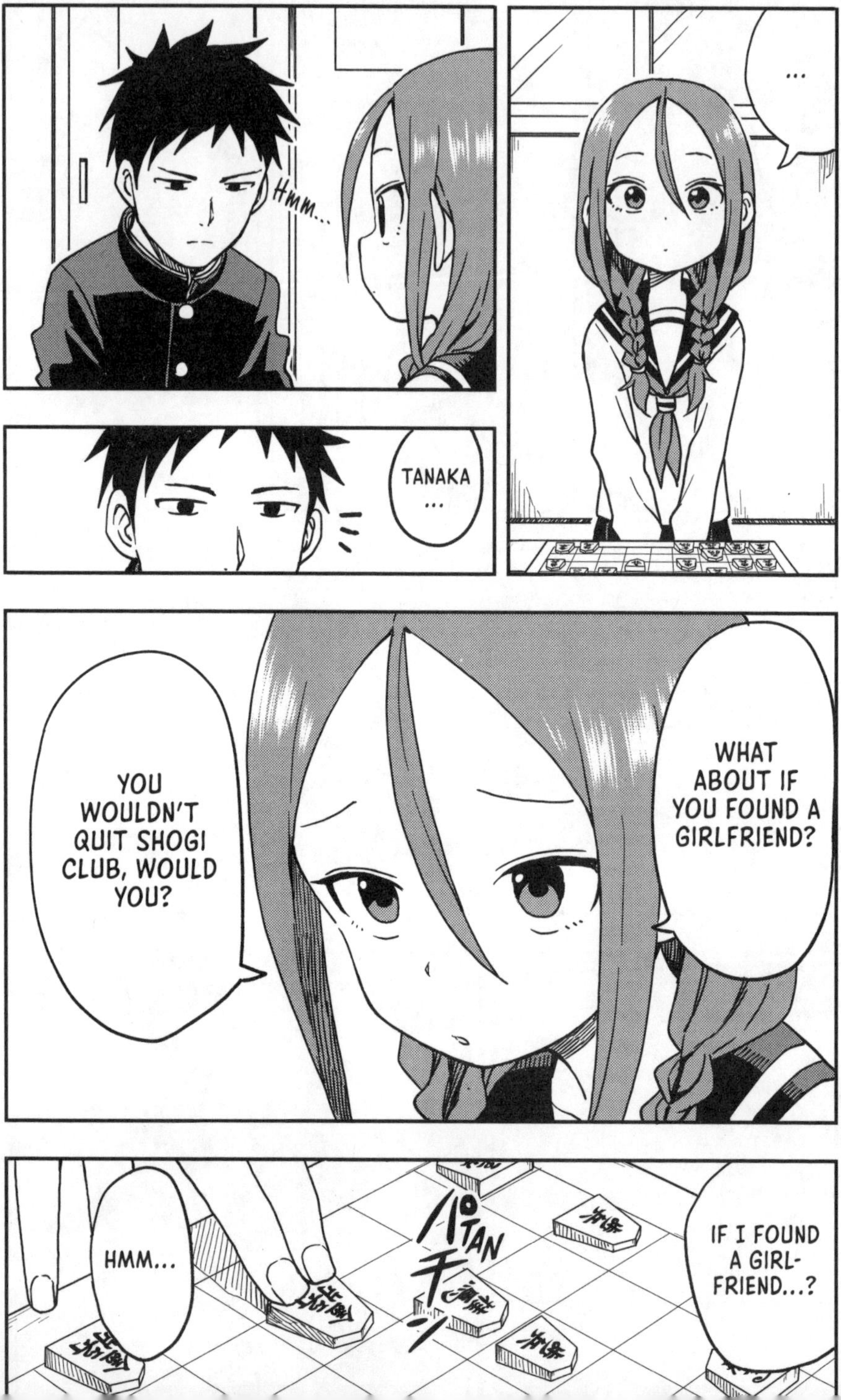
...
HMM...
TANAKA ...
WHAT ABOUT IF YOU FOUND A GIRLFRIEND?
YOU WOULDN'T QUIT SHOGI CLUB, WOULD YOU?
IF I FOUND A GIRL-FRIEND...?
パTAN
HMM...

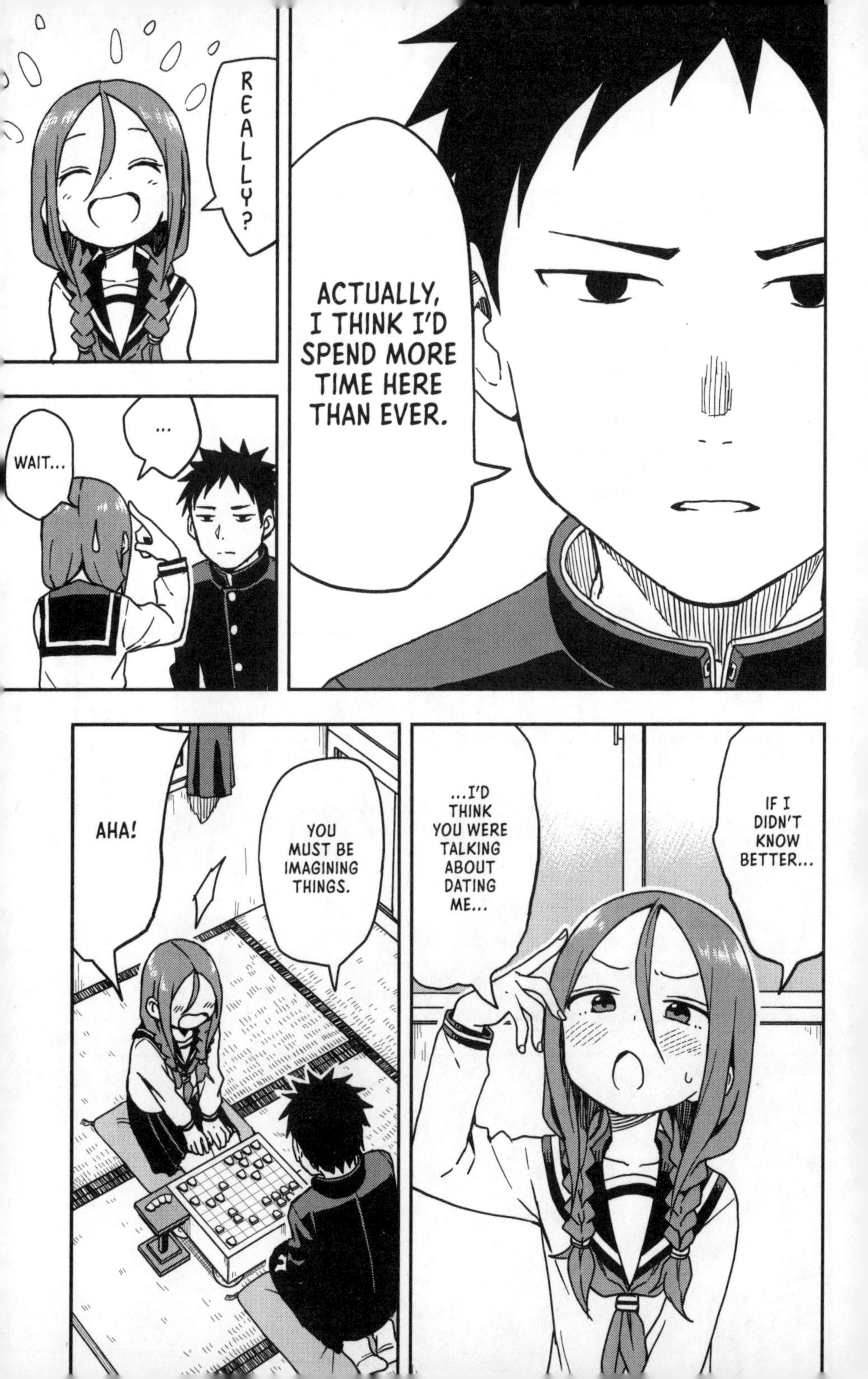
ACTUALLY, I THINK I'D SPEND MORE TIME HERE THAN EVER.
REALLY?
...
WAIT...
IF I DIDN'T KNOW BETTER...
...I'D THINK YOU WERE TALKING ABOUT DATING ME...
YOU MUST BE IMAGINING THINGS.
AHA!

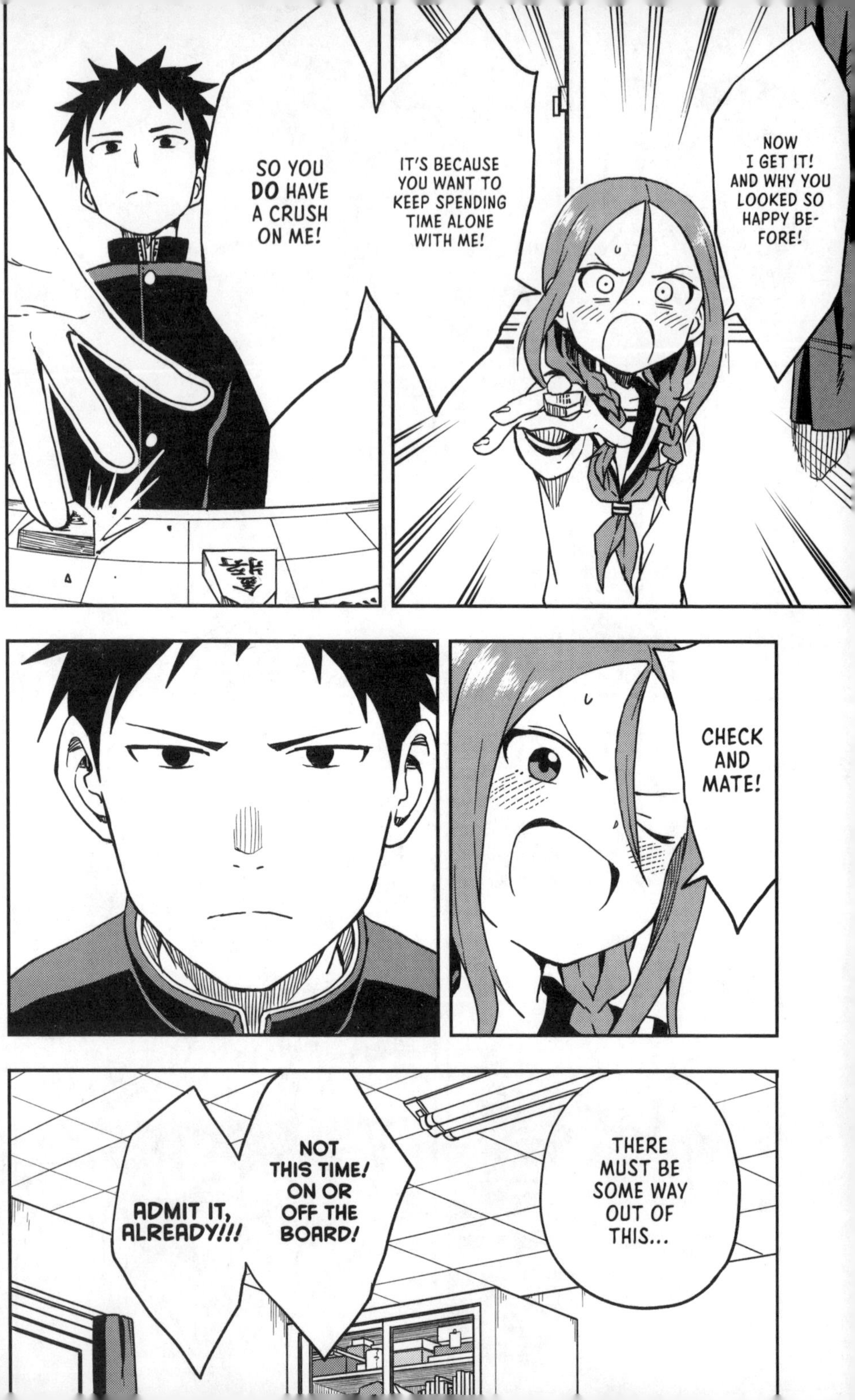
NOW I GET IT! AND WHY YOU LOOKED SO HAPPY BE-FORE!
IT'S BECAUSE YOU WANT TO KEEP SPENDING TIME ALONE WITH ME!
SO YOU **DO** HAVE A CRUSH ON ME!
CHECK AND MATE!
THERE MUST BE SOME WAY OUT OF THIS...
NOT THIS TIME! ON OR OFF THE BOARD!
ADMIT IT, ALREADY!!!

GAME 6 RECORD

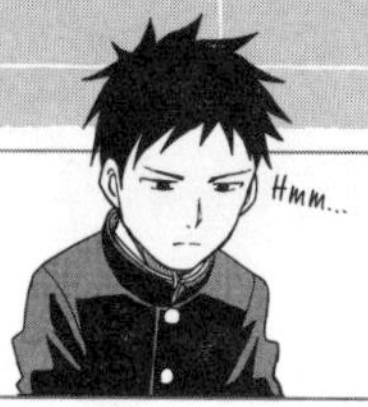
Hmm...

▲ BLACK (SENTE): AYUMU TANAKA △ WHITE (GOTE): URUSHI YAOTOME

(WHITE WINS ON MOVE 54, △ G×2H)

◁URUSHI: L, P×2

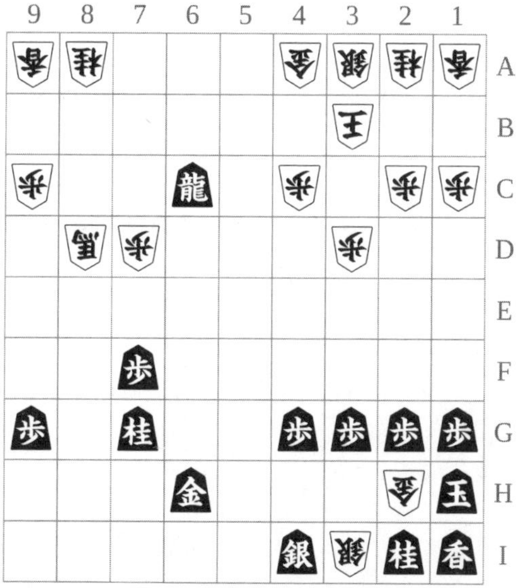
9 8 7 6 5 4 3 2 1
A
B
C
D
E
F
G
H
I

▲AAYUMU: R, B, G, S, P×3

▲ P-7F	△ P-3D
▲ P-6F	△ P-8D
▲ R-6H	△ P-8E
▲ B-7G	△ S-6B
▲ S-7H	△ P-5D
▲ K-4H	△ K-4B
▲ K-3H	△ K-3B
▲ K-2H	△ G6A-5B
▲ S-3H	△ P-7D
▲ S-6G	△ P-6D
▲ P-5F	△ P-6E
▲ P×6E	△ B×7G+
▲ N×7G	△ P-8F
▲ P×8F	△ R×8F
▲ S-6F	△ R-8I+
▲ P-5E	△ P×5E
▲ S×5E	△ +R×9I
▲ P-6D	△ B×5G
▲ R-6E	△ B-8D+
▲ S-5D	△ P×6H
▲ G4I-5H	△ P×6I+
▲ P-6C+	△ S×6C
▲ S×6C+	△ G×6C
▲ R×6C+	△ +P-6H
▲ G×6H	△ +R-4I
▲ S×4I	△ S×3I
▲ K-1H	△ G×2H

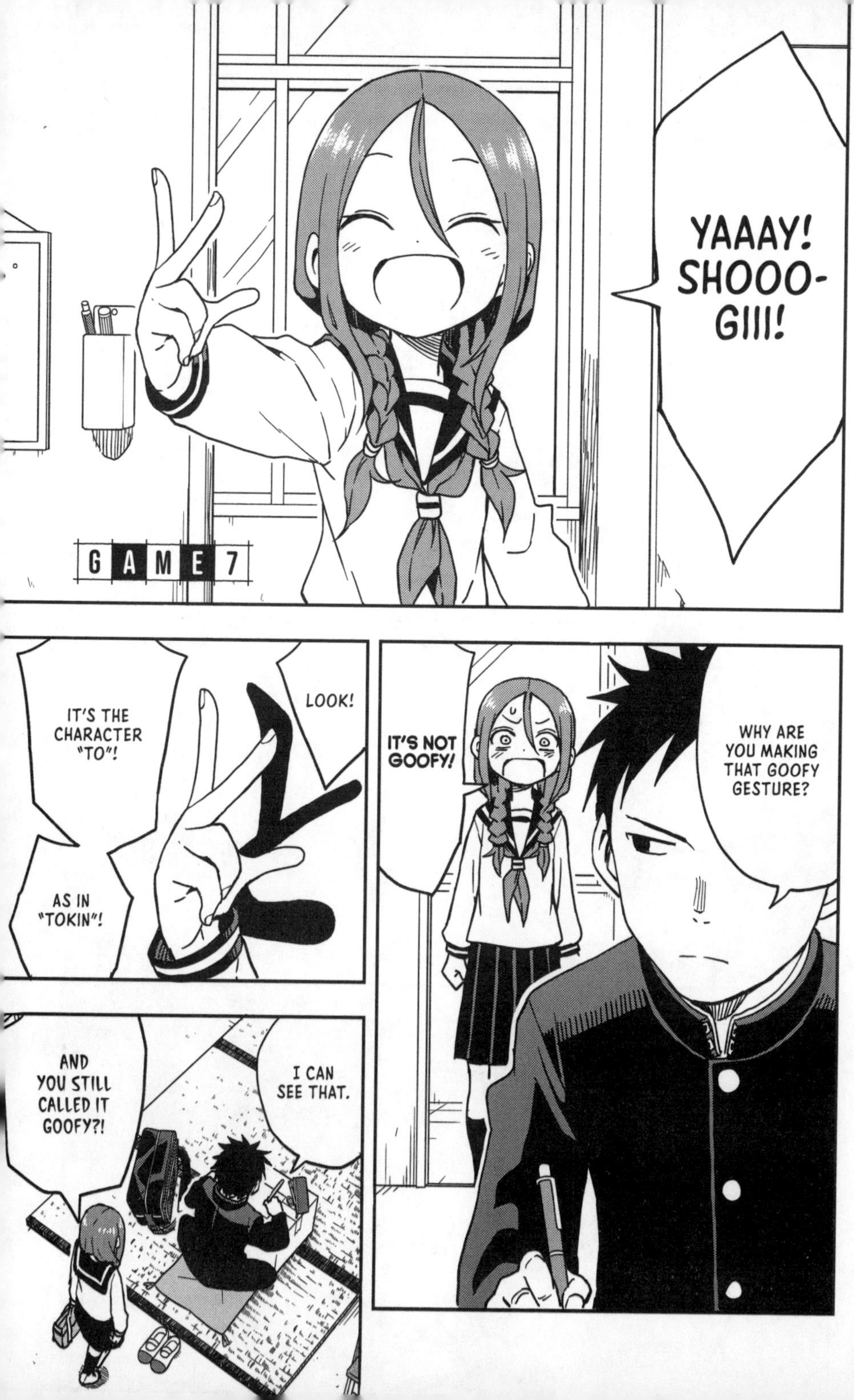
YAAAY! SHOOO-GIII!
GAME 7
WHY ARE YOU MAKING THAT GOOFY GESTURE?
IT'S NOT GOOFY!
LOOK!
IT'S THE CHARACTER "TO"!
AS IN "TOKIN"!
I CAN SEE THAT.
AND YOU STILL CALLED IT GOOFY?!

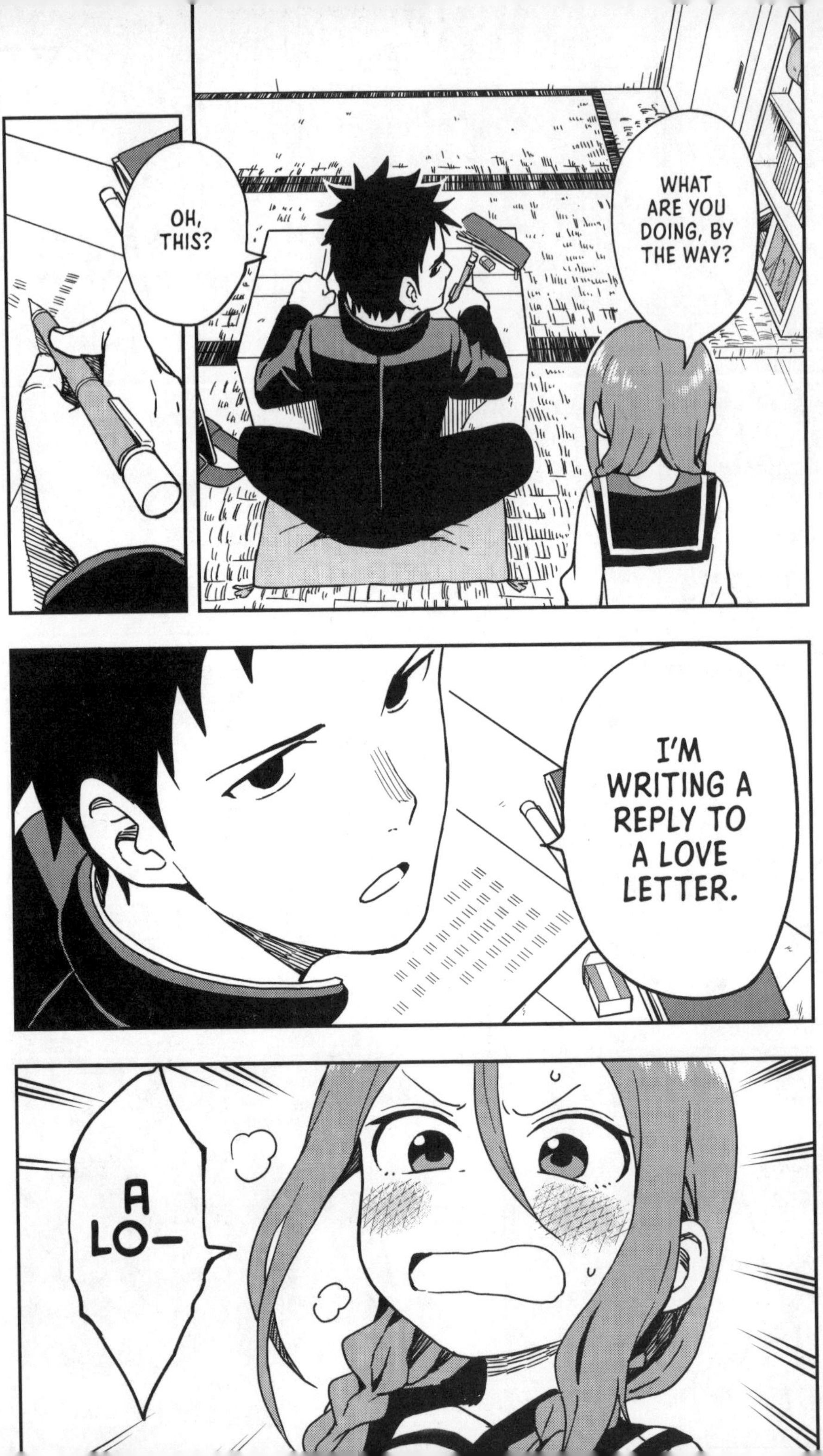
WHAT ARE YOU DOING, BY THE WAY?
OH, THIS?
I'M WRITING A REPLY TO A LOVE LETTER.
A LO—

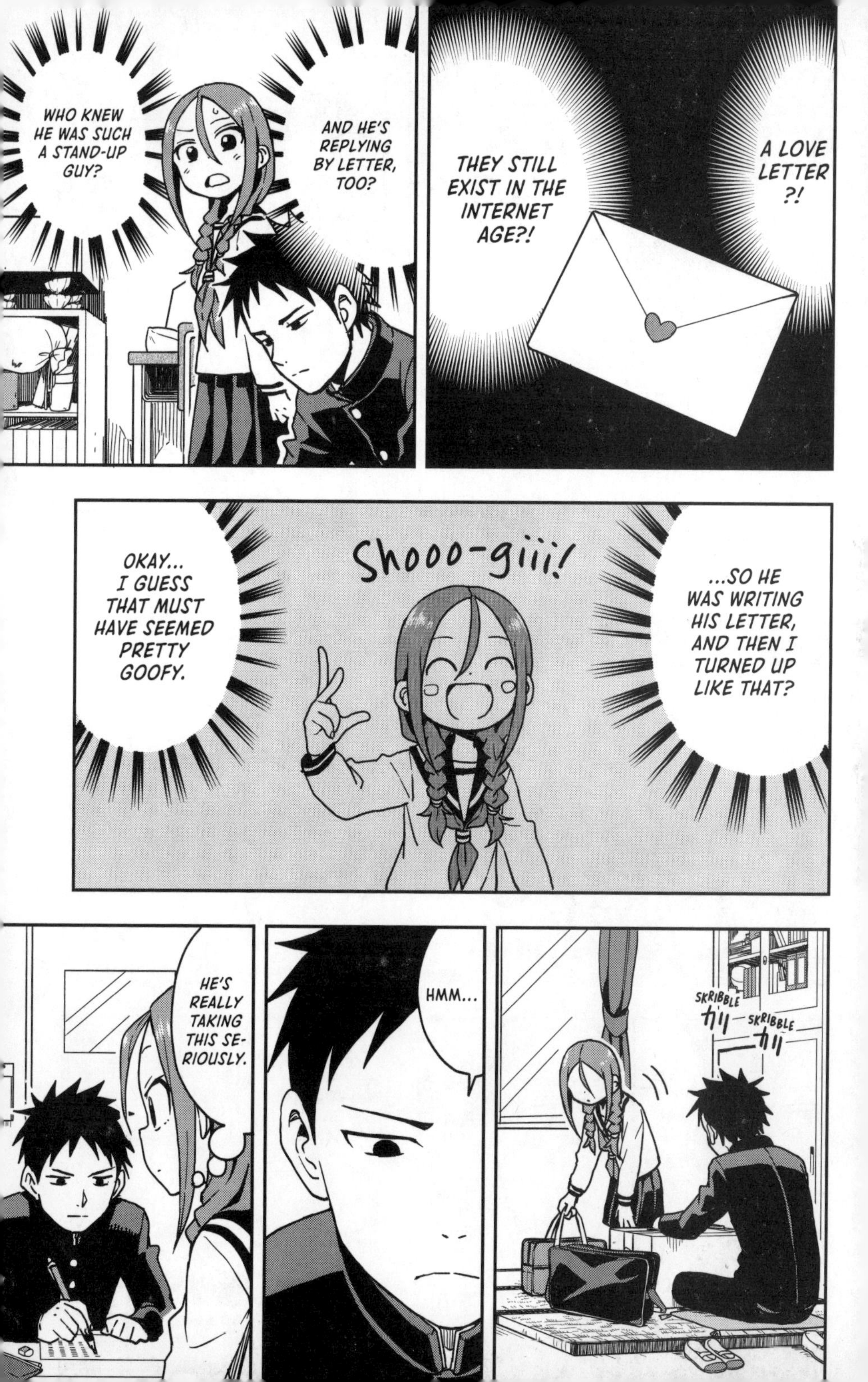
A LOVE LETTER ?!
THEY STILL EXIST IN THE INTERNET AGE?!
AND HE'S REPLYING BY LETTER, TOO?
WHO KNEW HE WAS SUCH A STAND-UP GUY?
...SO HE WAS WRITING HIS LETTER, AND THEN I TURNED UP LIKE THAT?
Shooo-giii!
OKAY... I GUESS THAT MUST HAVE SEEMED PRETTY GOOFY.
SKRIBBLE カリ
SKRIBBLE カリ
HMM...
HE'S REALLY TAKING THIS SE-RIOUSLY.

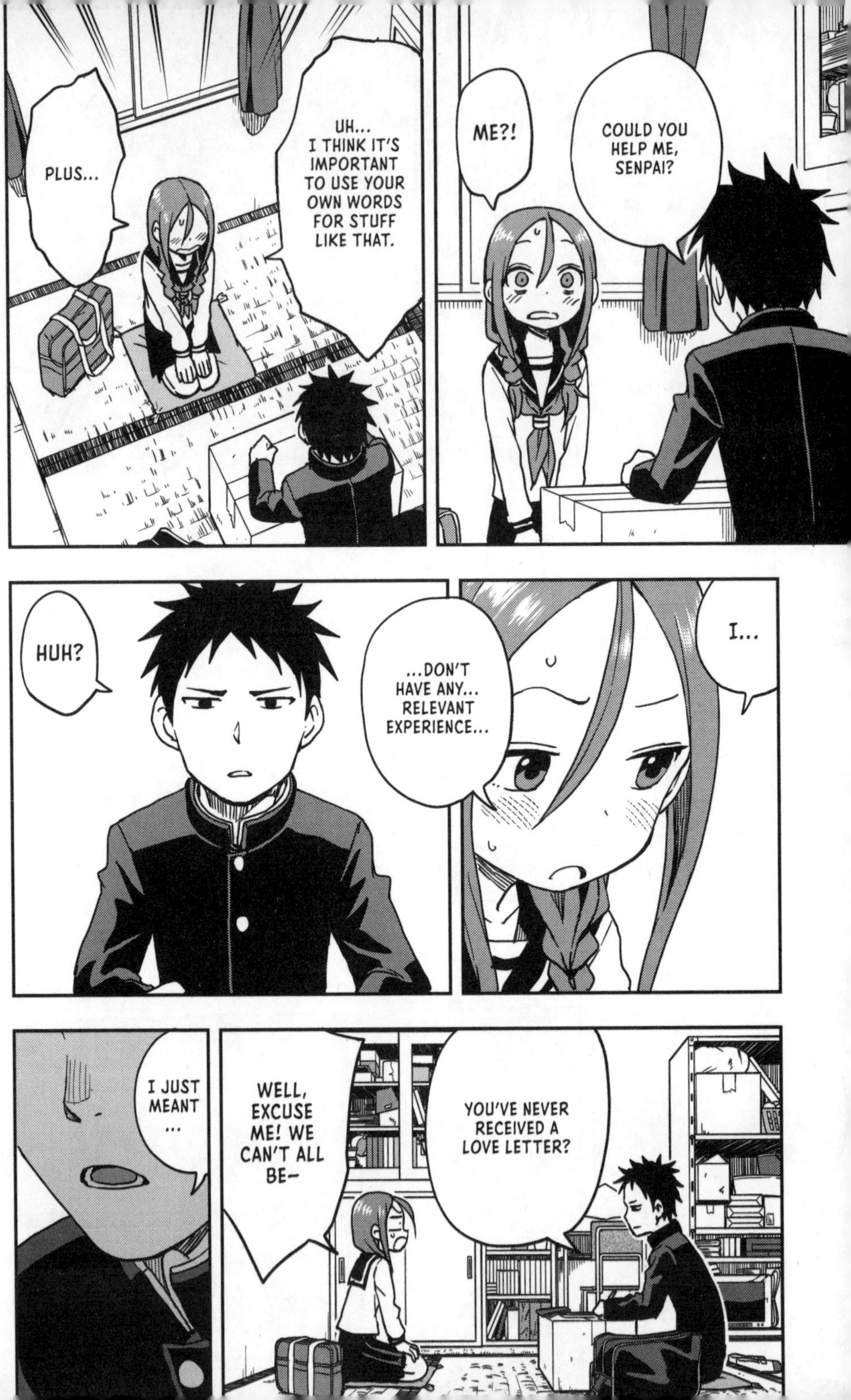
COULD YOU HELP ME, SENPAI?
ME?!
UH... I THINK IT'S IMPORTANT TO USE YOUR OWN WORDS FOR STUFF LIKE THAT.
PLUS...
I...
...DON'T HAVE ANY... RELEVANT EXPERIENCE...
HUH?
YOU'VE NEVER RECEIVED A LOVE LETTER?
WELL, EXCUSE ME! WE CAN'T ALL BE–
I JUST MEANT ...

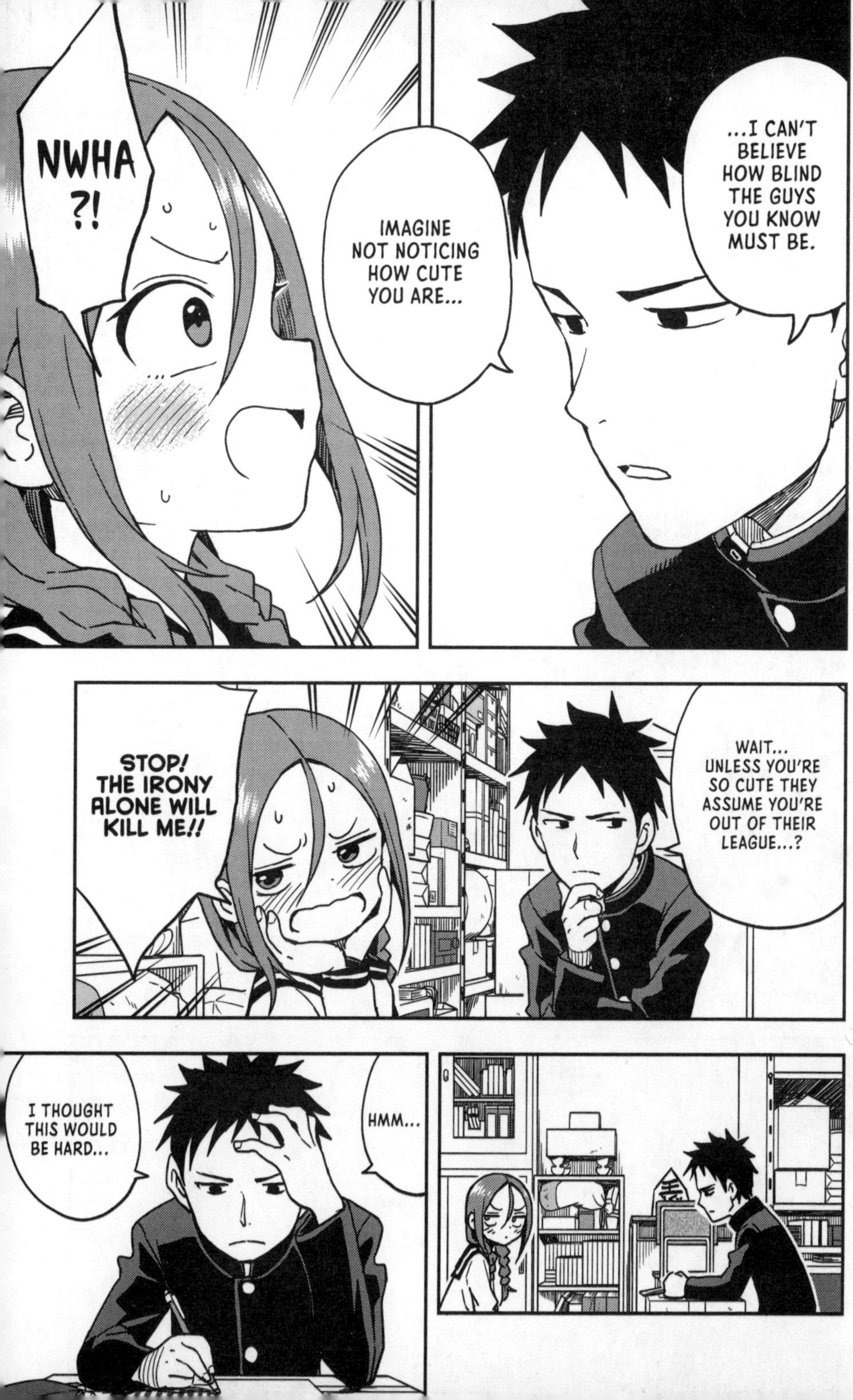
...I CAN'T BELIEVE HOW BLIND THE GUYS YOU KNOW MUST BE.
IMAGINE NOT NOTICING HOW CUTE YOU ARE...
NWHA ?!
WAIT... UNLESS YOU'RE SO CUTE THEY ASSUME YOU'RE OUT OF THEIR LEAGUE...?
STOP! THE IRONY ALONE WILL KILL ME!!
HMM...
I THOUGHT THIS WOULD BE HARD...

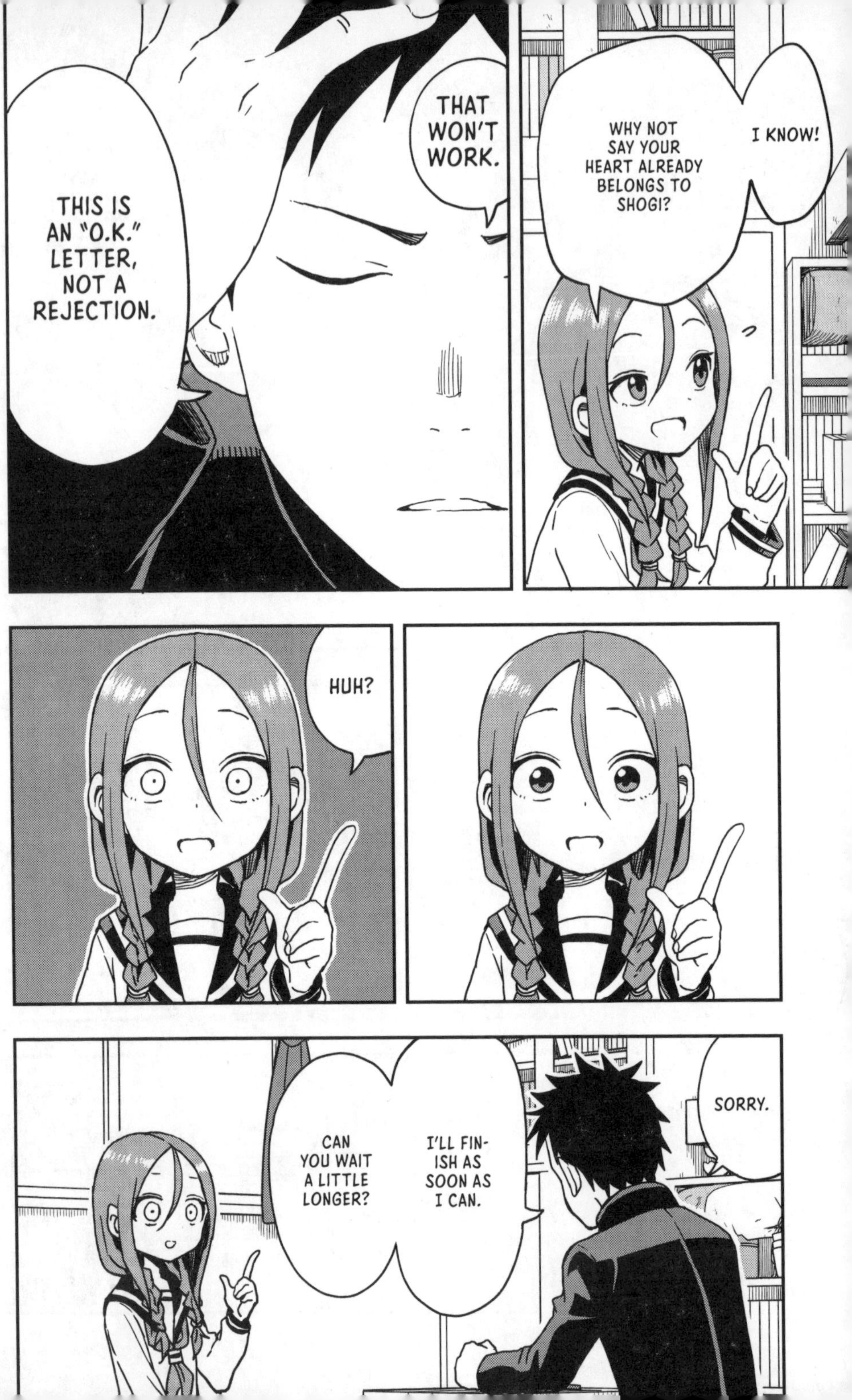
I KNOW!
WHY NOT SAY YOUR HEART ALREADY BELONGS TO SHOGI?
THAT WON'T WORK.
THIS IS AN "O.K." LETTER, NOT A REJECTION.
HUH?
SORRY.
I'LL FIN-ISH AS SOON AS I CAN.
CAN YOU WAIT A LITTLE LONGER?

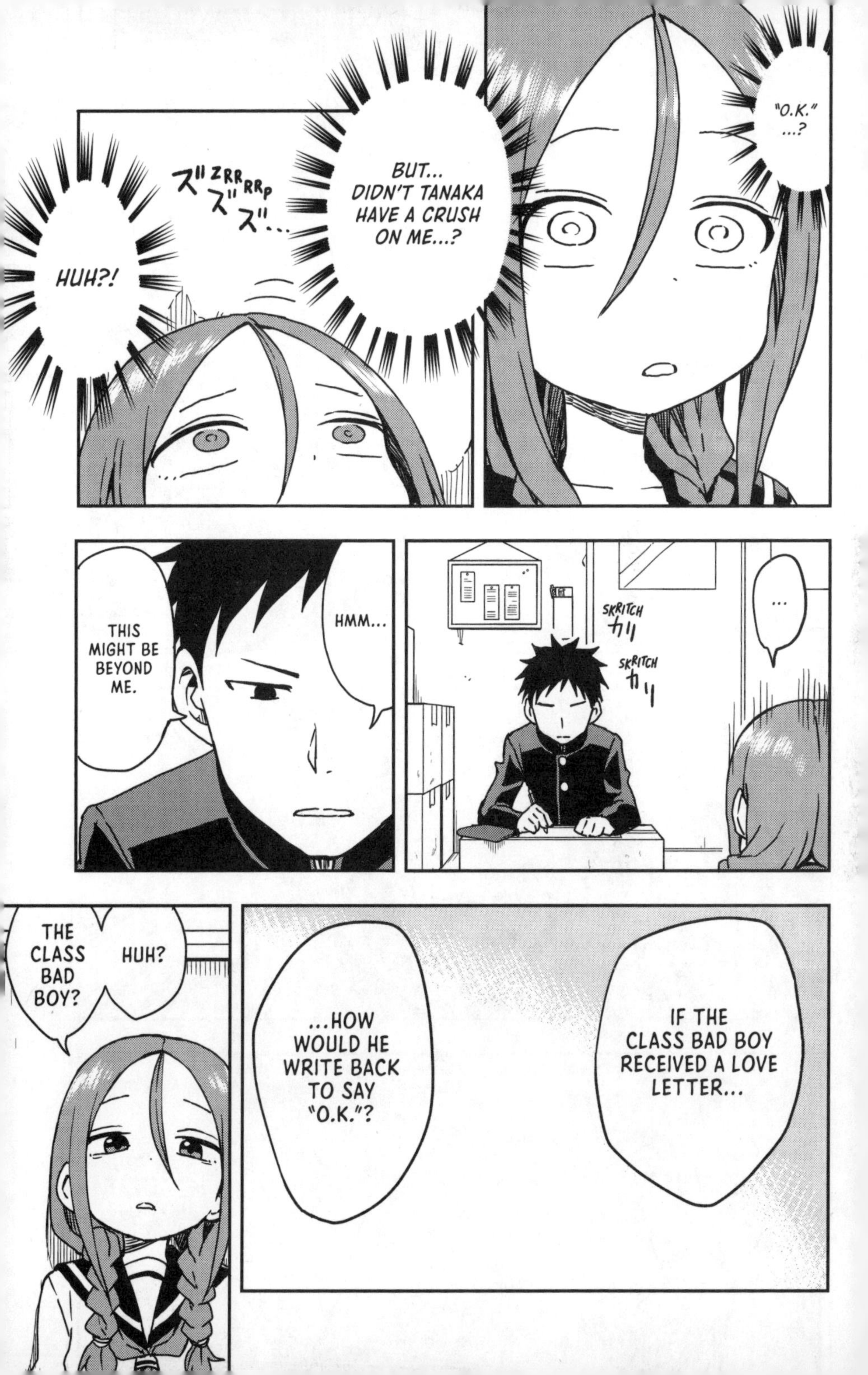
"O.K." ...?
BUT... DIDN'T TANAKA HAVE A CRUSH ON ME...?
ズ" ZRRRRRP ズ"ズ"...
HUH?!
...
SKRITCH カリ
SKRITCH カリ
HMM...
THIS MIGHT BE BEYOND ME.
IF THE CLASS BAD BOY RECEIVED A LOVE LETTER...
...HOW WOULD HE WRITE BACK TO SAY "O.K."?
HUH?
THE CLASS BAD BOY?

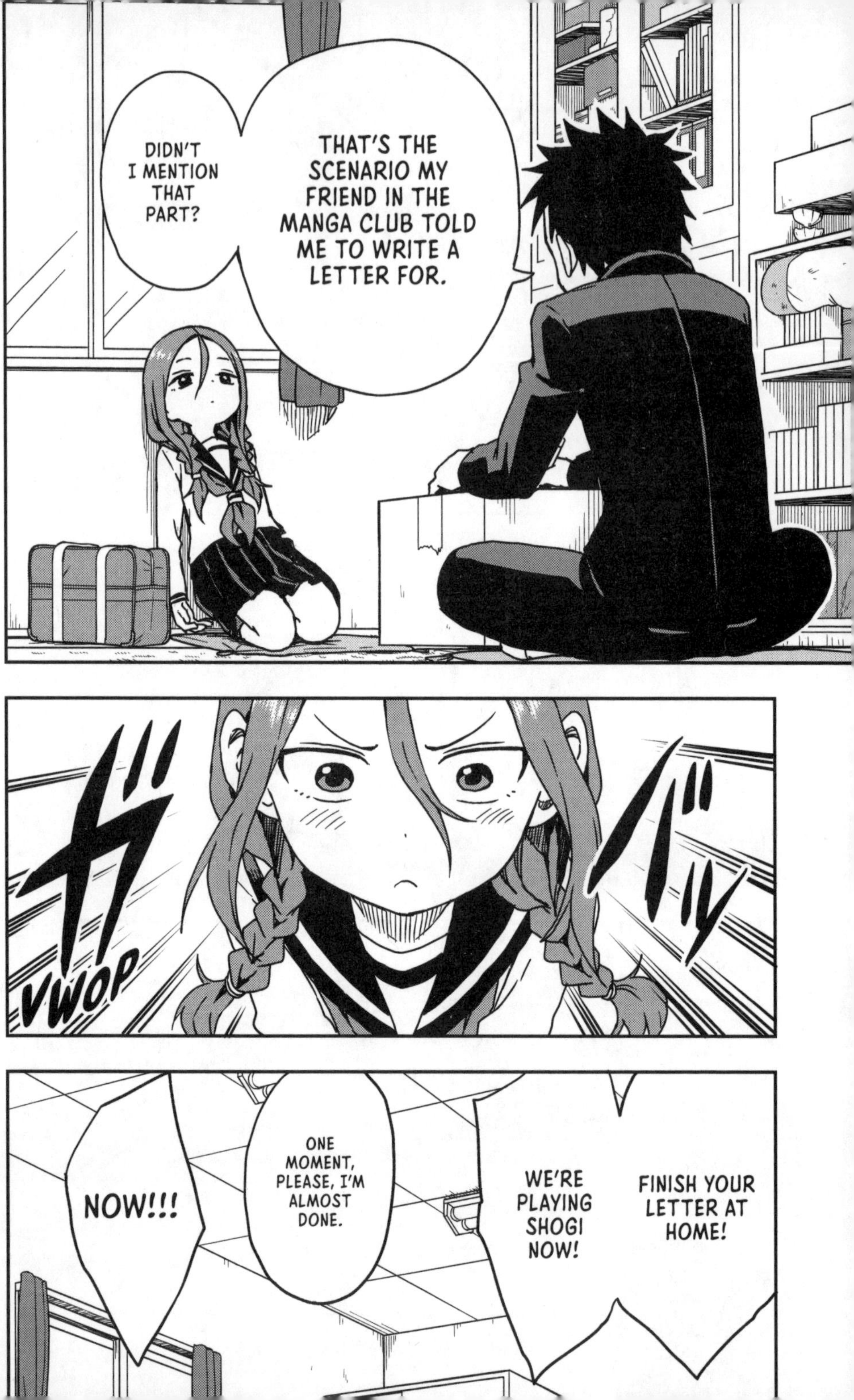
THAT'S THE SCENARIO MY FRIEND IN THE MANGA CLUB TOLD ME TO WRITE A LETTER FOR.
DIDN'T I MENTION THAT PART?
VWOP
FINISH YOUR LETTER AT HOME!
WE'RE PLAYING SHOGI NOW!
ONE MOMENT, PLEASE, I'M ALMOST DONE.
NOW!!!

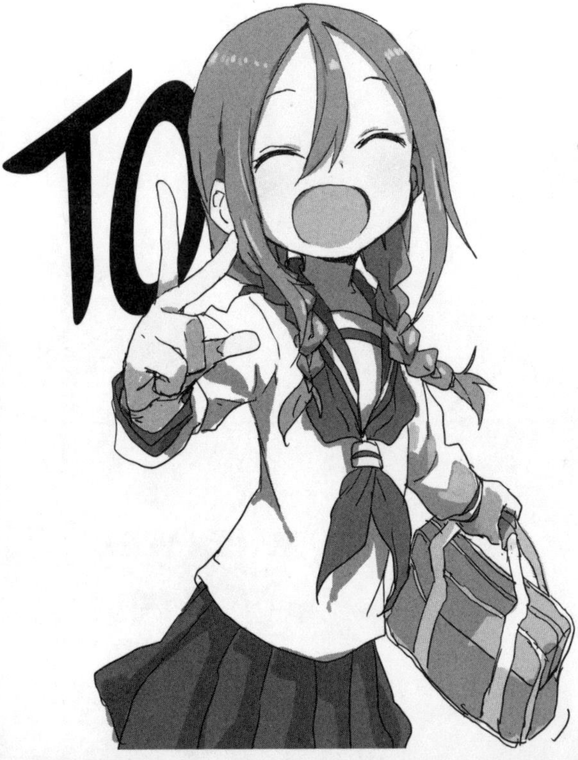
TO

WHEN WILL
AYUMU
MAKE HIS
MOVE?

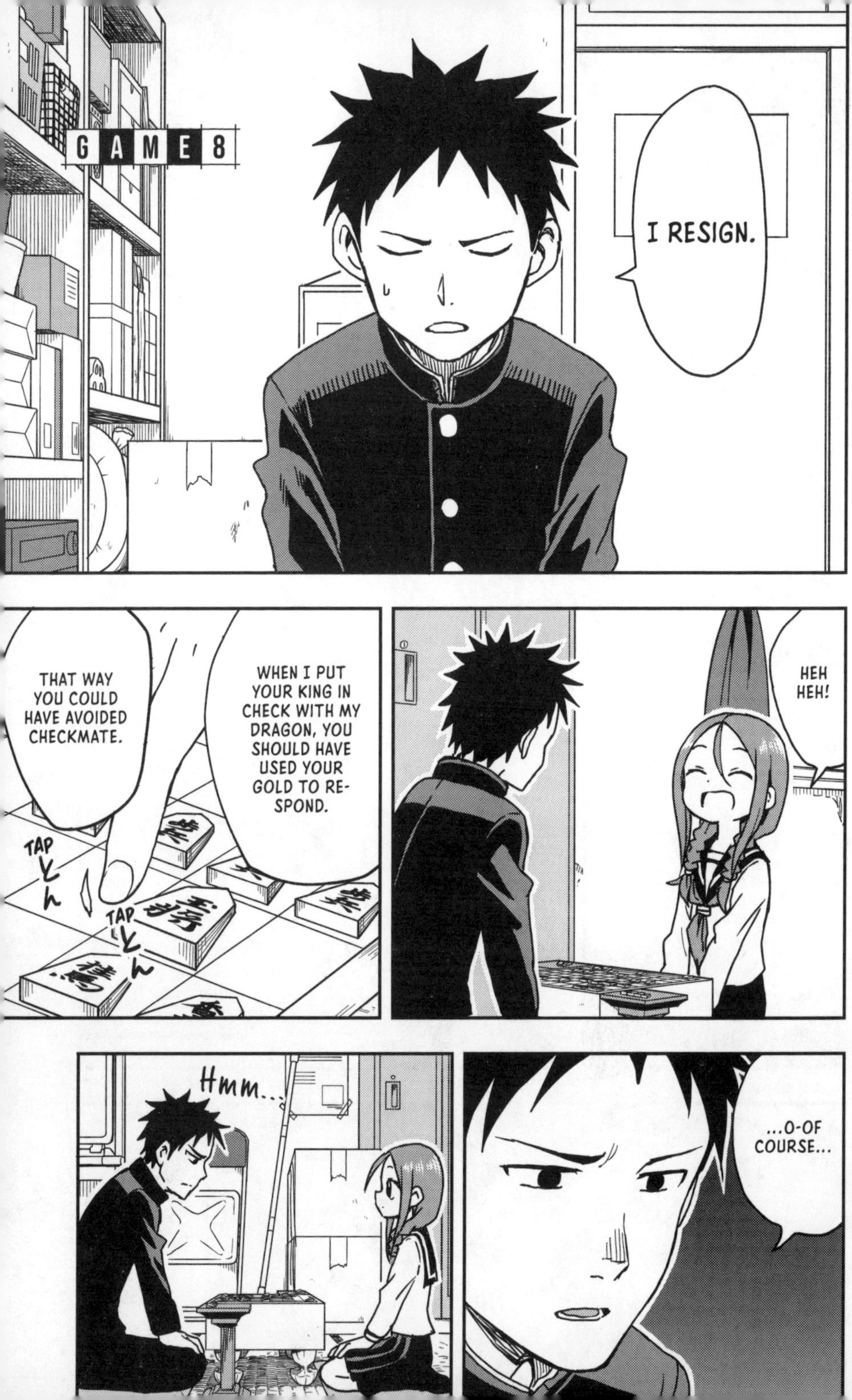
GAME 8
I RESIGN.
HEH HEH!
WHEN I PUT YOUR KING IN CHECK WITH MY DRAGON, YOU SHOULD HAVE USED YOUR GOLD TO RE-SPOND.
THAT WAY YOU COULD HAVE AVOIDED CHECKMATE.
TAP とん
TAP とん
...O-OF COURSE...
Hmm...

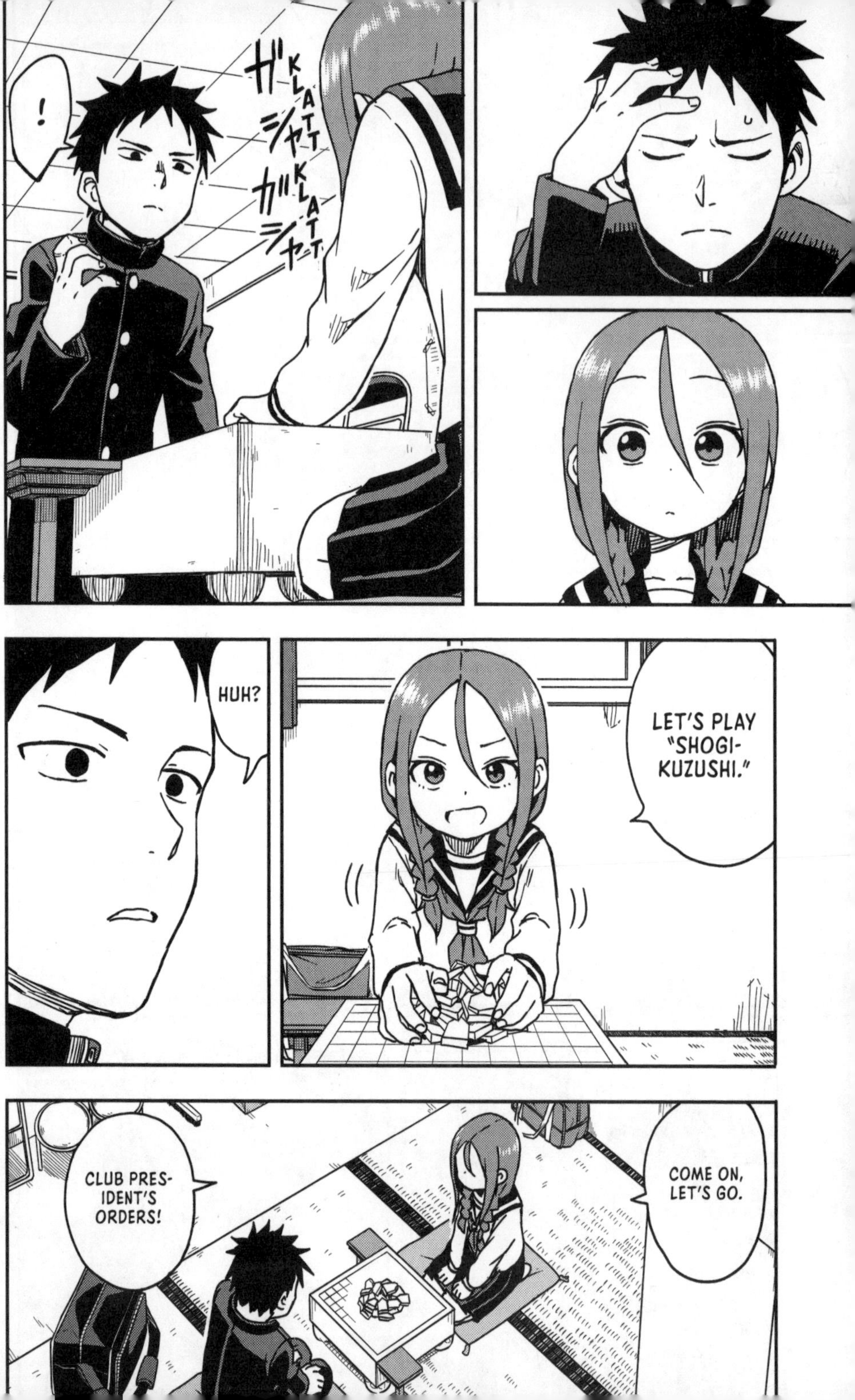
!
ガシャ
KLATT
ガシャ
KLATT
LET'S PLAY "SHOGI-KUZUSHI."
HUH?
COME ON, LET'S GO.
CLUB PRESIDENT'S ORDERS!

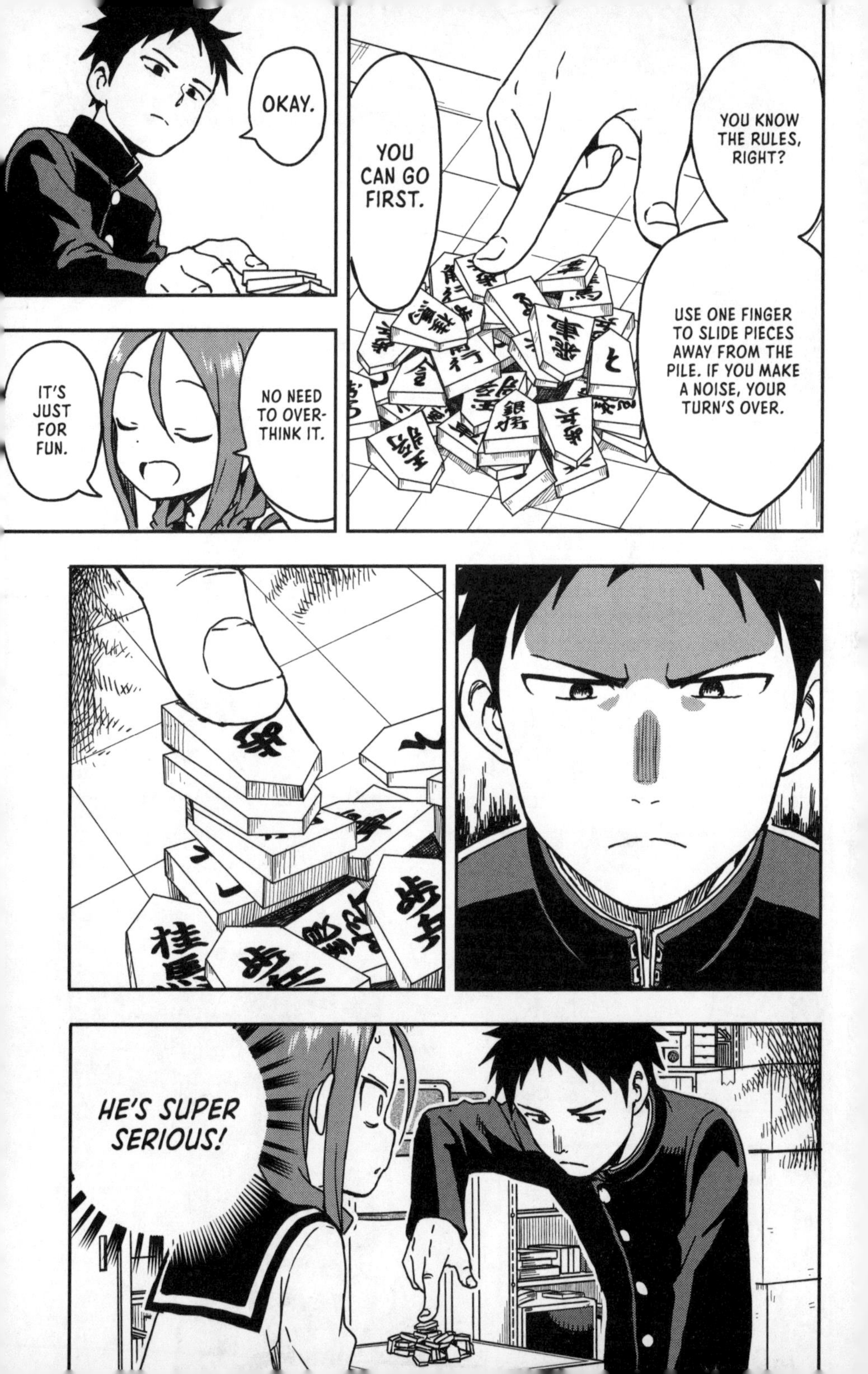
YOU KNOW THE RULES, RIGHT?
YOU CAN GO FIRST.
USE ONE FINGER TO SLIDE PIECES AWAY FROM THE PILE. IF YOU MAKE A NOISE, YOUR TURN'S OVER.
OKAY.
NO NEED TO OVER-THINK IT.
IT'S JUST FOR FUN.
HE'S SUPER SERIOUS!

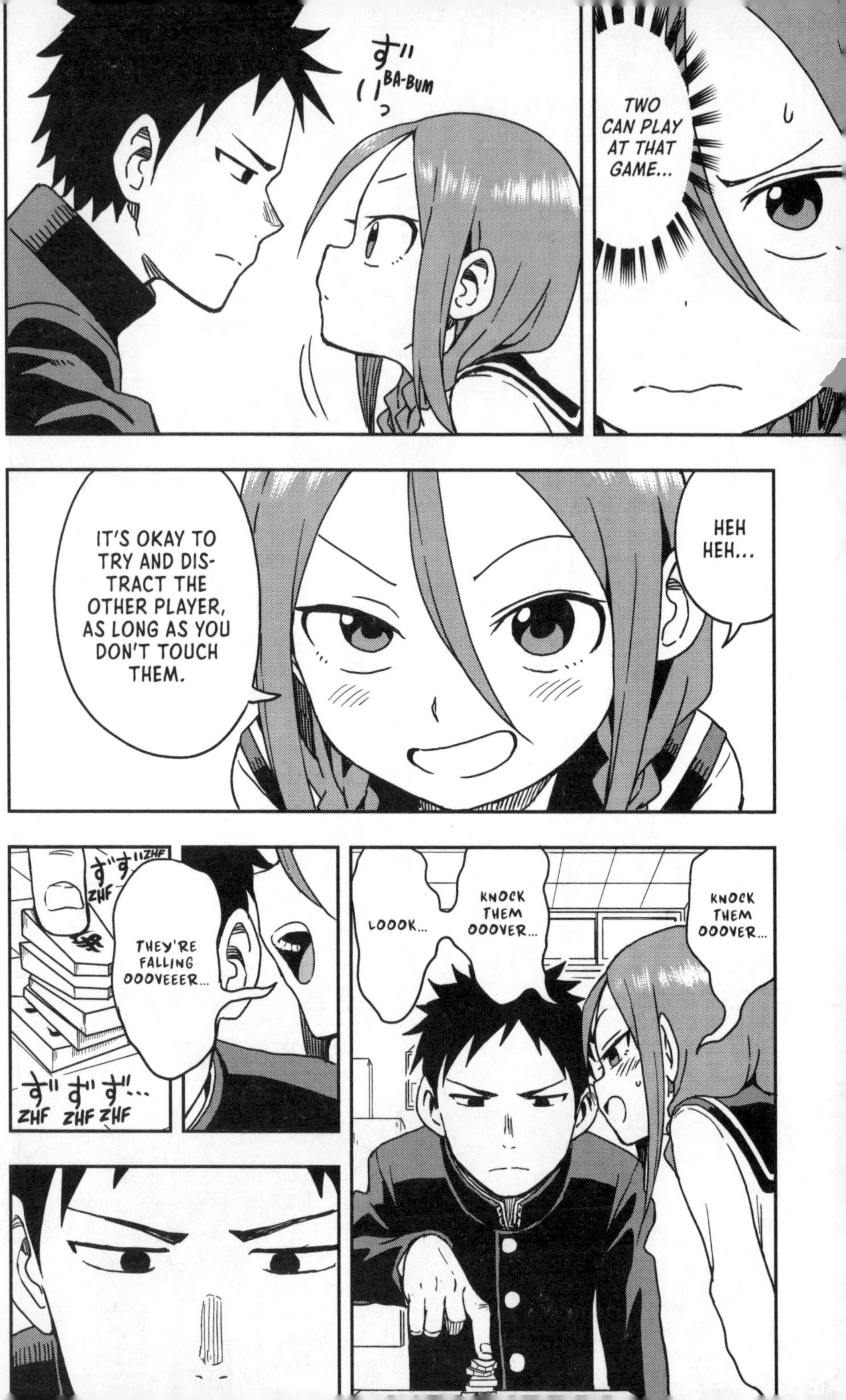
TWO CAN PLAY AT THAT GAME...
ず BA-BUM
HEH HEH...
IT'S OKAY TO TRY AND DIS-TRACT THE OTHER PLAYER, AS LONG AS YOU DON'T TOUCH THEM.
KNOCK THEM OOOVER...
KNOCK THEM OOOVER...
LOOOK...
ずず ZHF ZHF
THEY'RE FALLING OOOVEEER...
ずずず… ZHF ZHF ZHF

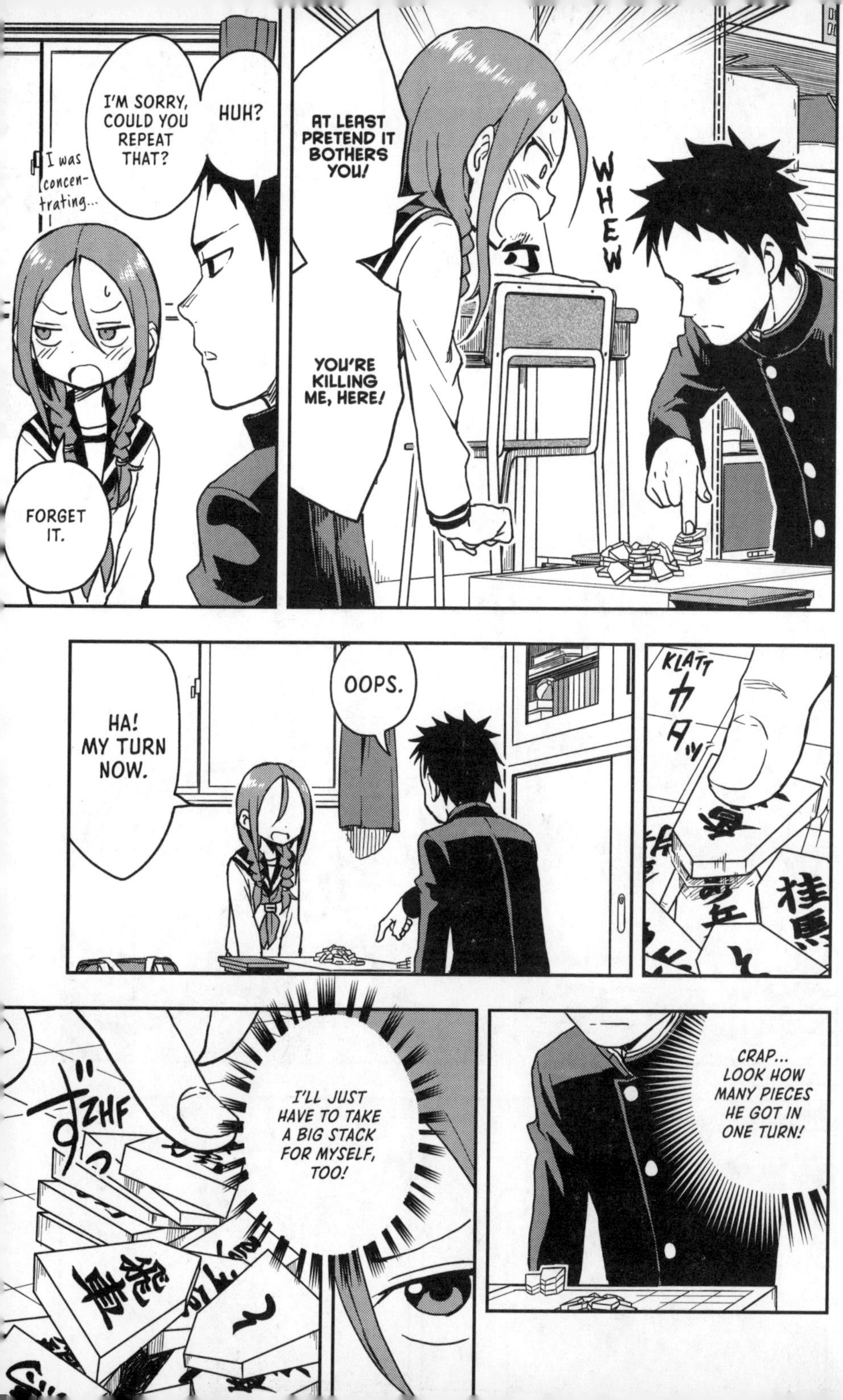

WHEW
AT LEAST PRETEND IT BOTHERS YOU!
YOU'RE KILLING ME, HERE!
HUH?
I'M SORRY, COULD YOU REPEAT THAT?
I was concen-trating...
FORGET IT.
KLATT
カタッ
OOPS.
HA! MY TURN NOW.
CRAP... LOOK HOW MANY PIECES HE GOT IN ONE TURN!
ZHF
I'LL JUST HAVE TO TAKE A BIG STACK FOR MYSELF, TOO!

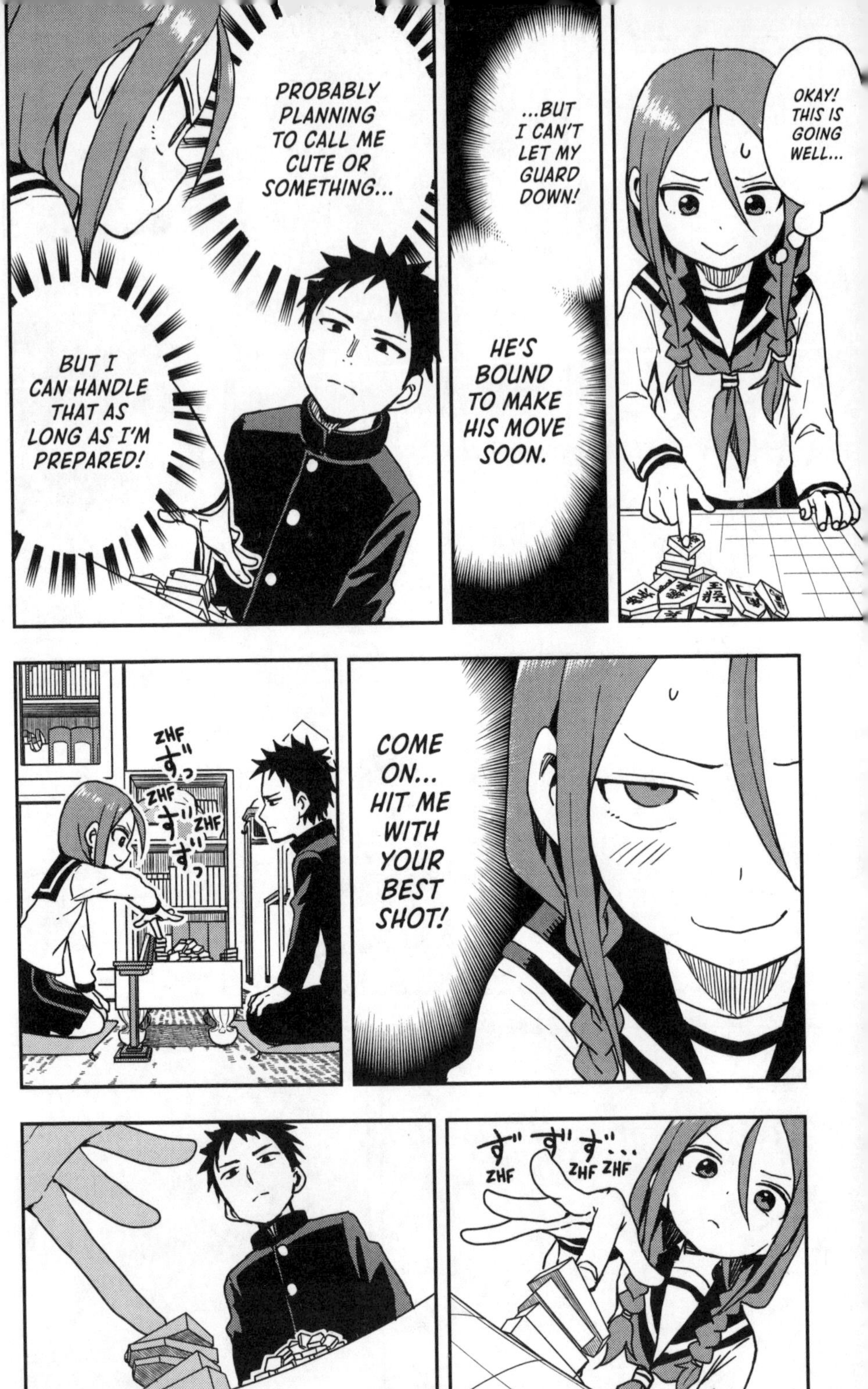
OKAY! THIS IS GOING WELL...
...BUT I CAN'T LET MY GUARD DOWN!
HE'S BOUND TO MAKE HIS MOVE SOON.
PROBABLY PLANNING TO CALL ME CUTE OR SOMETHING...
BUT I CAN HANDLE THAT AS LONG AS I'M PREPARED!
COME ON... HIT ME WITH YOUR BEST SHOT!
ZHF ずっ
ZHF ずっ
ZHF ずっ
ず ZHF
ず ZHF
ず... ZHF

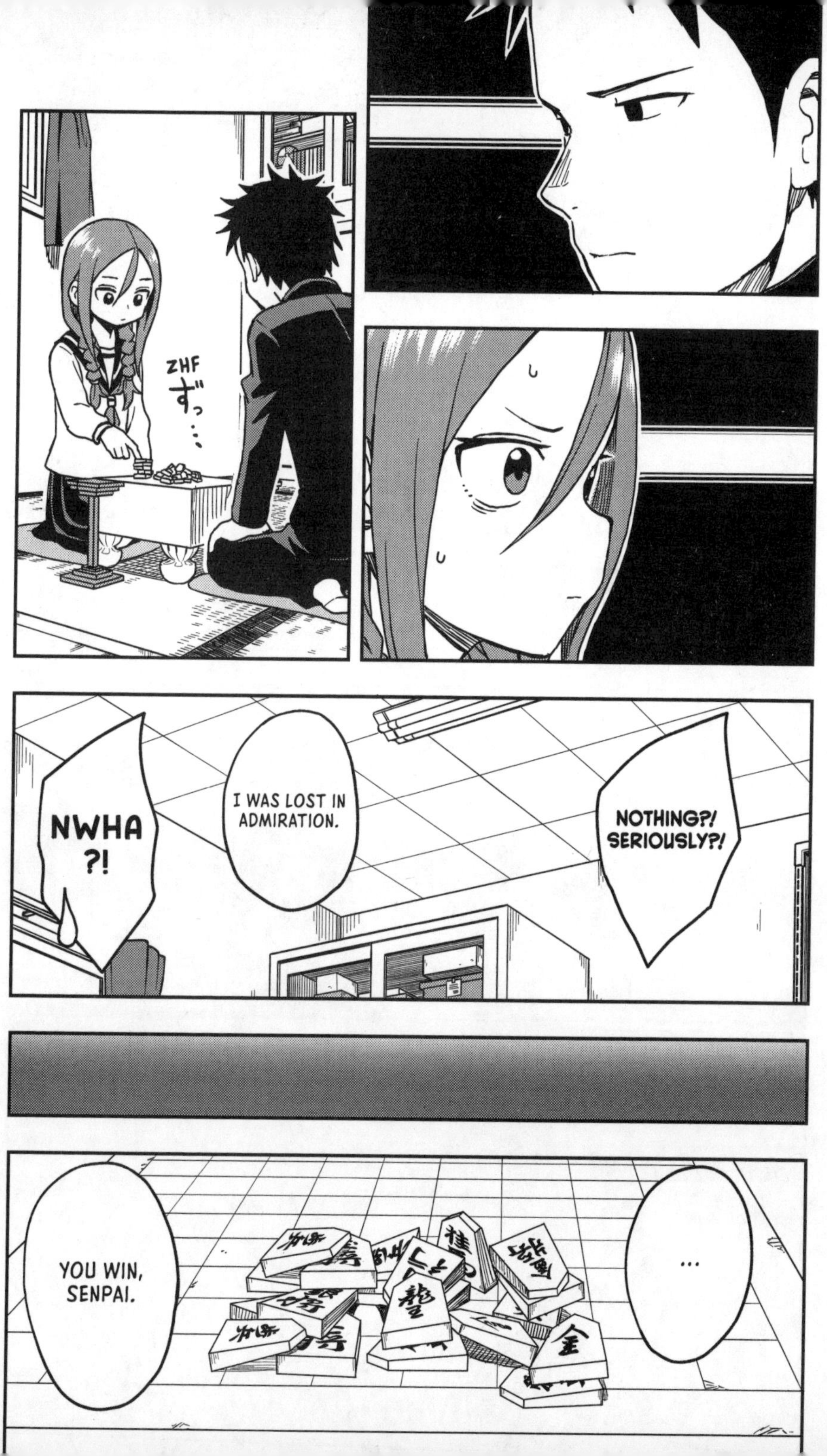
ZHF
ずっ…
NOTHING?! SERIOUSLY?!
I WAS LOST IN ADMIRATION.
NWHA ?!
...
YOU WIN, SENPAI.

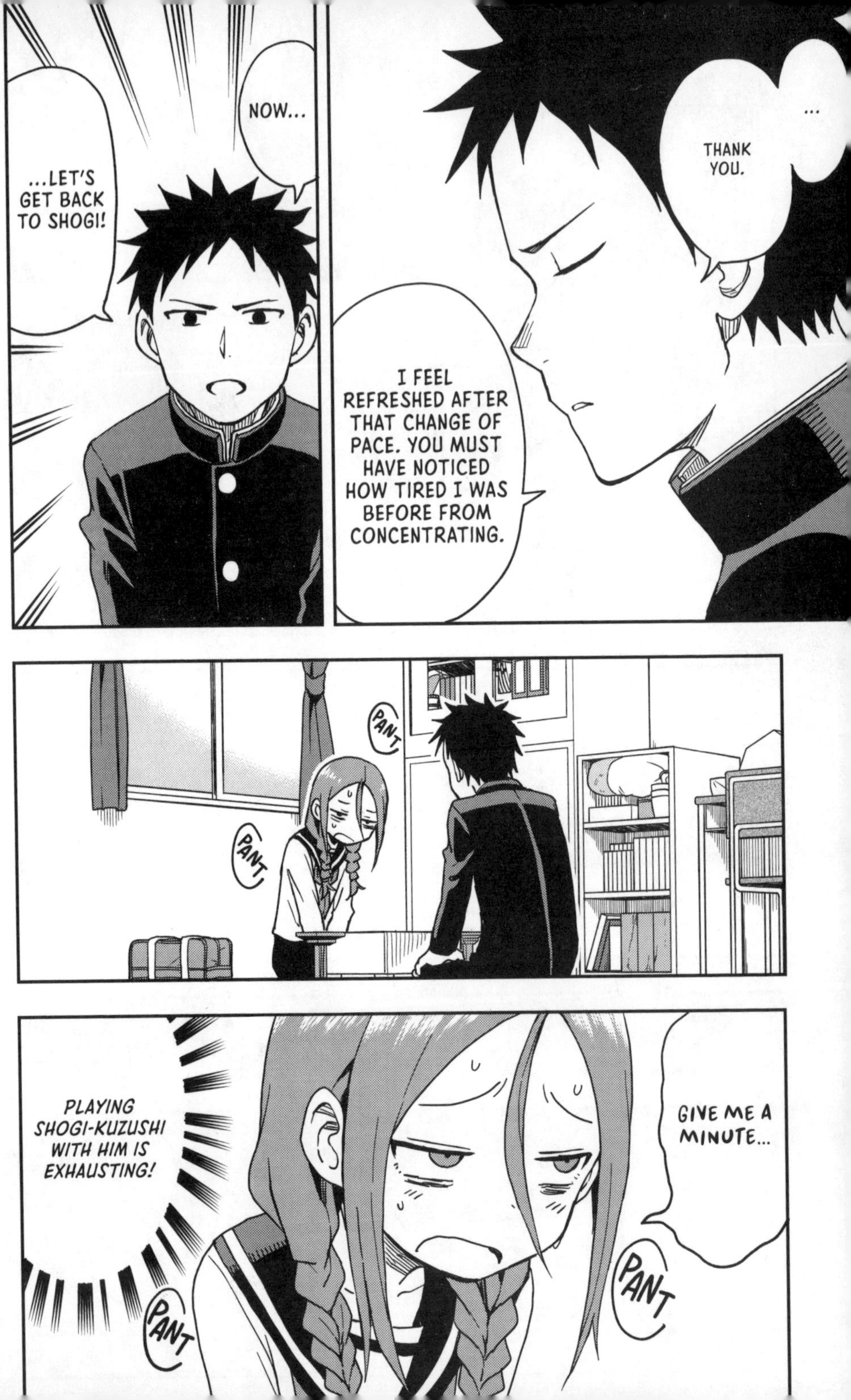
...
THANK YOU.
I FEEL REFRESHED AFTER THAT CHANGE OF PACE. YOU MUST HAVE NOTICED HOW TIRED I WAS BEFORE FROM CONCENTRATING.
NOW...
...LET'S GET BACK TO SHOGI!
PANT
PANT
GIVE ME A MINUTE...
PANT
PLAYING SHOGI-KUZUSHI WITH HIM IS EXHAUSTING!
PANT

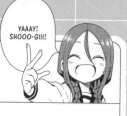

GAME 8 RECORD

▲ BLACK (SENTE): AYUMU TANAKA △ WHITE (GOTE): URUSHI YAOTOME

(WHITE WINS ON MOVE 94, △ G×3H)

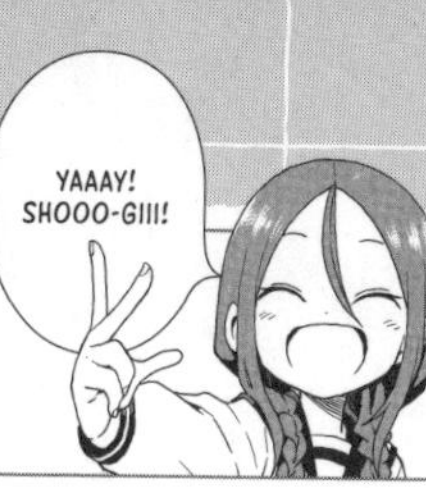
YAAAY! SHOOO-GIII!

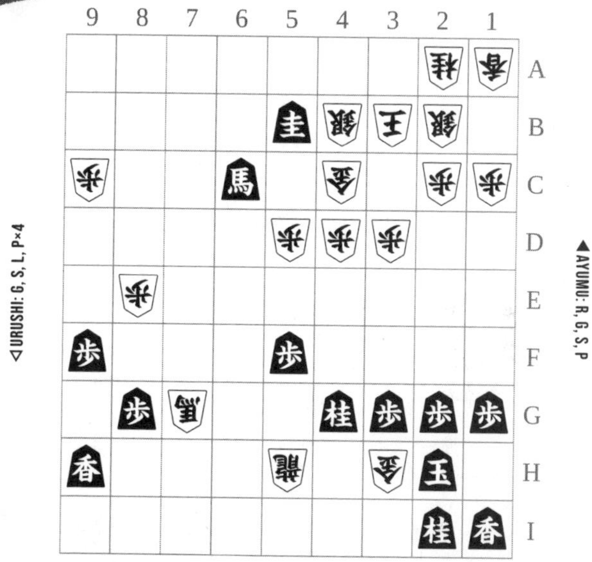
9 8 7 6 5 4 3 2 1
A B C D E F G H I
◁URUSHI: G, S, L, P×4
▲AYUMU: R, G, S, P

▲ P-7F	△ P-8D	▲ S×7F	△ R-7B	▲ P×4B	△ G×4B
▲ P-6F	△ P-3D	▲ G-6G	△ S-2B	▲ N×6D	△ G×4A
▲ R-6H	△ P-8E	▲ P-6D	△ S-7E	▲ P×4D	△ P×4D
▲ B-7G	△ S-7B	▲ S×7E	△ R×7E	▲ P×4C	△ G×4C
▲ S-7H	△ S-8C	▲ B×8B	△ P×6F	▲ G×5B	△ G×4B
▲ S-6G	△ S-8D	▲ G×6F	△ R×7G+	▲ G×4B	△ G4A×4B
▲ P-9F	△ P-7D	▲ G-6G	△ +R-7I	▲ S×5A	△ S×4A
▲ K-4H	△ K-4B	▲ B×9A+	△ N×3E	▲ S×4B+	△ S×4B
▲ K-3H	△ K-3B	▲ +B×8A	△ N×4G+	▲ G×4A	△ S×5A
▲ K-2H	△ P-5D	▲ S×4G	△ +R×4I	▲ G×4B	△ S×4B
▲ S-3H	△ G6A-5B	▲ N×3I	△ P×6B	▲ N-5B+	△ R×6H
▲ G6I-5H	△ P-6D	▲ P-6C+	△ P×6C	▲ L×5H	△ +R×4G
▲ P-5F	△ P-7E	▲ G-7G	△ B×5I	▲ N×4G	△ R×5H+
▲ L-9H	△ P-6E	▲ R×6C+	△ G×6C	▲ S×3H	△ S×3I
▲ P×6E	△ B×7G+	▲ +B×6C	△ B×7G+	▲ K×3I	△ G×4H
▲ N×7G	△ P×7F	▲ P×4B	△ G×4B	▲ K-2H	△ G×3H

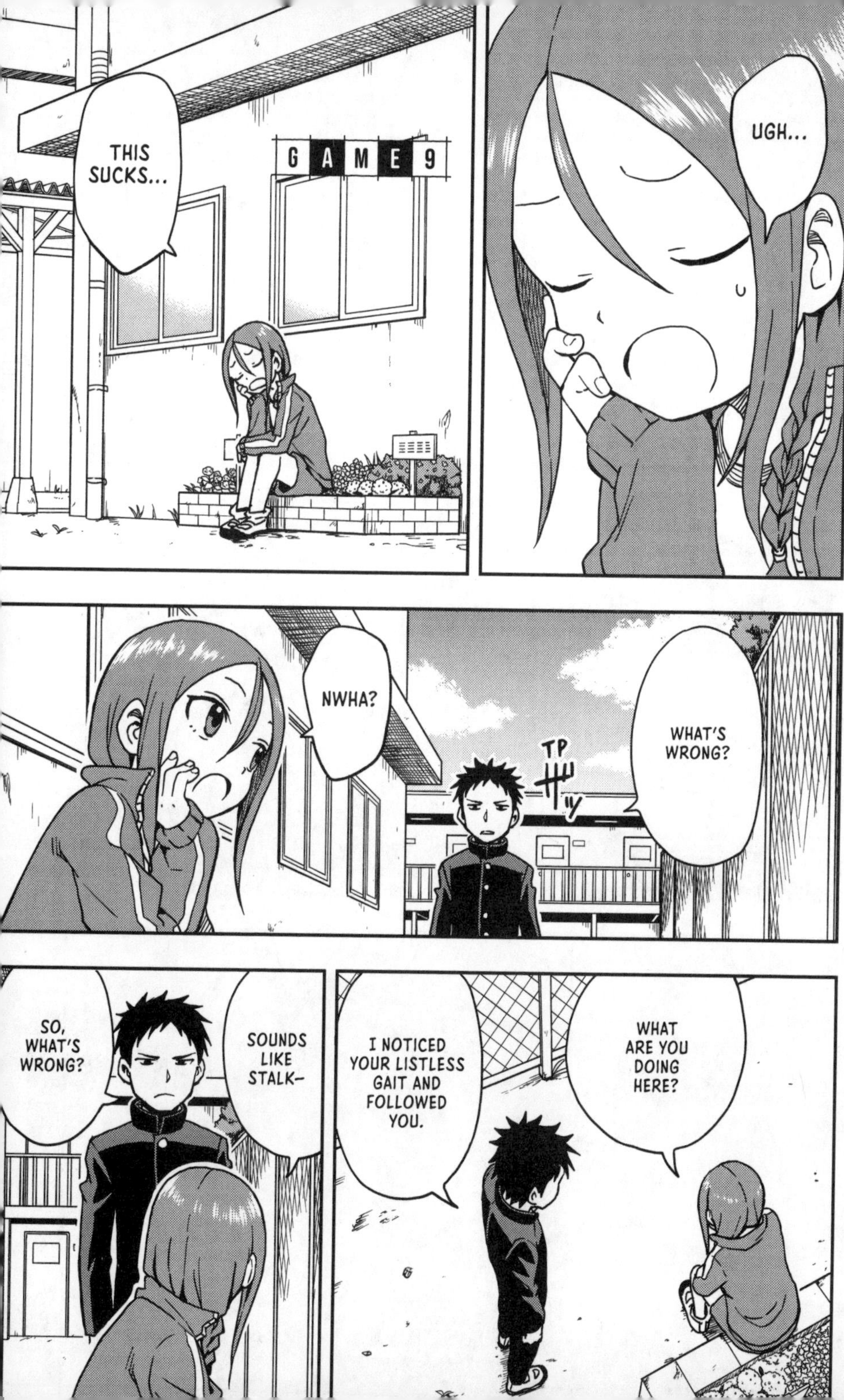
UGH...
GAME 9
THIS SUCKS...
WHAT'S WRONG?
TP
NWHA?
WHAT ARE YOU DOING HERE?
I NOTICED YOUR LISTLESS GAIT AND FOLLOWED YOU.
SOUNDS LIKE STALK–
SO, WHAT'S WRONG?

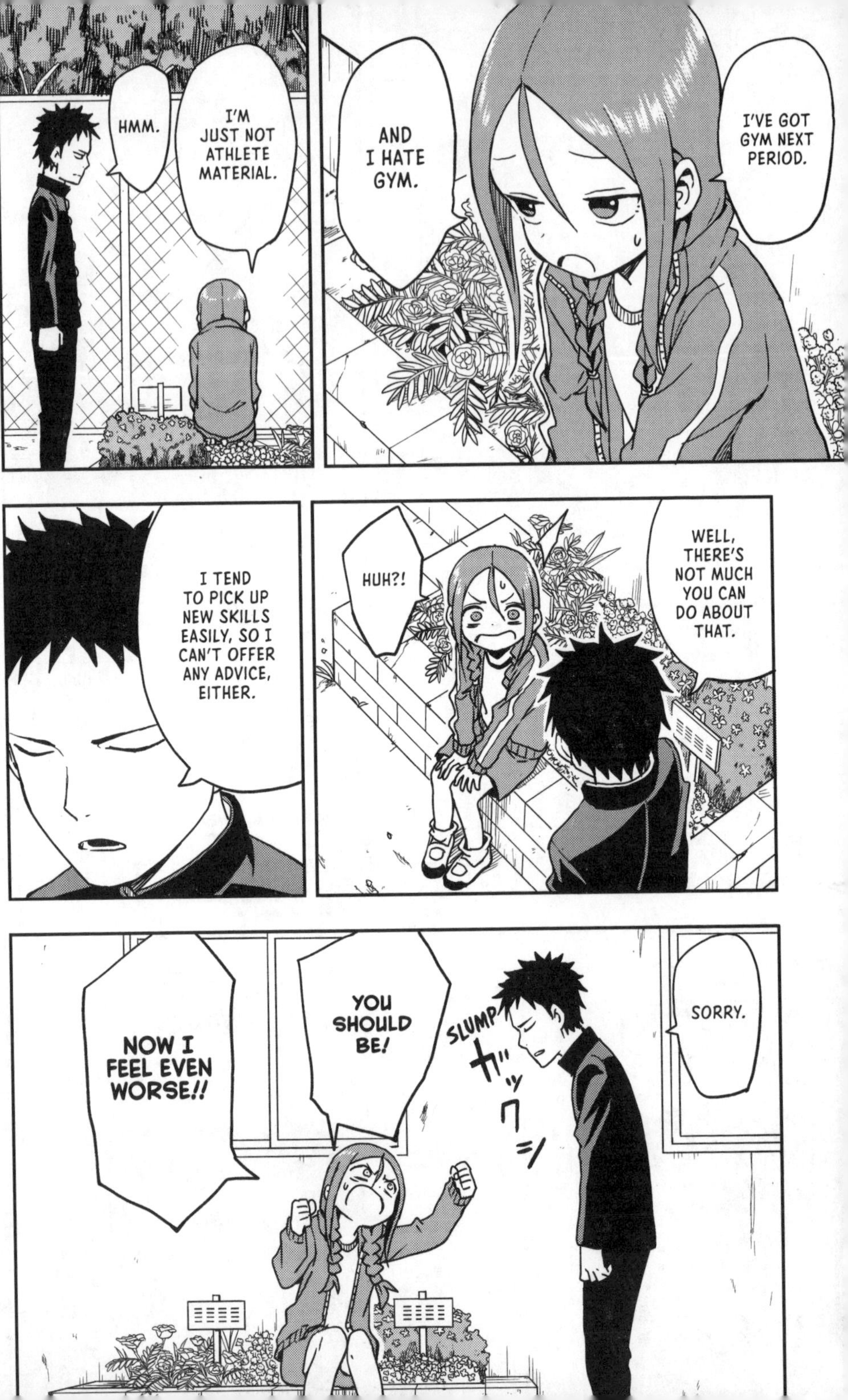
I'VE GOT GYM NEXT PERIOD.
AND I HATE GYM.
I'M JUST NOT ATHLETE MATERIAL.
HMM.
WELL, THERE'S NOT MUCH YOU CAN DO ABOUT THAT.
HUH?!
I TEND TO PICK UP NEW SKILLS EASILY, SO I CAN'T OFFER ANY ADVICE, EITHER.
SORRY.
SLUMP
YOU SHOULD BE!
NOW I FEEL EVEN WORSE!!

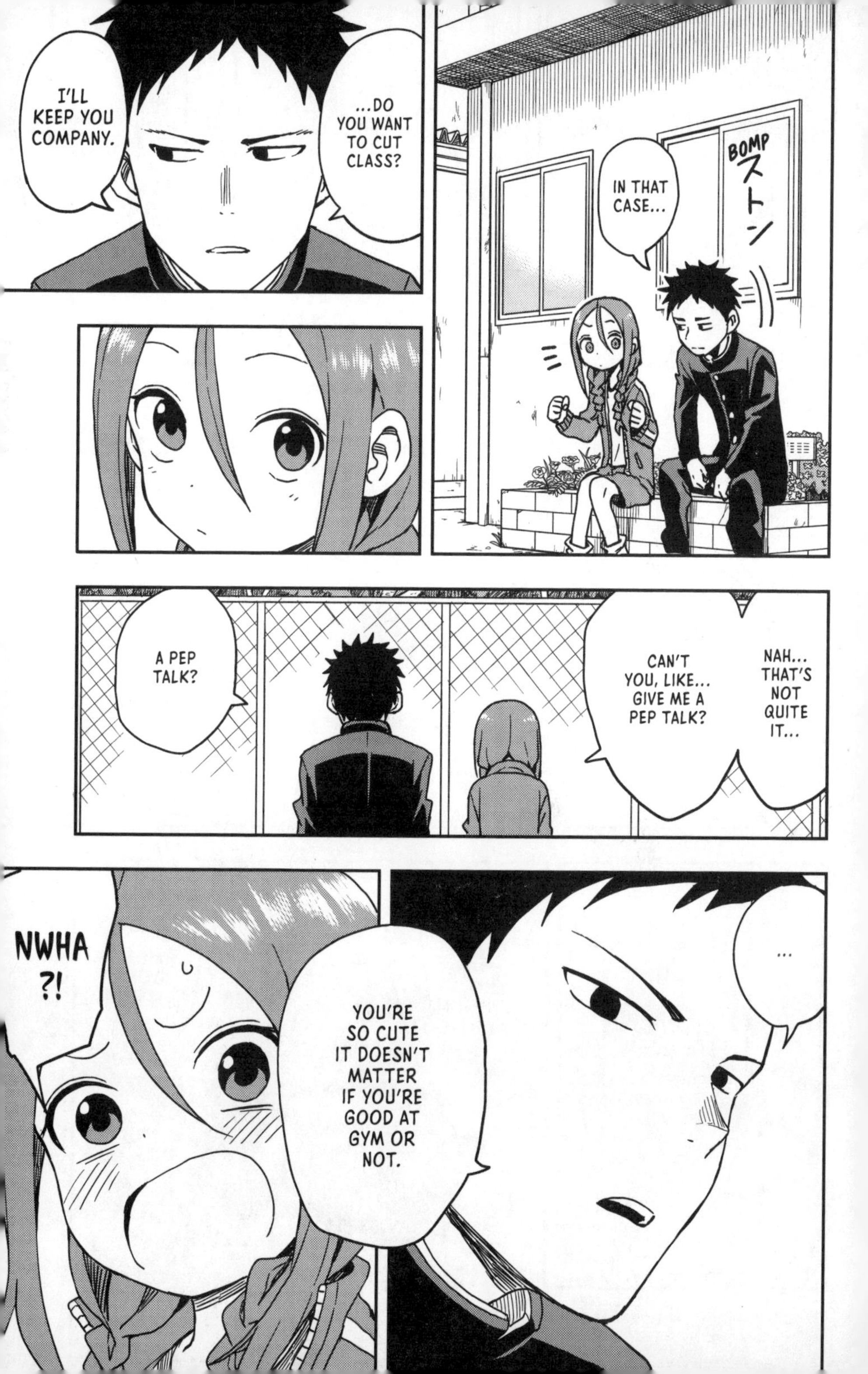

IN THAT CASE...
BOMP
ストン
...DO YOU WANT TO CUT CLASS?
I'LL KEEP YOU COMPANY.
NAH... THAT'S NOT QUITE IT...
CAN'T YOU, LIKE... GIVE ME A PEP TALK?
A PEP TALK?
...
YOU'RE SO CUTE IT DOESN'T MATTER IF YOU'RE GOOD AT GYM OR NOT.
NWHA ?!

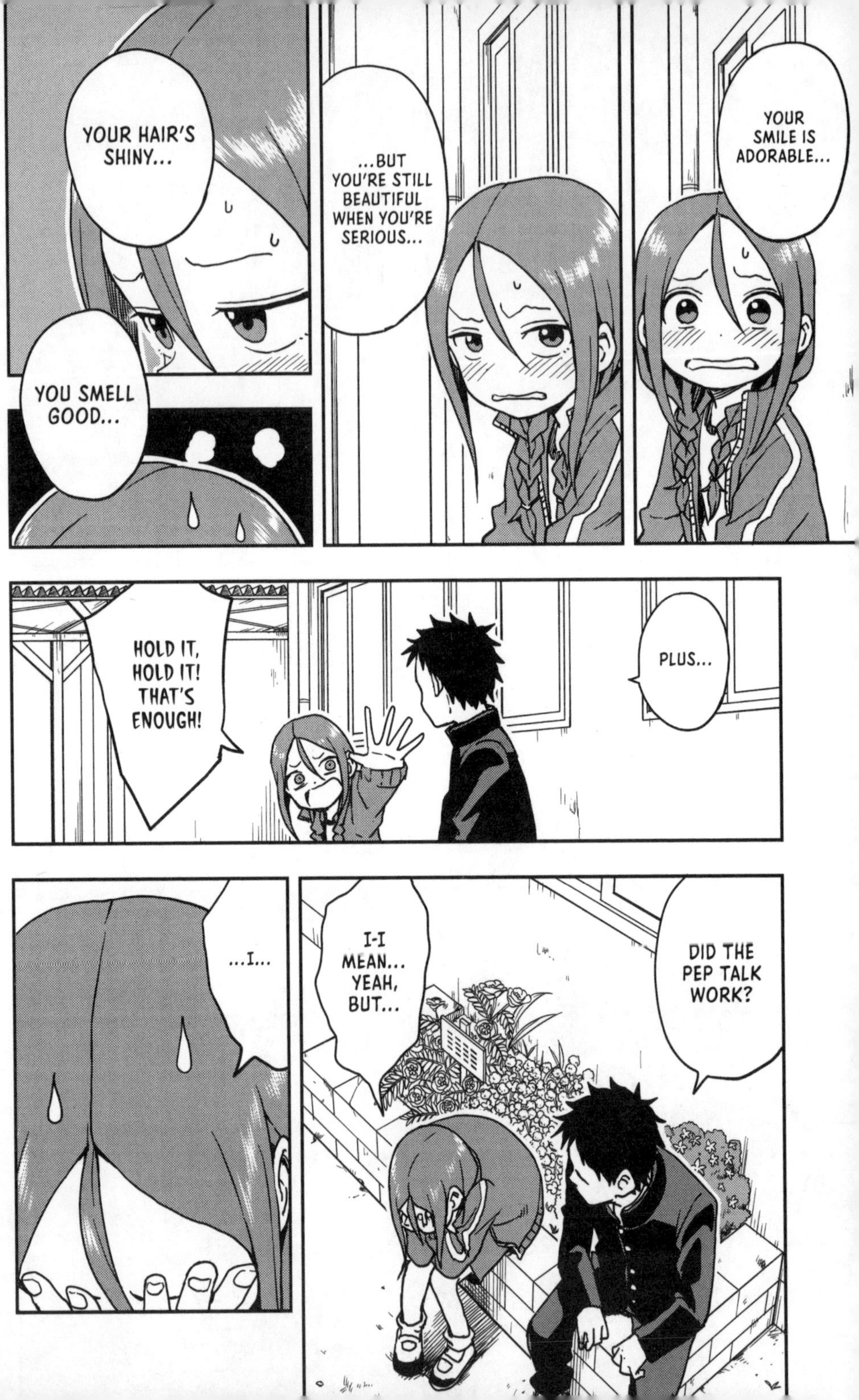
YOUR SMILE IS ADORABLE...
...BUT YOU'RE STILL BEAUTIFUL WHEN YOU'RE SERIOUS...
YOUR HAIR'S SHINY...
YOU SMELL GOOD...
PLUS...
HOLD IT, HOLD IT! THAT'S ENOUGH!
DID THE PEP TALK WORK?
I-I MEAN... YEAH, BUT...
...I...

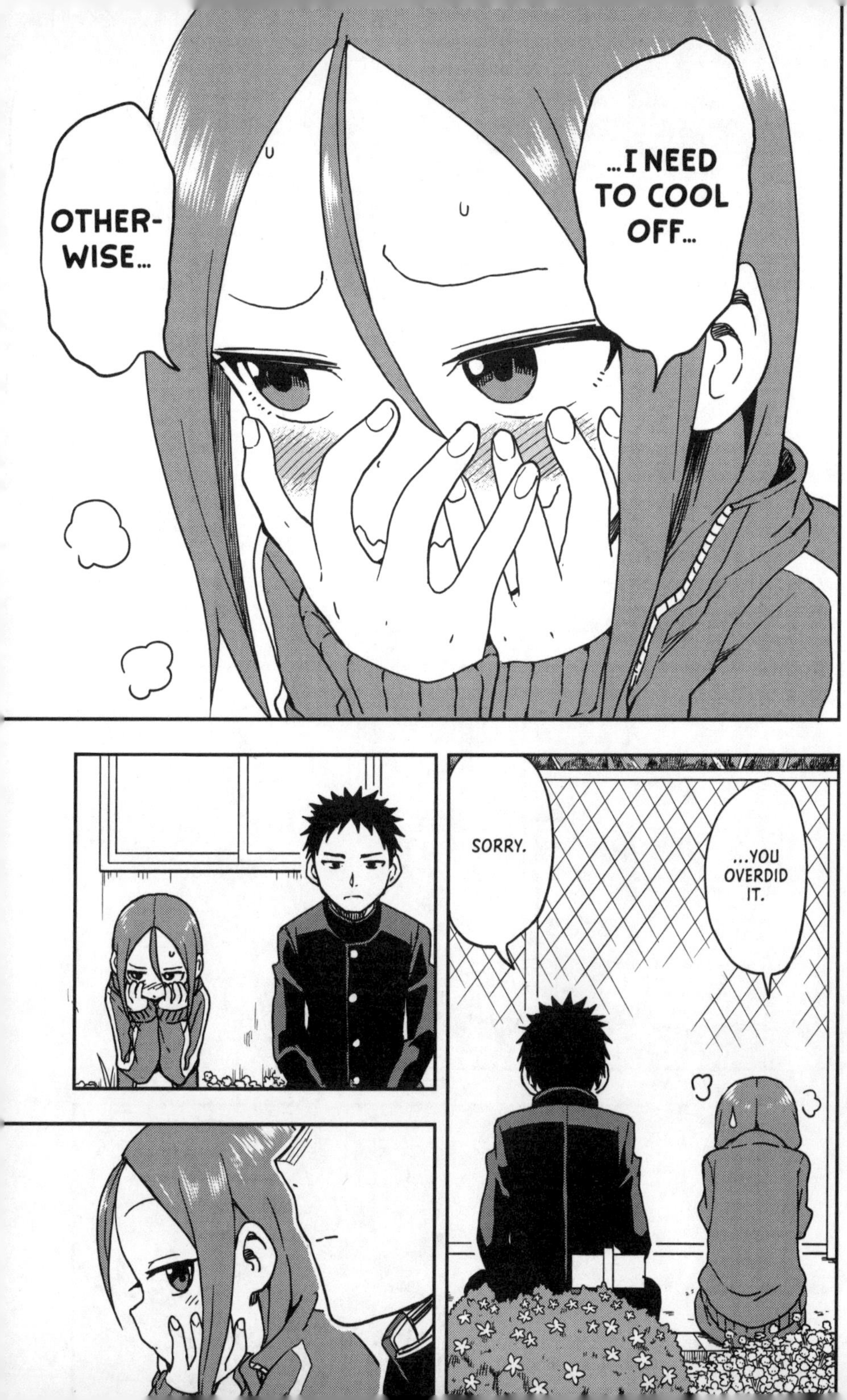
...I NEED TO COOL OFF...
OTHER-WISE...
...YOU OVERDID IT.
SORRY.

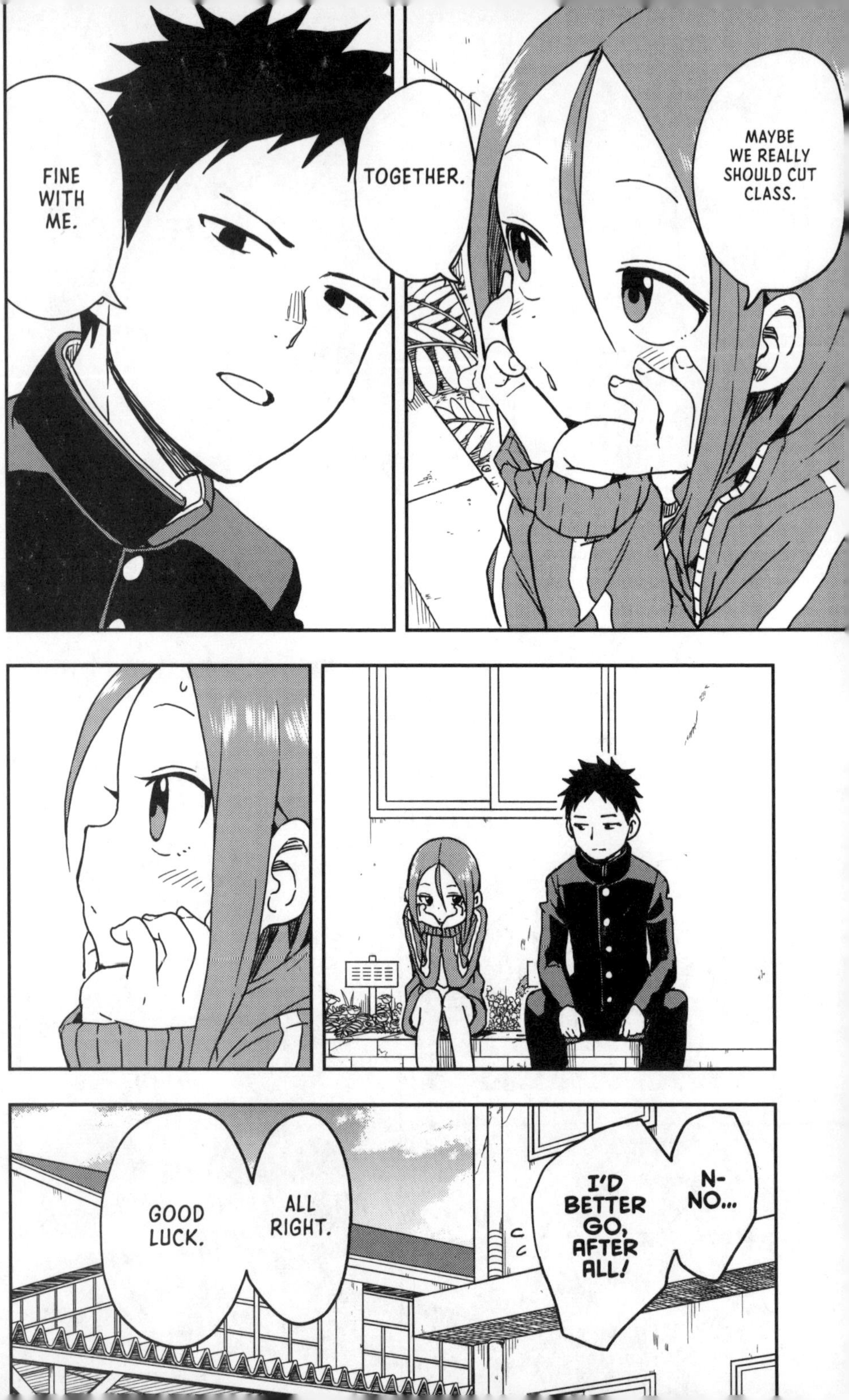
MAYBE WE REALLY SHOULD CUT CLASS.
TOGETHER.
FINE WITH ME.
N-NO...
I'D BETTER GO, AFTER ALL!
ALL RIGHT.
GOOD LUCK.

WHEN WILL AYUMU MAKE HIS MOVE?

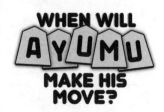

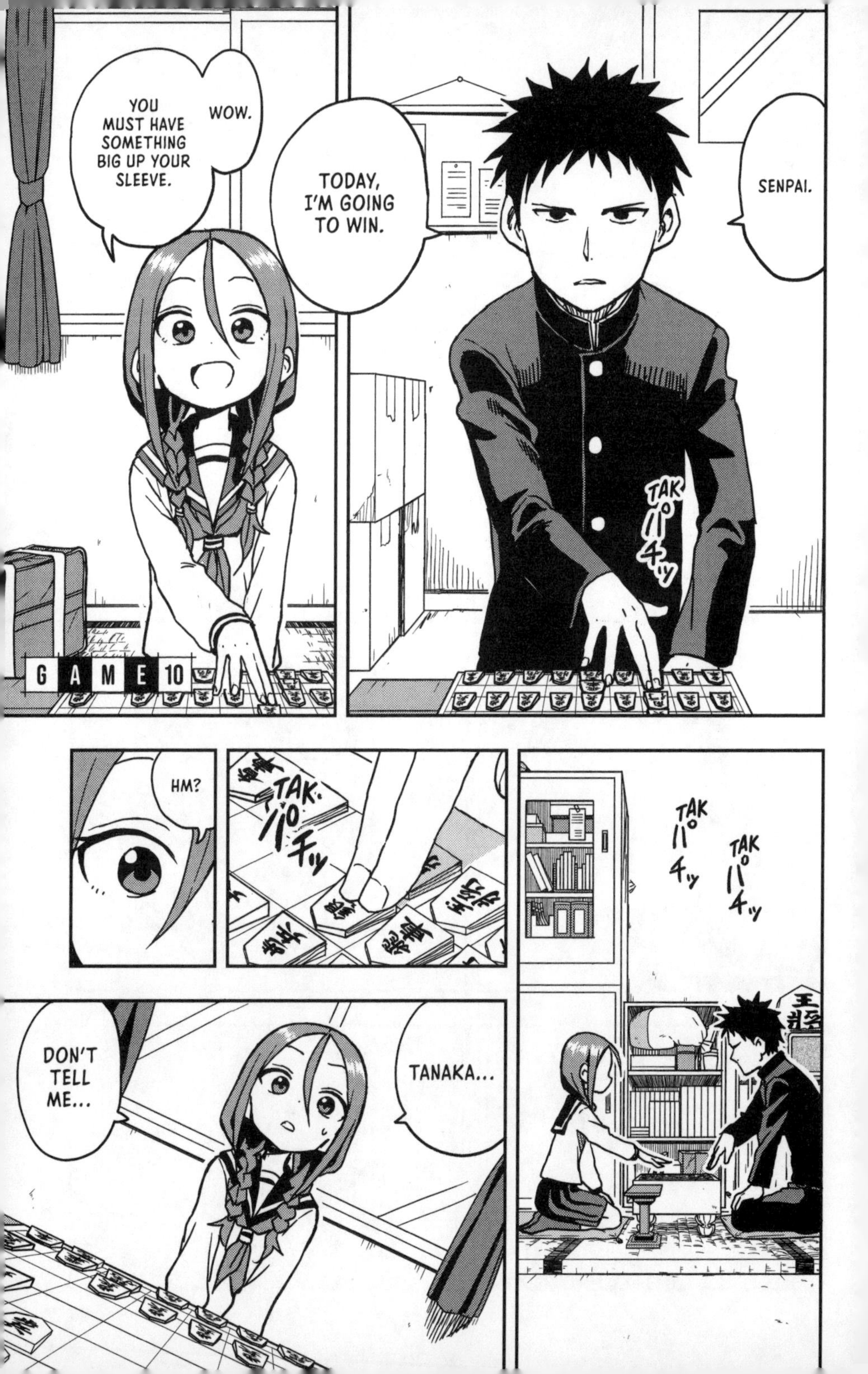
SENPAI.
TODAY, I'M GOING TO WIN.
TAK パチッ
WOW.
YOU MUST HAVE SOMETHING BIG UP YOUR SLEEVE.
GAME 10
TAK パチッ
TAK パチッ
TAK パチッ
HM?
TANAKA...
DON'T TELL ME...

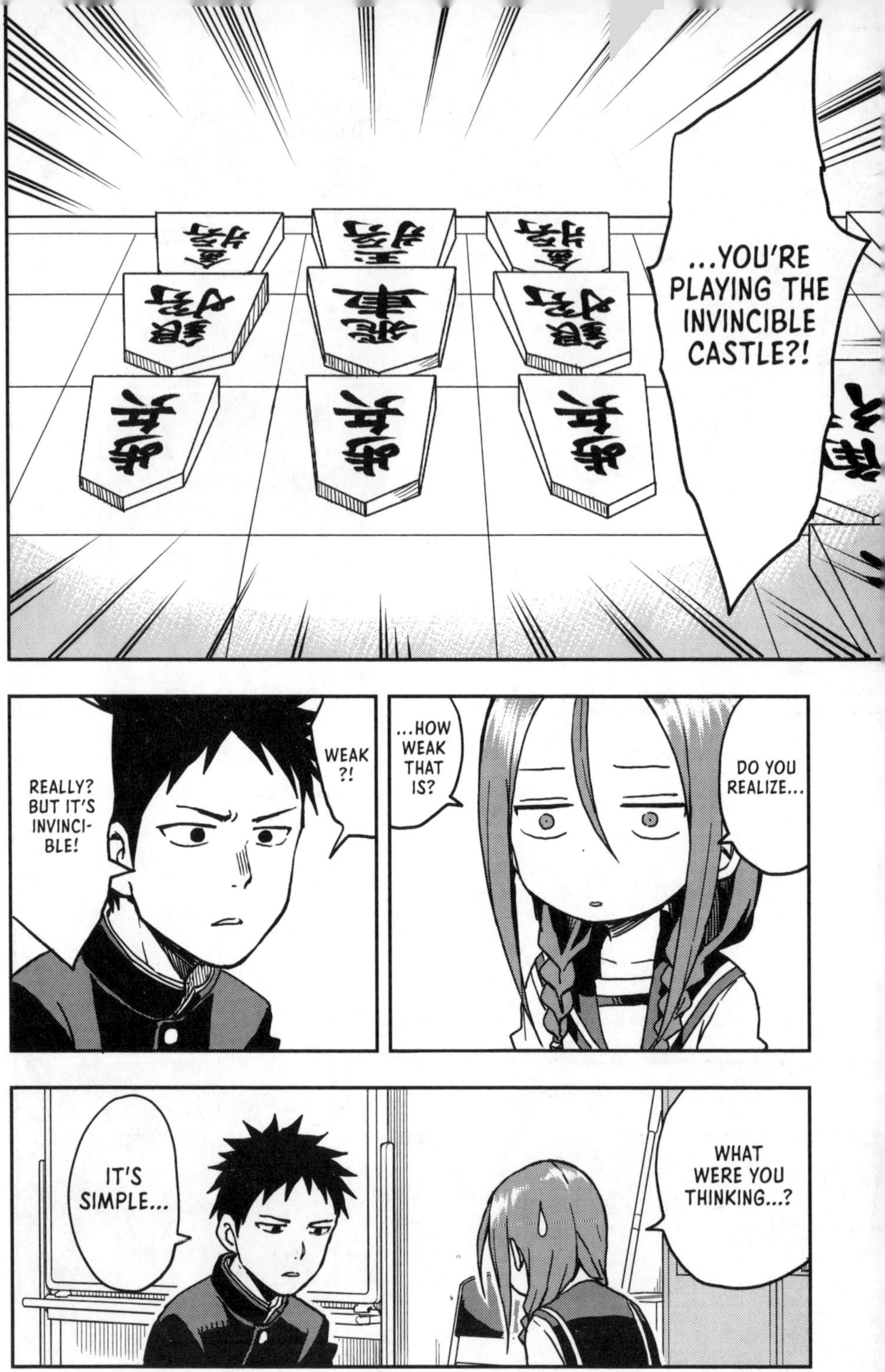
...YOU'RE PLAYING THE INVINCIBLE CASTLE?!
DO YOU REALIZE...
...HOW WEAK THAT IS?
WEAK ?!
REALLY? BUT IT'S INVINCI-BLE!
WHAT WERE YOU THINKING...?
IT'S SIMPLE...

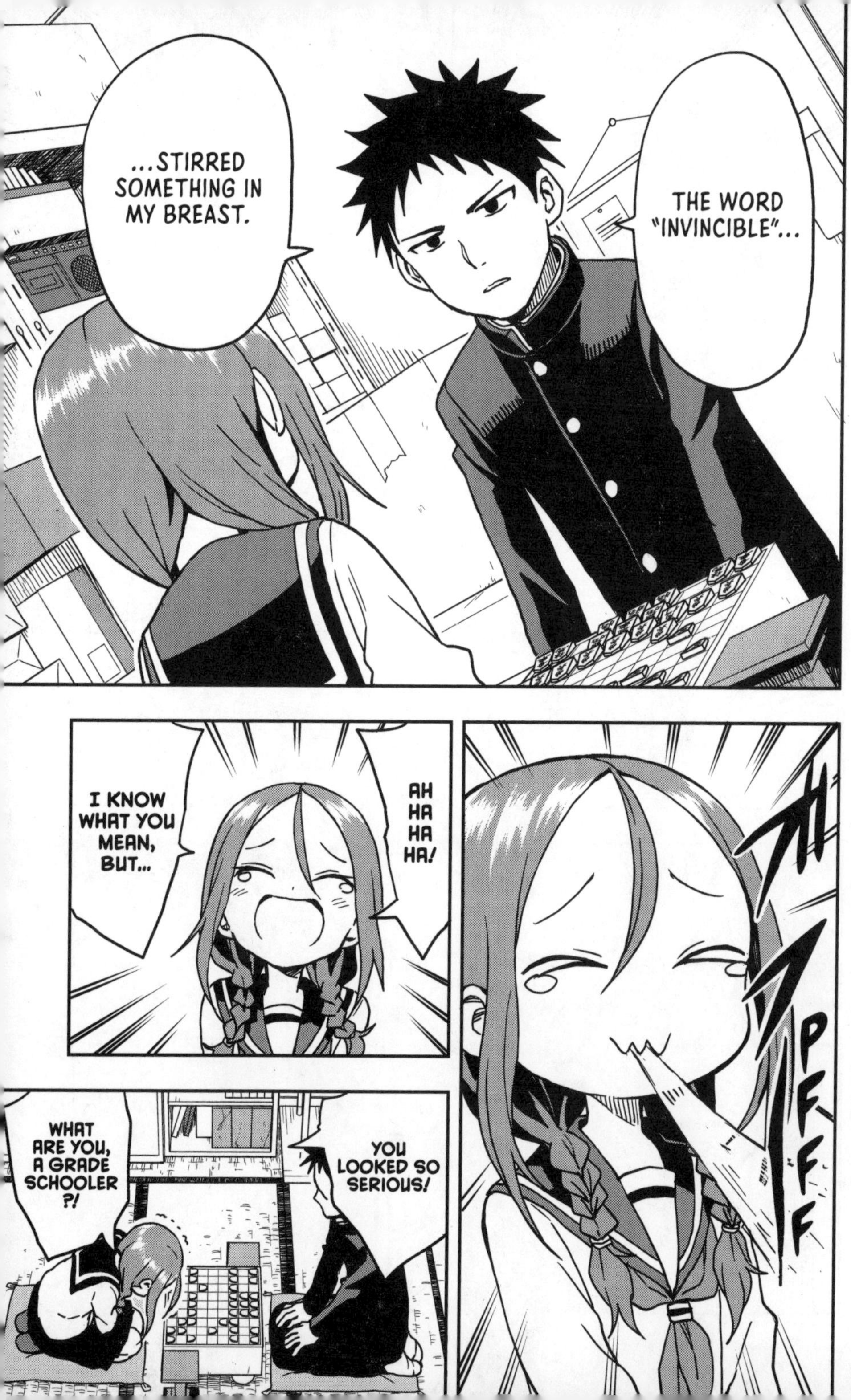
THE WORD "INVINCIBLE"...
...STIRRED SOMETHING IN MY BREAST.
PFFFF
AH HA HA HA!
I KNOW WHAT YOU MEAN, BUT...
YOU LOOKED SO SERIOUS!
WHAT ARE YOU, A GRADE SCHOOLER?!

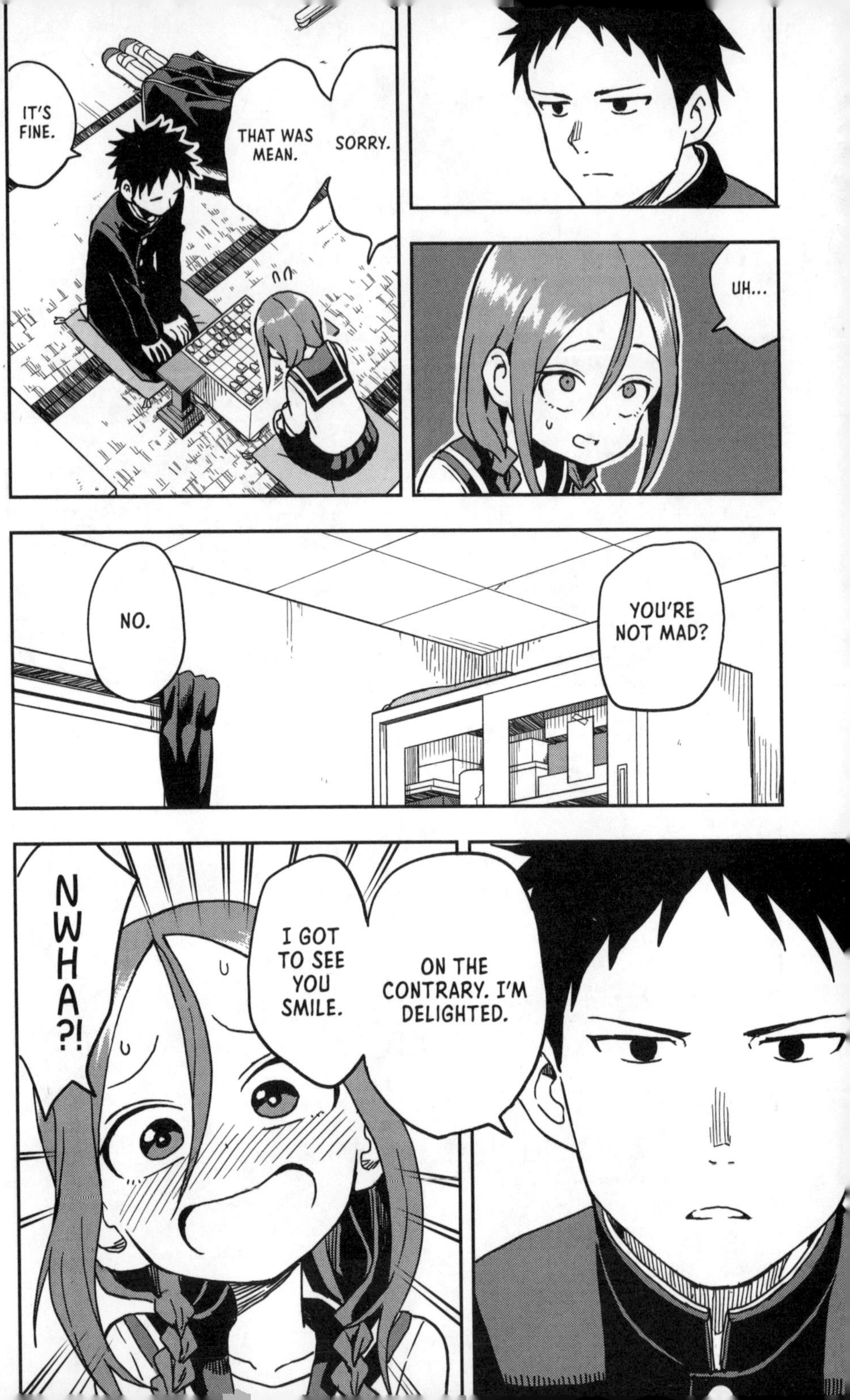
UH...
SORRY.
THAT WAS MEAN.
IT'S FINE.
YOU'RE NOT MAD?
NO.
ON THE CONTRARY. I'M DELIGHTED.
I GOT TO SEE YOU SMILE.
NWHA?!

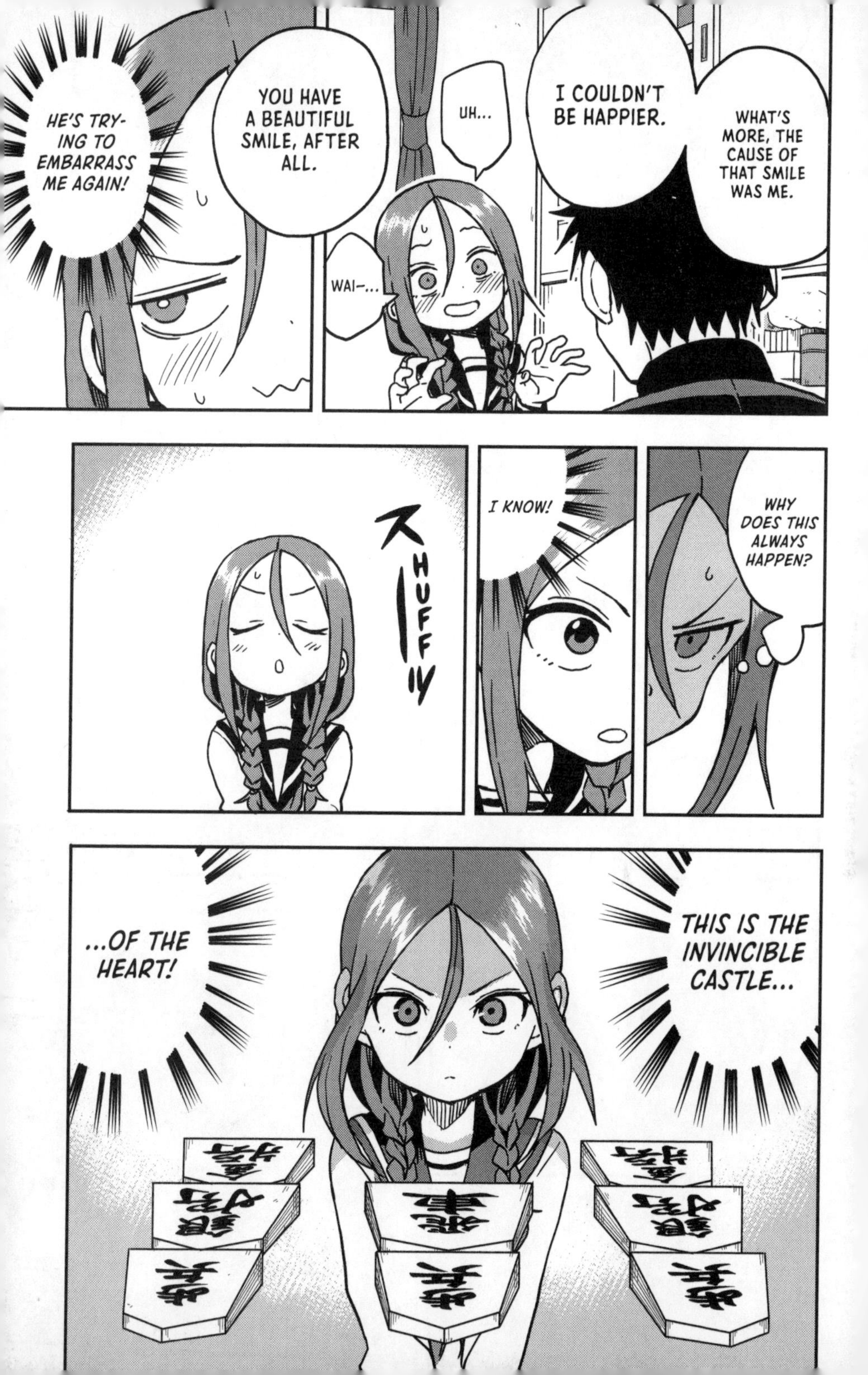
WHAT'S MORE, THE CAUSE OF THAT SMILE WAS ME.
I COULDN'T BE HAPPIER.
UH...
WAI—...
YOU HAVE A BEAUTIFUL SMILE, AFTER ALL.
HE'S TRY-ING TO EMBARRASS ME AGAIN!
WHY DOES THIS ALWAYS HAPPEN?
I KNOW!
スHUFFLY
THIS IS THE INVINCIBLE CASTLE...
...OF THE HEART!

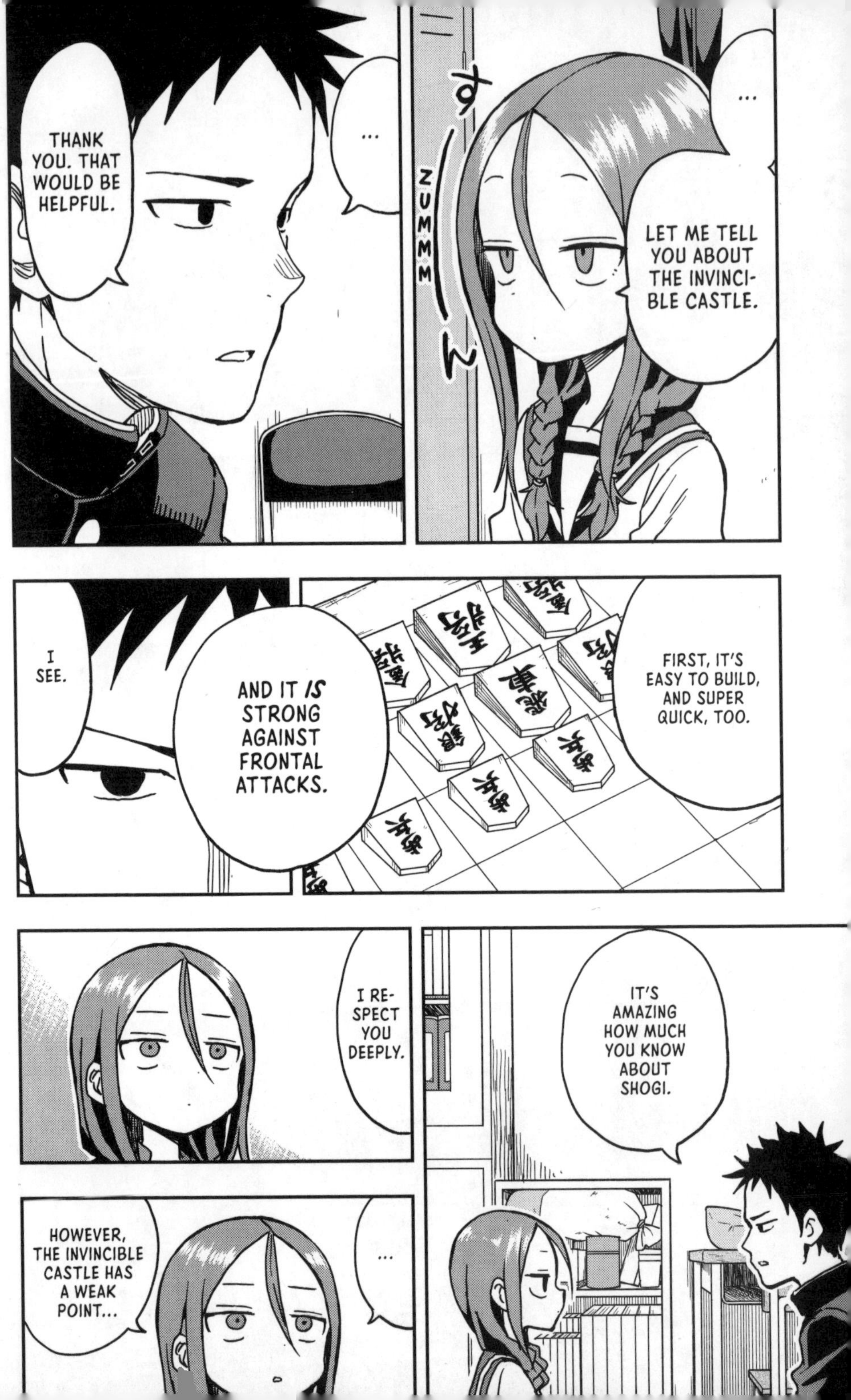
...
LET ME TELL YOU ABOUT THE INVINCIBLE CASTLE.
す―ん
ZUMMMM
...
THANK YOU. THAT WOULD BE HELPFUL.
FIRST, IT'S EASY TO BUILD, AND SUPER QUICK, TOO.
AND IT *IS* STRONG AGAINST FRONTAL ATTACKS.
I SEE.
IT'S AMAZING HOW MUCH YOU KNOW ABOUT SHOGI.
I RE-SPECT YOU DEEPLY.
...
HOWEVER, THE INVINCIBLE CASTLE HAS A WEAK POINT...

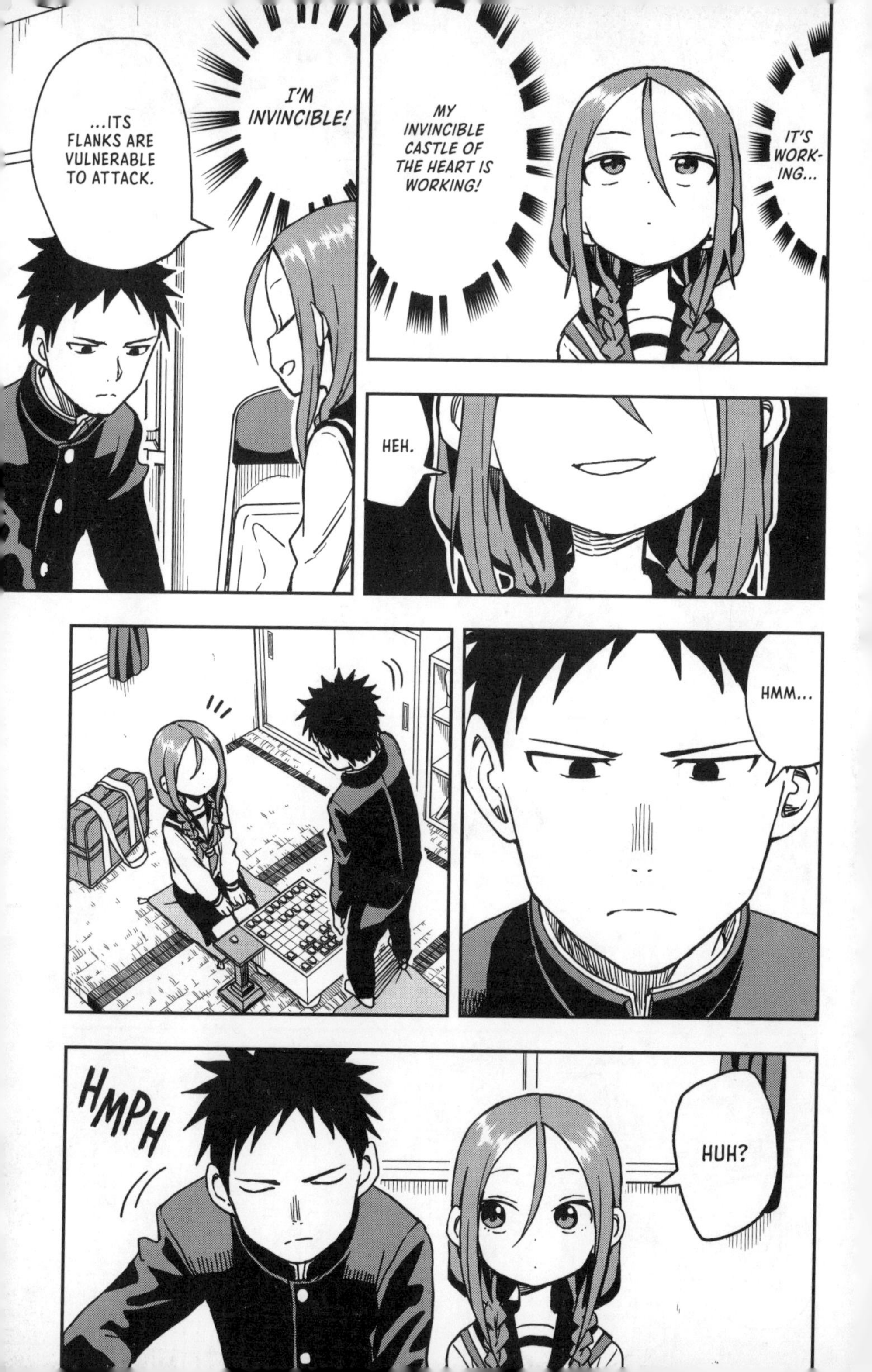
IT'S WORKING...
MY INVINCIBLE CASTLE OF THE HEART IS WORKING!
HEH.
I'M INVINCIBLE!
...ITS FLANKS ARE VULNERABLE TO ATTACK.
HMM...
HUH?
HMPH

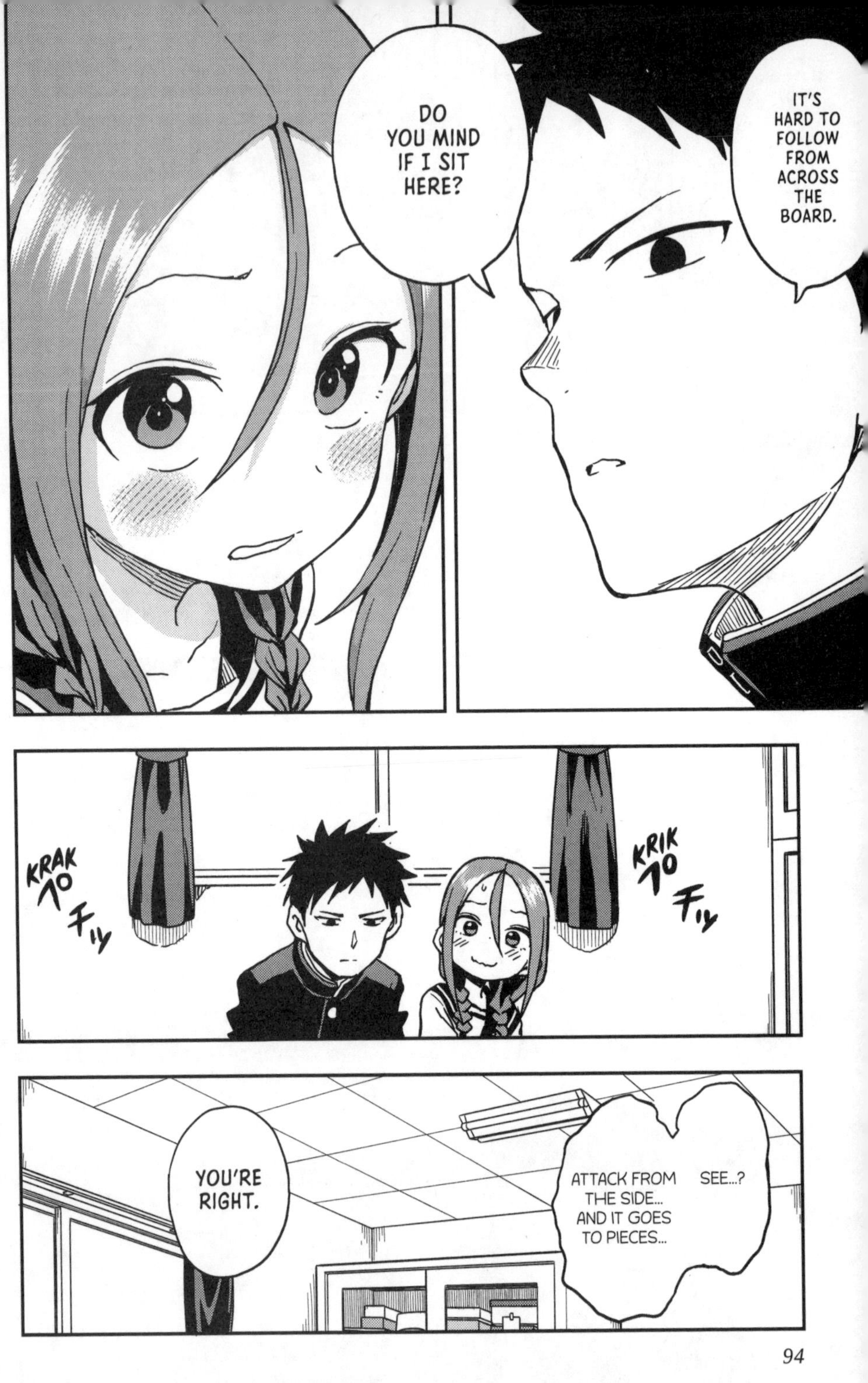
IT'S HARD TO FOLLOW FROM ACROSS THE BOARD.
DO YOU MIND IF I SIT HERE?
KRIK
KRAK
SEE...?
ATTACK FROM THE SIDE... AND IT GOES TO PIECES...
YOU'RE RIGHT.

GAME 10 RECORD

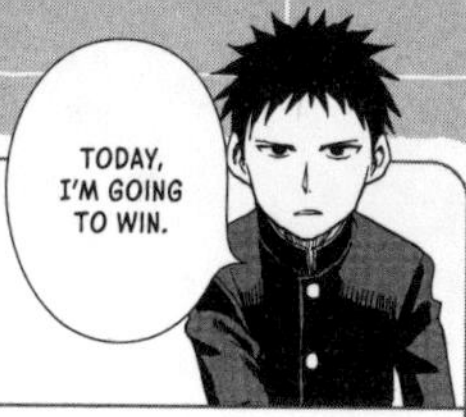
TODAY, I'M GOING TO WIN.

▲ BLACK (SENTE): AYUMU TANAKA △ WHITE (GOTE): URUSHI YAOTOME

(WHITE WINS ON MOVE 18, △ P×7H)

◁ URUSHI: P

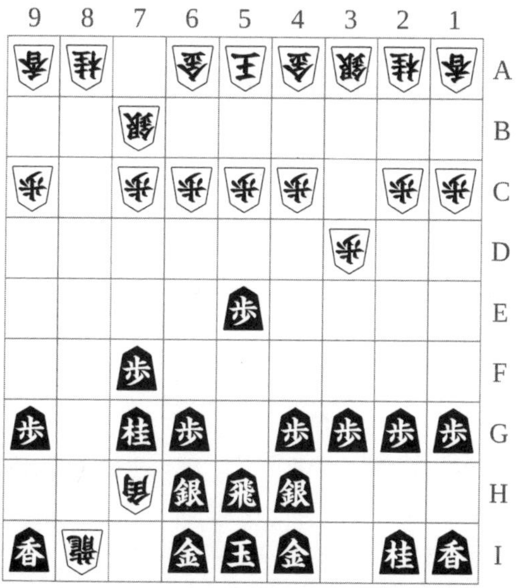

▲ AYUMU: B, P

▲ R-5H	△ P-8D
▲ P-7F	△ P-8E
▲ B-7G	△ P-3D
▲ S-6H	△ S-7B
▲ S-4H	△ B×7G+
▲ N×7G	△ P-8F
▲ P×8F	△ R×8F
▲ P-5F	△ R-8I+
▲ P-5E	△ B×7H

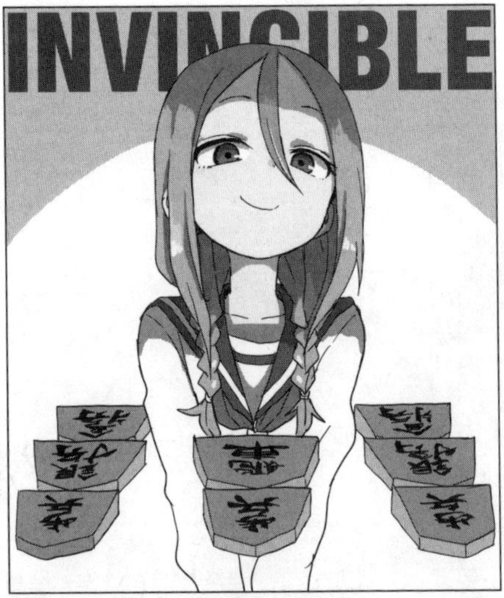
INVINCIBLE

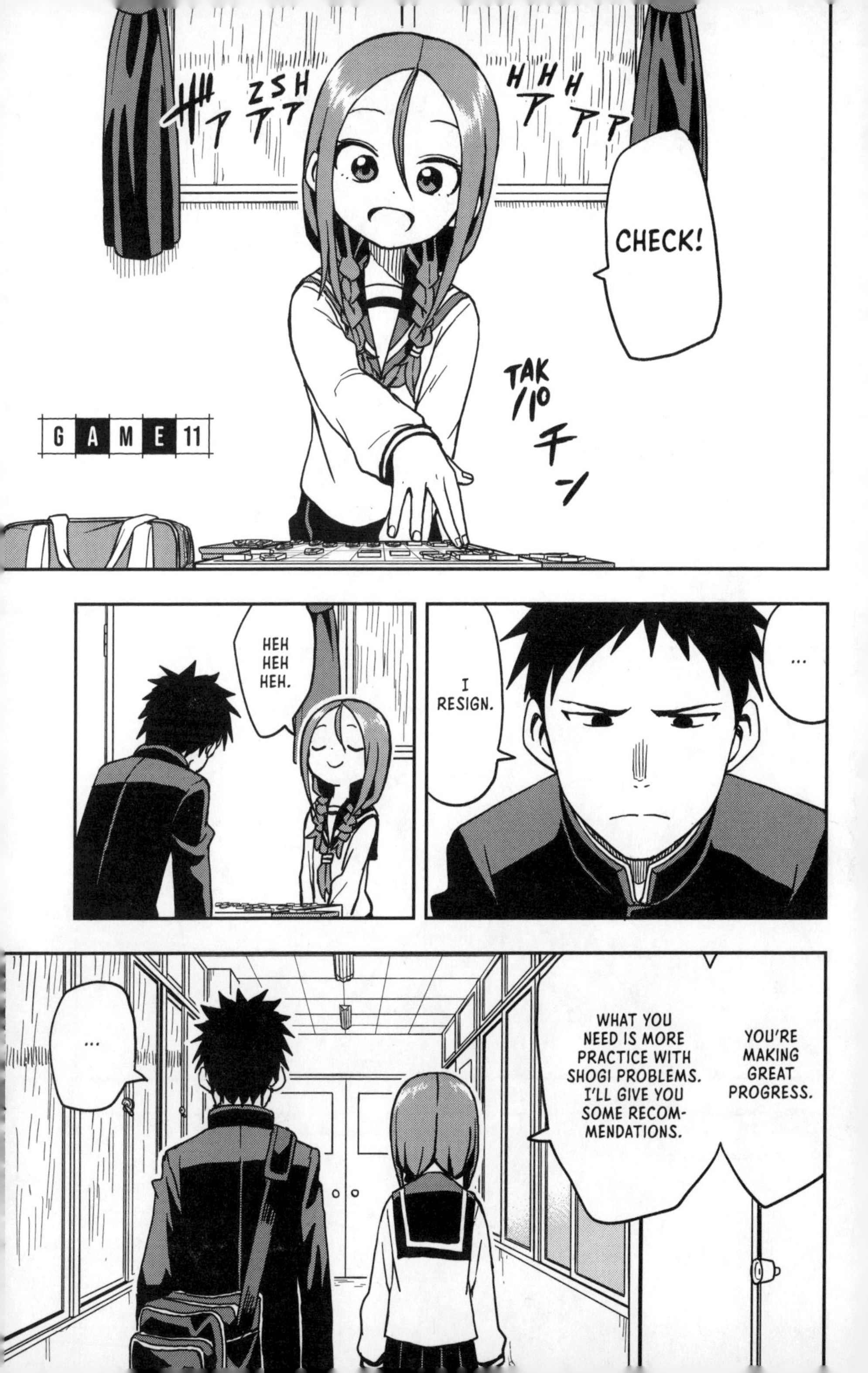
HHH
CHECK!
ZSH
TAK
GAME 11
...
I RESIGN.
HEH HEH HEH.
YOU'RE MAKING GREAT PROGRESS.
WHAT YOU NEED IS MORE PRACTICE WITH SHOGI PROBLEMS. I'LL GIVE YOU SOME RECOM-MENDATIONS.
...

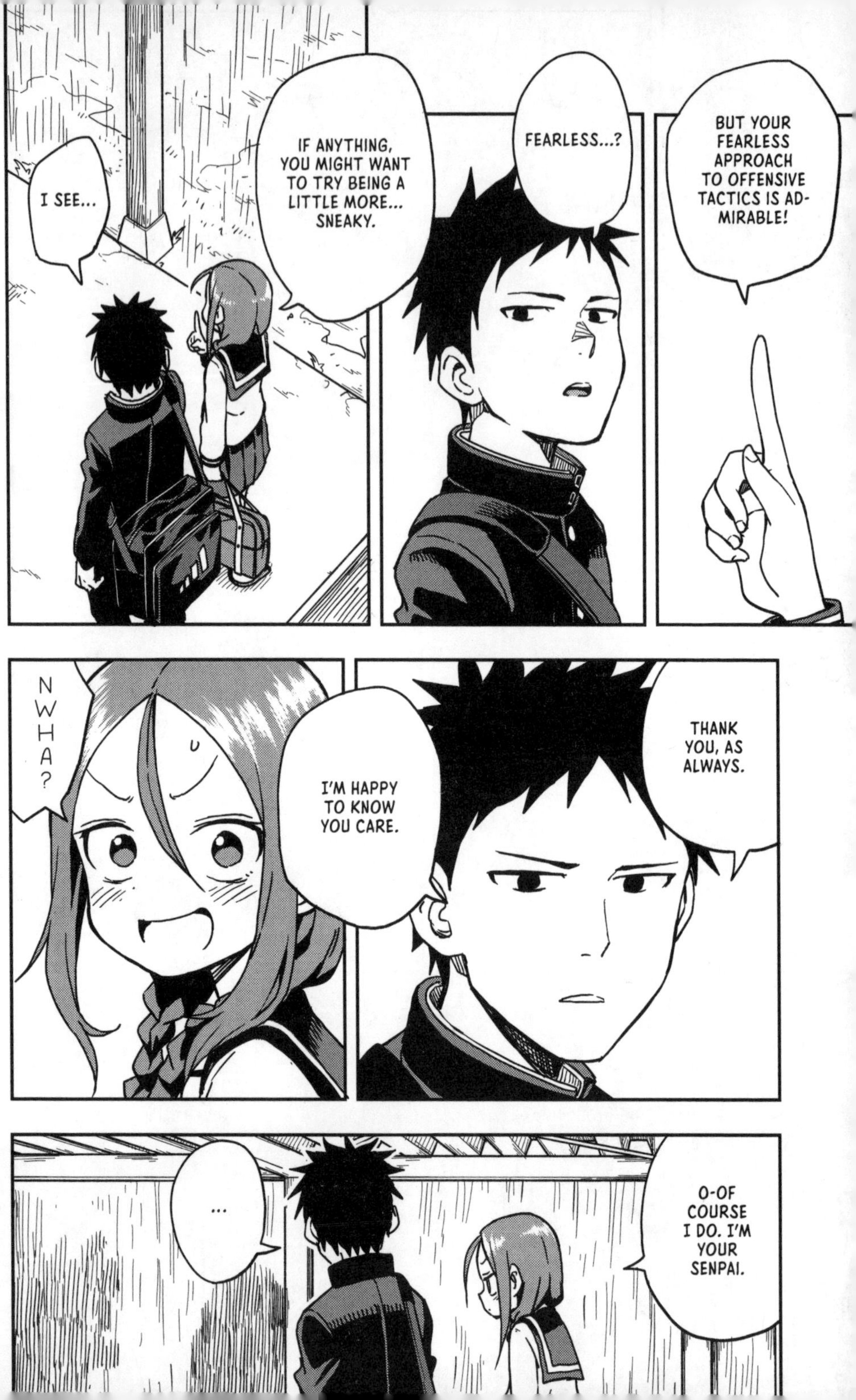
BUT YOUR FEARLESS APPROACH TO OFFENSIVE TACTICS IS ADMIRABLE!
FEARLESS...?
IF ANYTHING, YOU MIGHT WANT TO TRY BEING A LITTLE MORE... SNEAKY.
I SEE...
THANK YOU, AS ALWAYS.
I'M HAPPY TO KNOW YOU CARE.
NWHA?
O-OF COURSE I DO. I'M YOUR SENPAI.
...

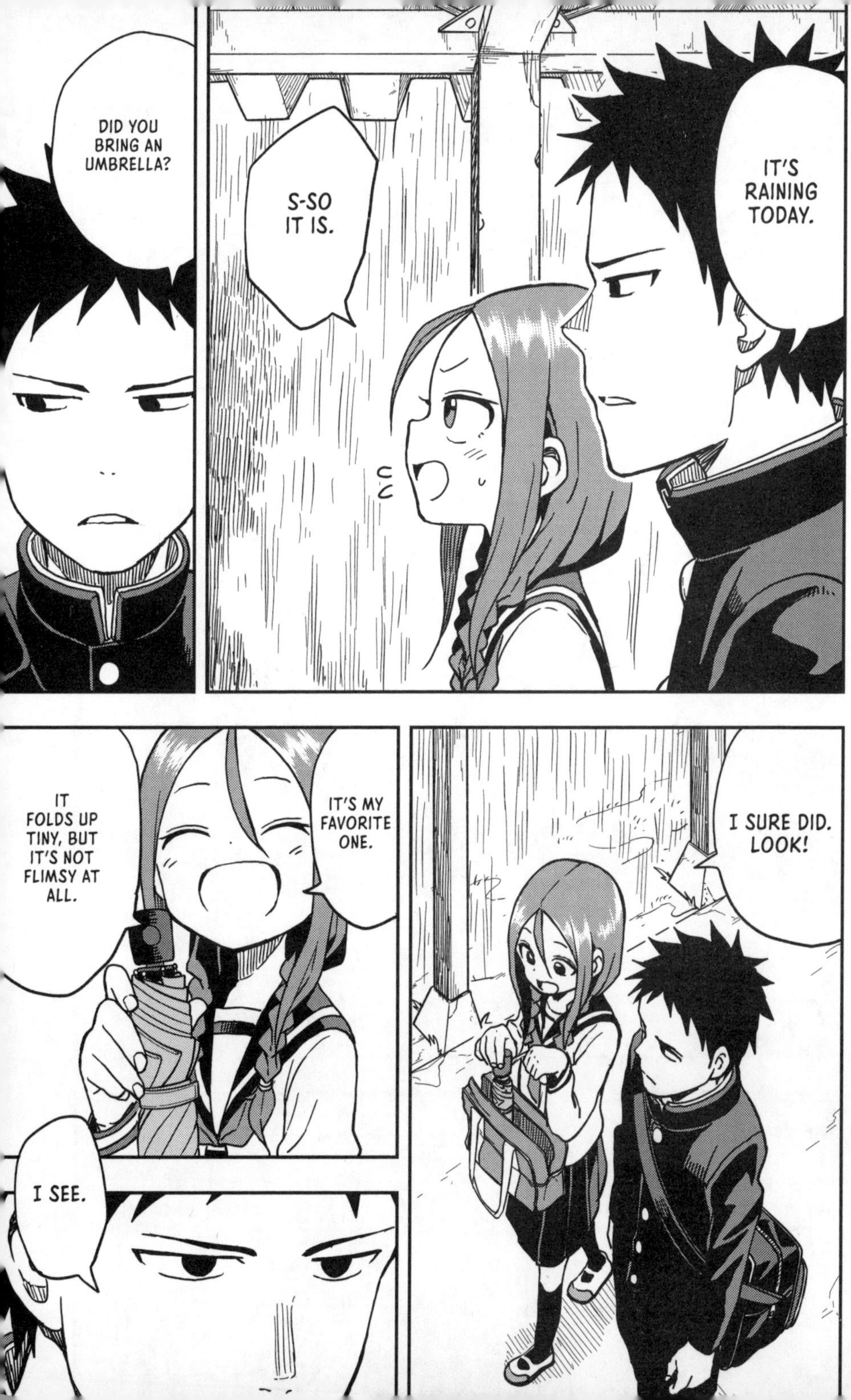
IT'S RAINING TODAY.
S-SO IT IS.
DID YOU BRING AN UMBRELLA?
I SURE DID. LOOK!
IT'S MY FAVORITE ONE.
IT FOLDS UP TINY, BUT IT'S NOT FLIMSY AT ALL.
I SEE.

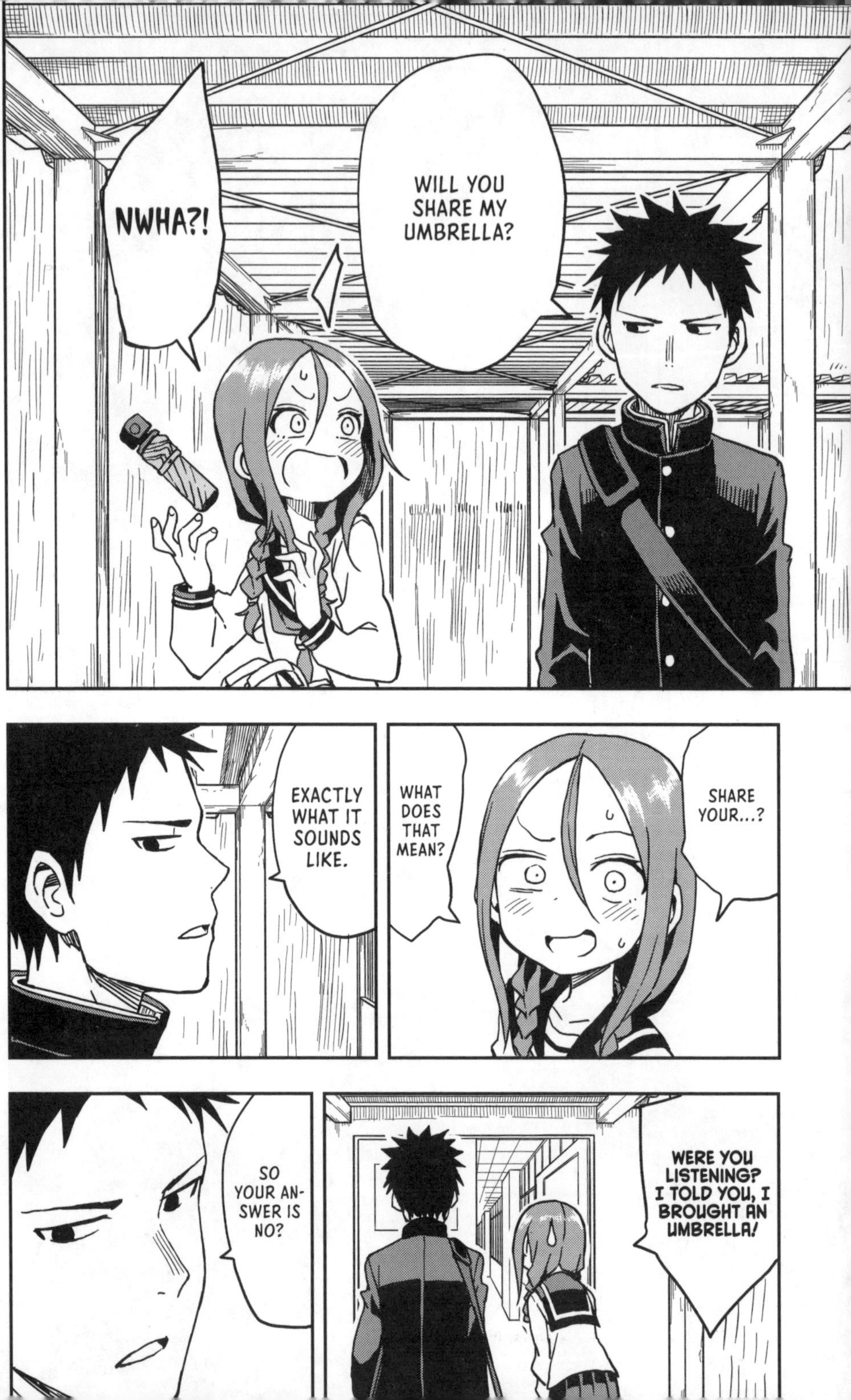
WILL YOU SHARE MY UMBRELLA?
NWHA?!
SHARE YOUR...?
WHAT DOES THAT MEAN?
EXACTLY WHAT IT SOUNDS LIKE.
WERE YOU LISTENING? I TOLD YOU, I BROUGHT AN UMBRELLA!
SO YOUR AN-SWER IS NO?

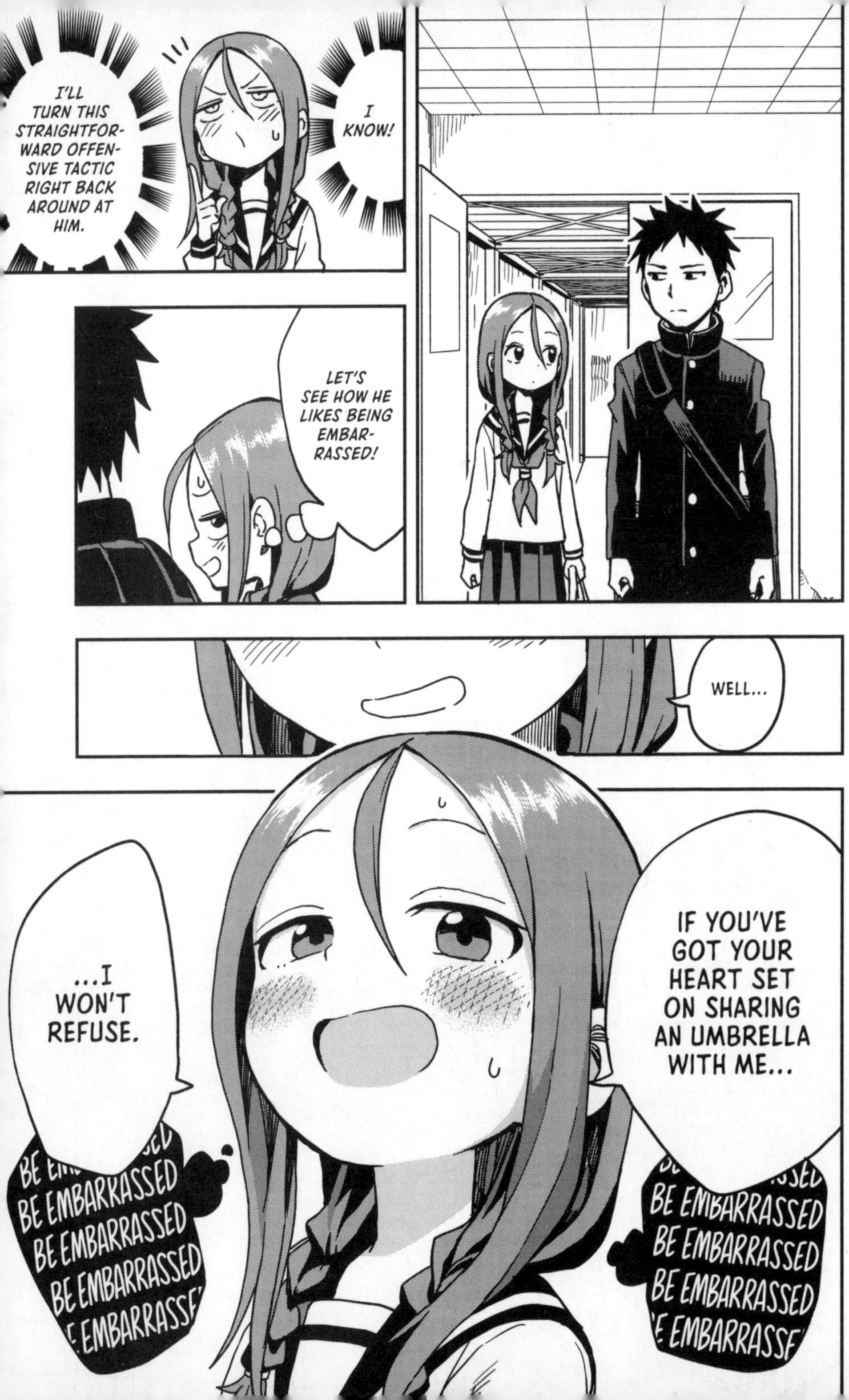
I KNOW!
I'LL TURN THIS STRAIGHTFORWARD OFFENSIVE TACTIC RIGHT BACK AROUND AT HIM.
LET'S SEE HOW HE LIKES BEING EMBARRASSED!
WELL...
IF YOU'VE GOT YOUR HEART SET ON SHARING AN UMBRELLA WITH ME...
...I WON'T REFUSE.
BE EMBARRASSED
BE EMBARRASSED
BE EMBARRASSED
BE EMBARRASSED
BE EMBARRASSED
BE EMBARRASSED
BE EMBARRASSED
BE EMBARRASSED

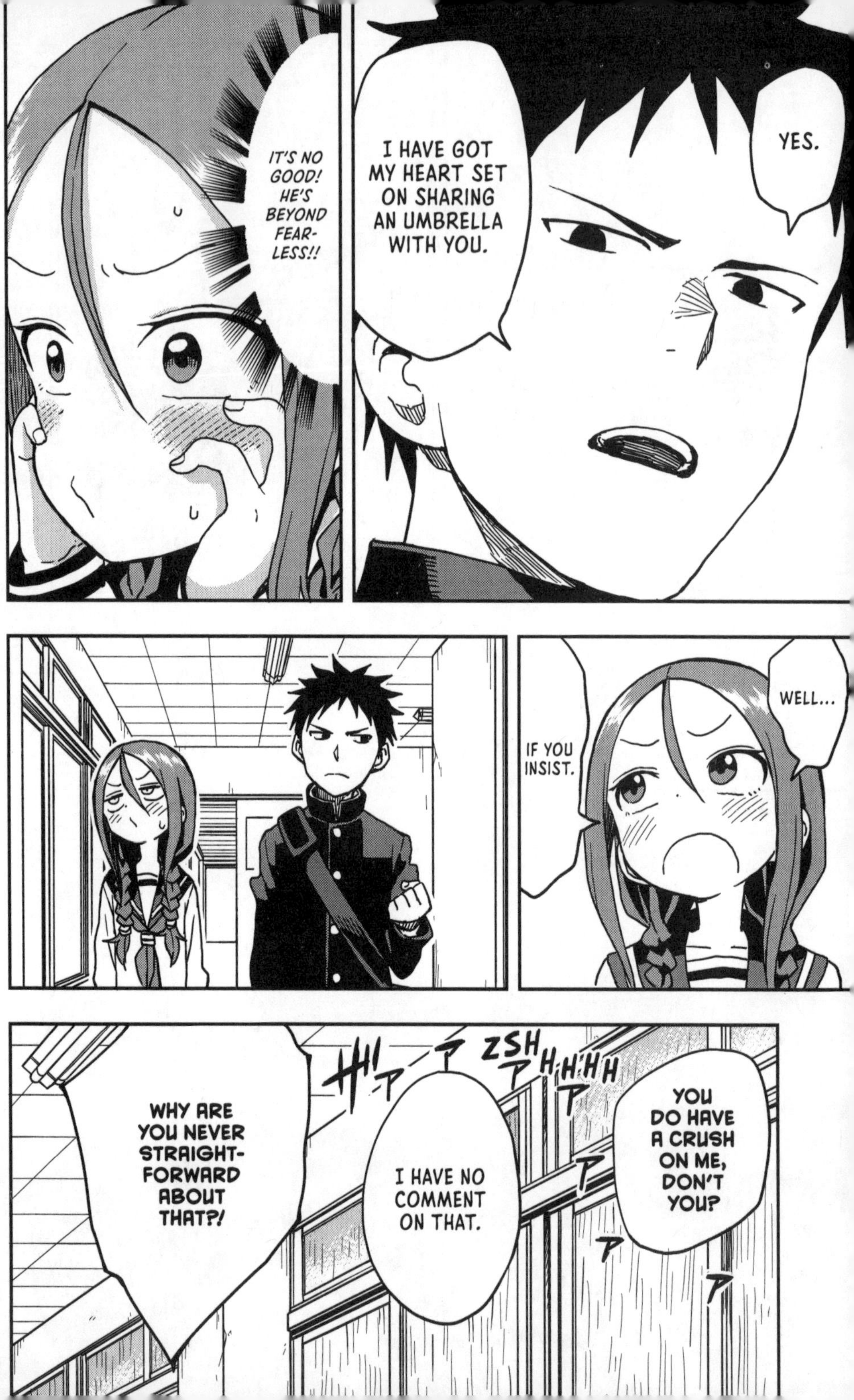
YES.
I HAVE GOT MY HEART SET ON SHARING AN UMBRELLA WITH YOU.
IT'S NO GOOD! HE'S BEYOND FEAR-LESS!!
WELL...
IF YOU INSIST.
YOU DO HAVE A CRUSH ON ME, DON'T YOU?
I HAVE NO COMMENT ON THAT.
ZSHHHHH
WHY ARE YOU NEVER STRAIGHT-FORWARD ABOUT THAT?!

WHEN WILL AYUMU MAKE HIS MOVE?

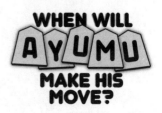

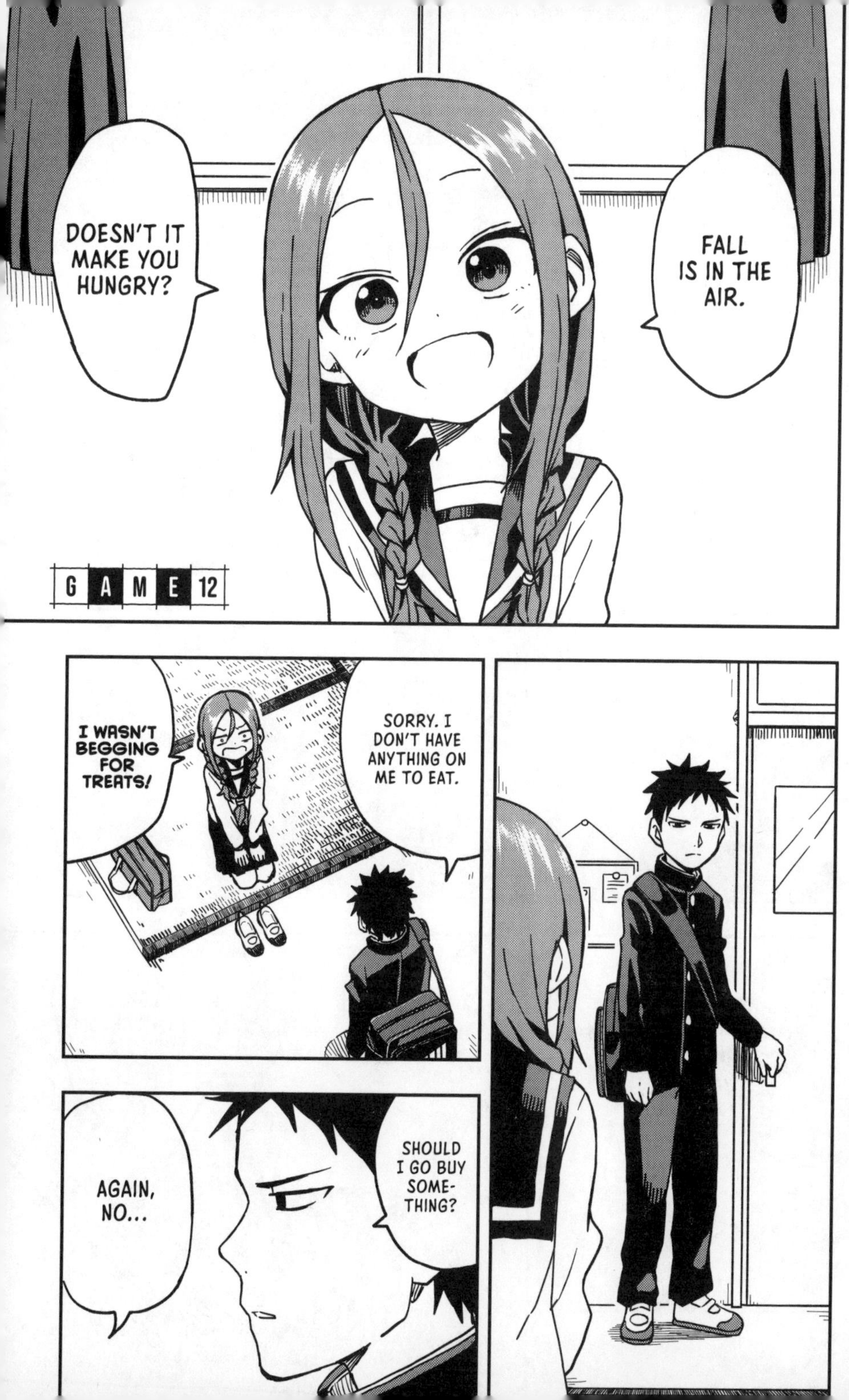
FALL IS IN THE AIR.
DOESN'T IT MAKE YOU HUNGRY?
GAME 12
SORRY. I DON'T HAVE ANYTHING ON ME TO EAT.
I WASN'T BEGGING FOR TREATS!
SHOULD I GO BUY SOME-THING?
AGAIN, NO...

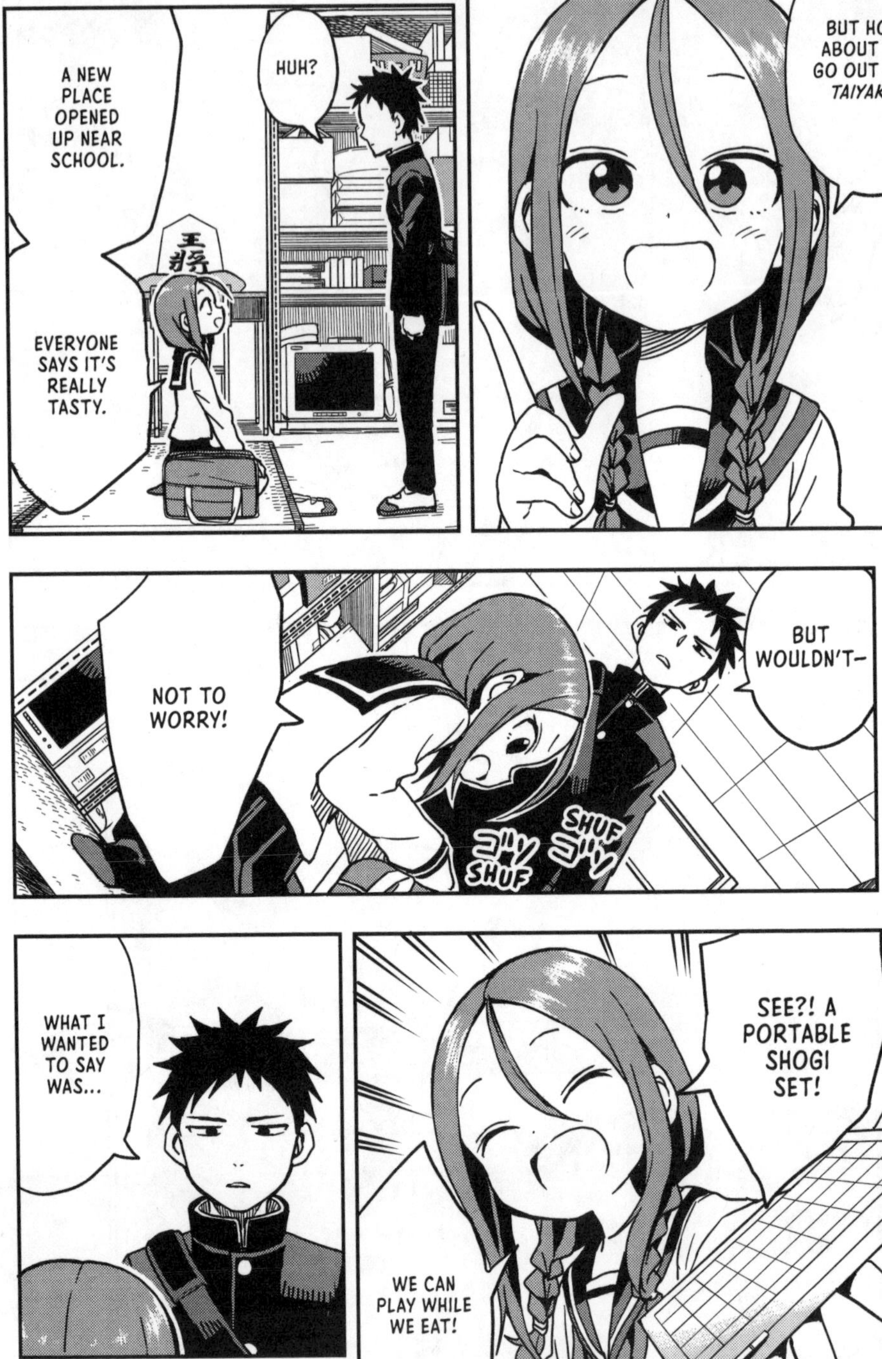
BUT HOW ABOUT WE GO OUT FOR *TAIYAKI?*
HUH?
A NEW PLACE OPENED UP NEAR SCHOOL.
EVERYONE SAYS IT'S REALLY TASTY.
BUT WOULDN'T-
NOT TO WORRY!
SHUF
SHUF
SEE?! A PORTABLE SHOGI SET!
WE CAN PLAY WHILE WE EAT!
WHAT I WANTED TO SAY WAS...

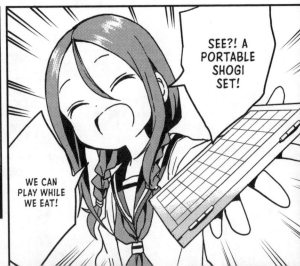

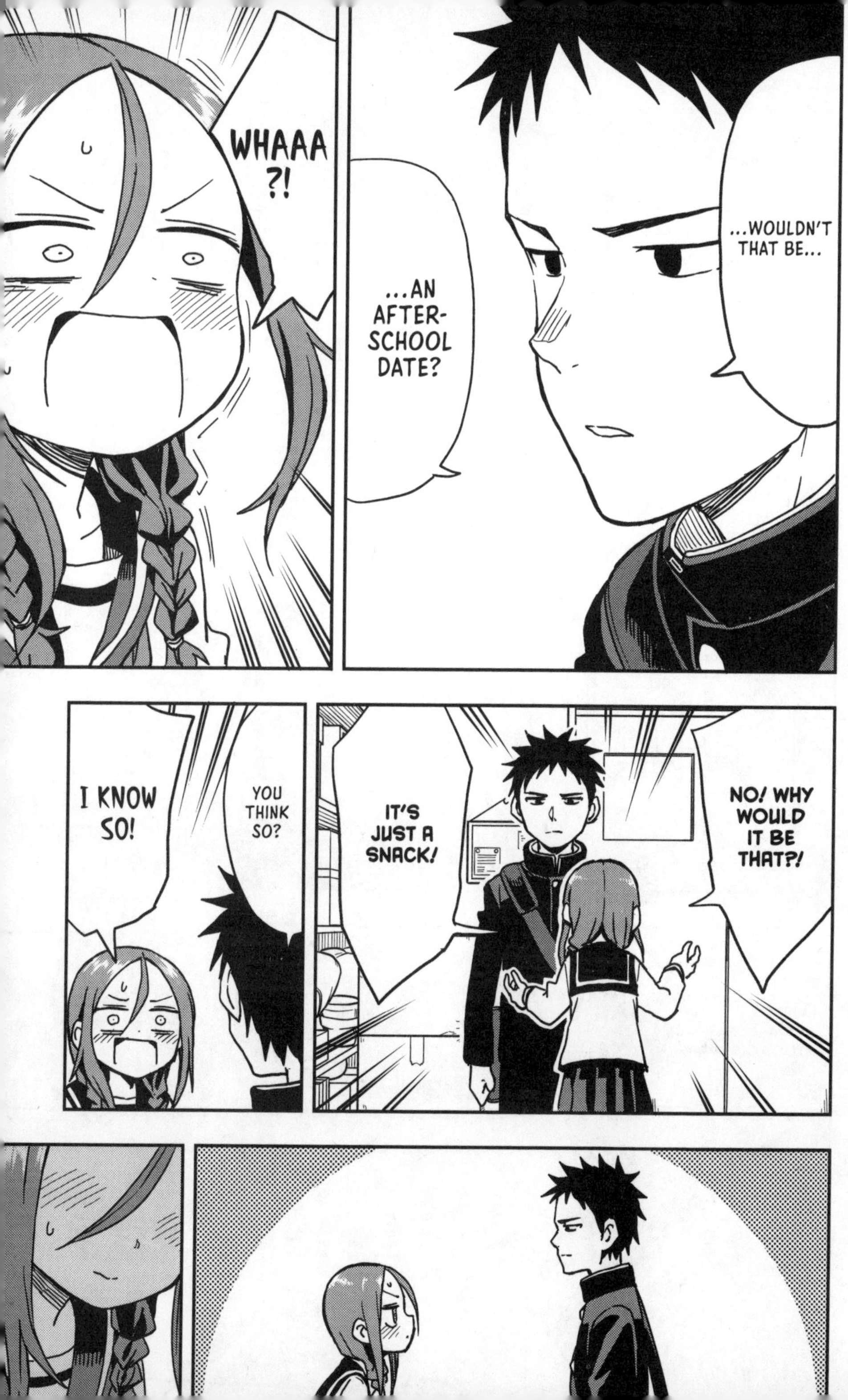
...WOULDN'T THAT BE...
...AN AFTER-SCHOOL DATE?
WHAAA ?!
NO! WHY WOULD IT BE THAT?!
IT'S JUST A SNACK!
YOU THINK SO?
I KNOW SO!

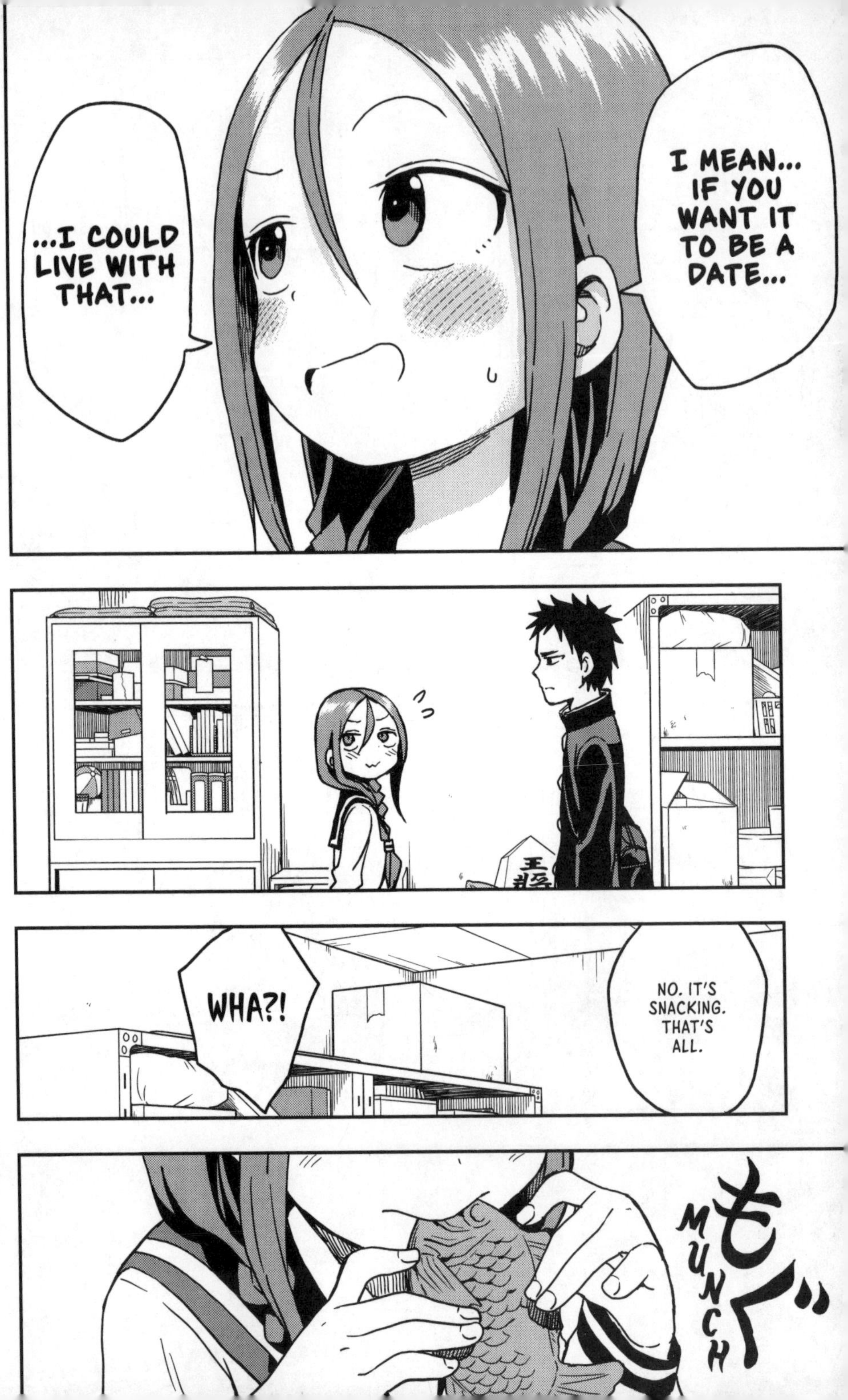
I MEAN... IF YOU WANT IT TO BE A DATE...
...I COULD LIVE WITH THAT...
NO. IT'S SNACKING. THAT'S ALL.
WHA?!
MUNCH

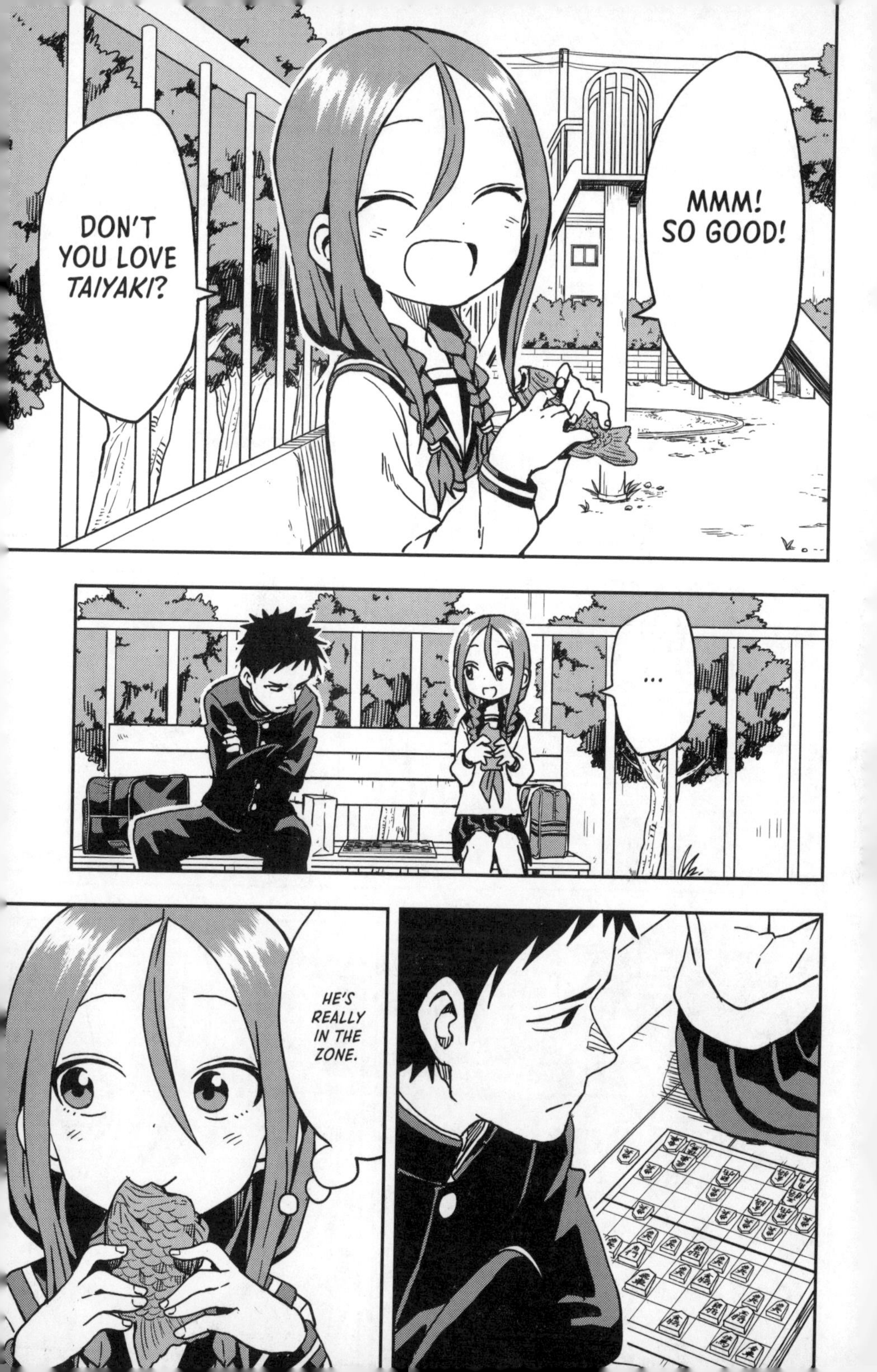
MMM! SO GOOD!
DON'T YOU LOVE *TAIYAKI*?
...
HE'S REALLY IN THE ZONE.

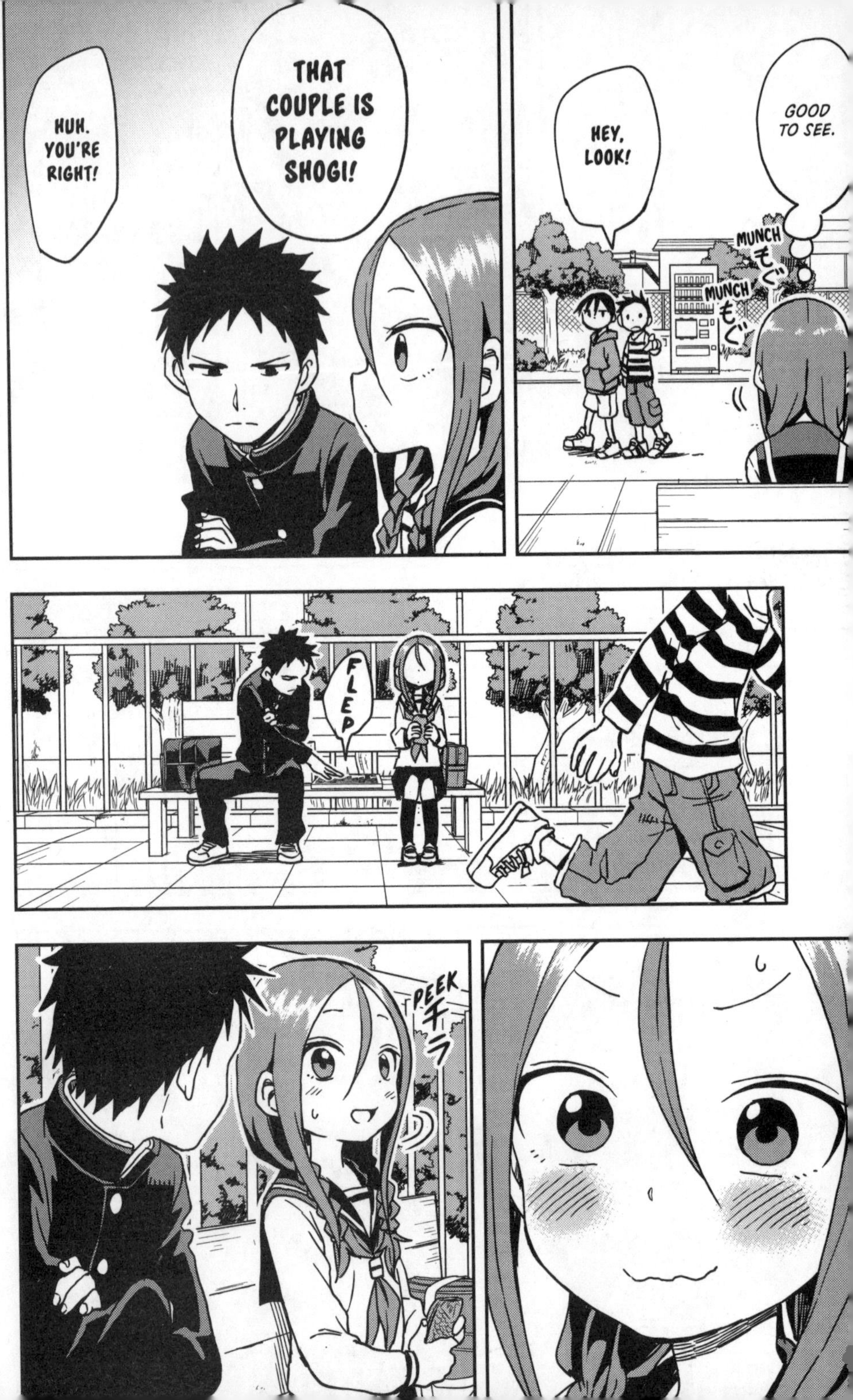
GOOD TO SEE.
HEY, LOOK!
MUNCH もぐ
MUNCH もぐ
THAT COUPLE IS PLAYING SHOGI!
HUH. YOU'RE RIGHT!
FLEP
PEEK チラ

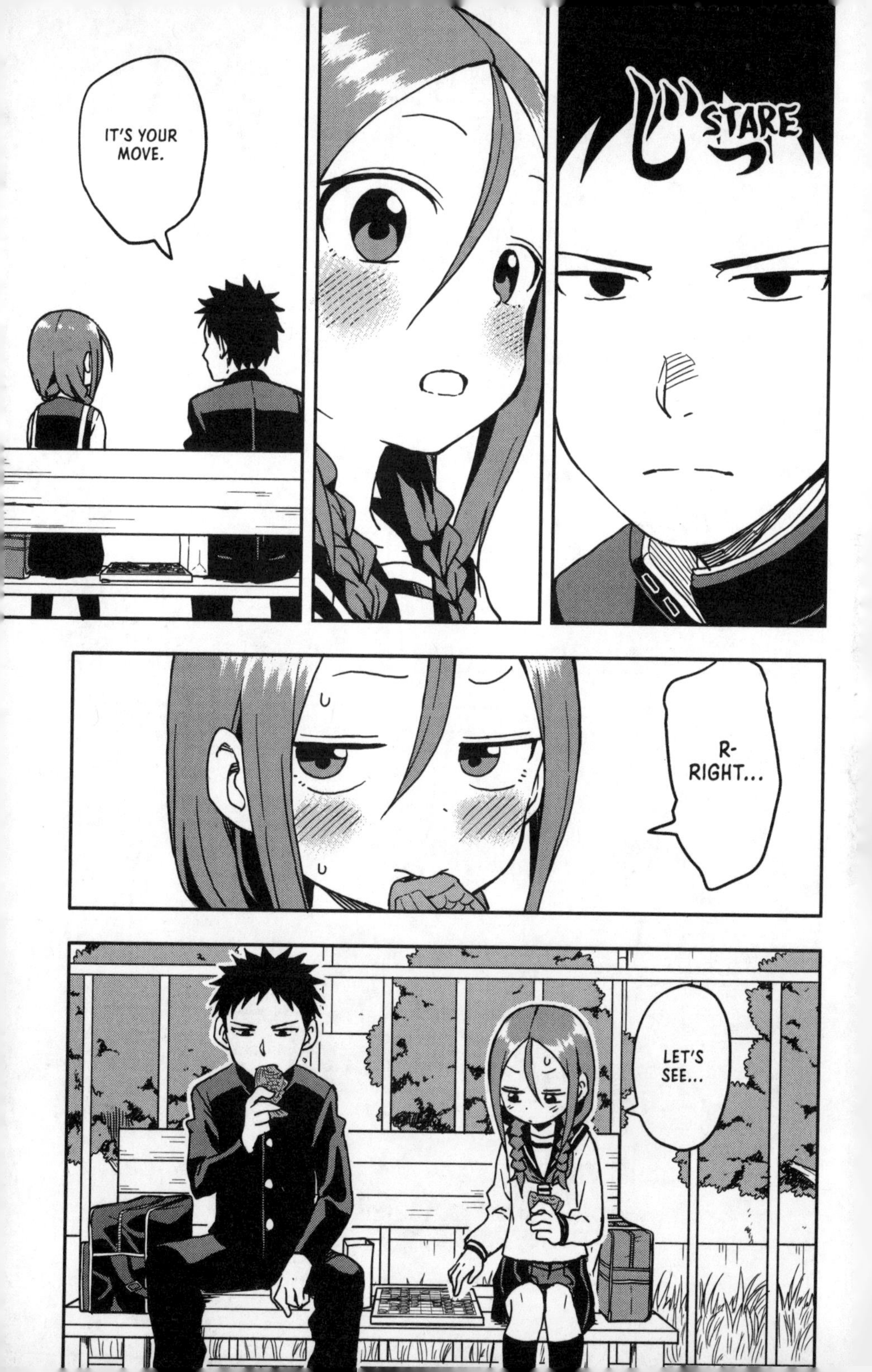
STARE
IT'S YOUR MOVE.
R-RIGHT...
LET'S SEE...

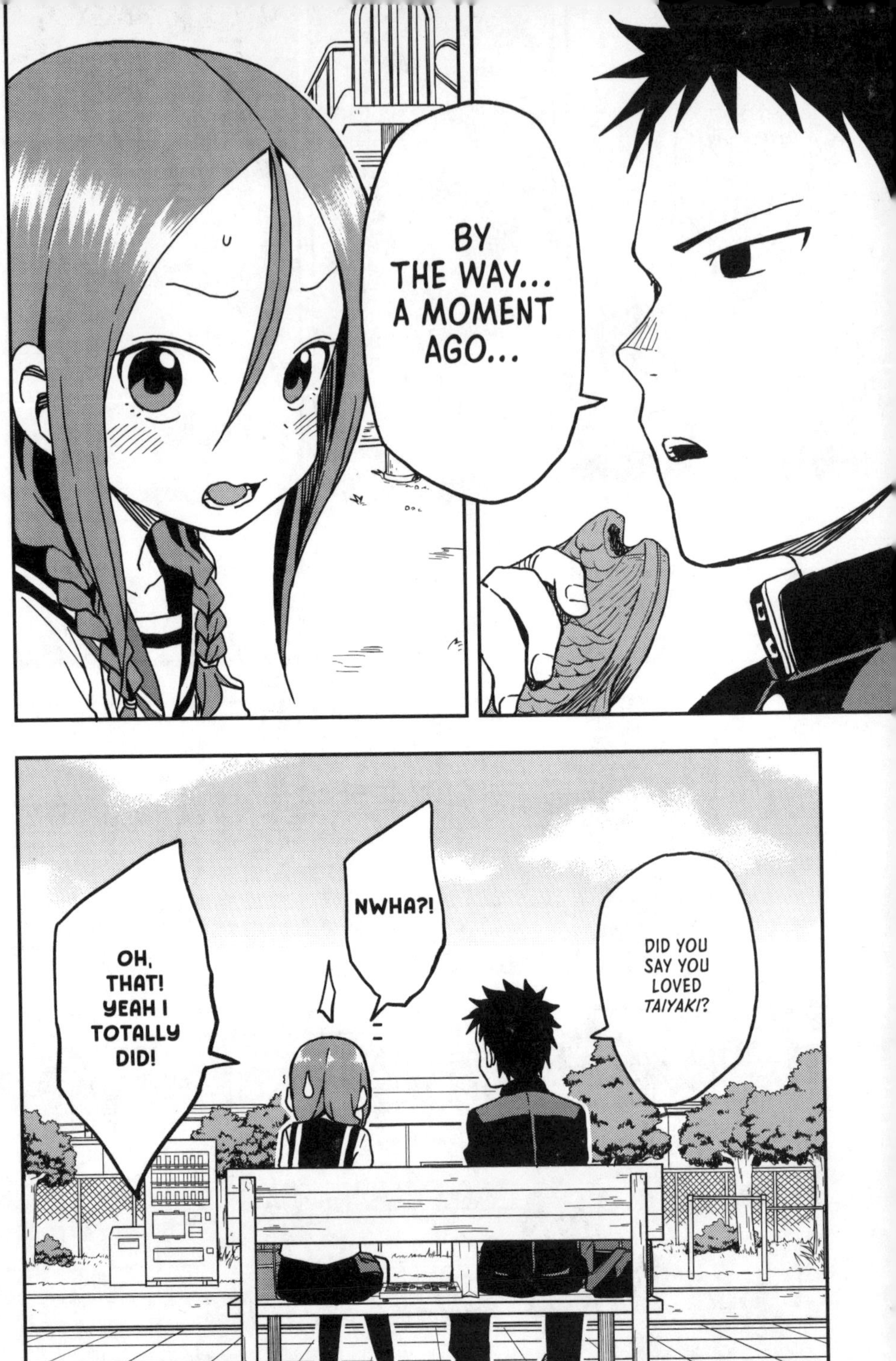
BY THE WAY... A MOMENT AGO...
DID YOU SAY YOU LOVED *TAIYAKI*?
NWHA?!
OH, THAT! YEAH I TOTALLY DID!

GAME 12 RECORD

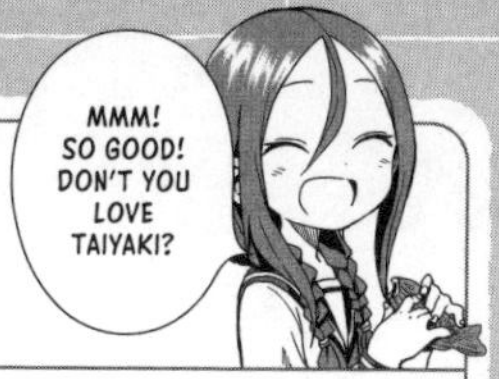
MMM! SO GOOD! DON'T YOU LOVE TAIYAKI?

▲ BLACK (SENTE): AYUMU TANAKA △ WHITE (GOTE): URUSHI YAOTOME

(WHITE WINS ON MOVE 35, △ N-3G)

◁URUSHI: P

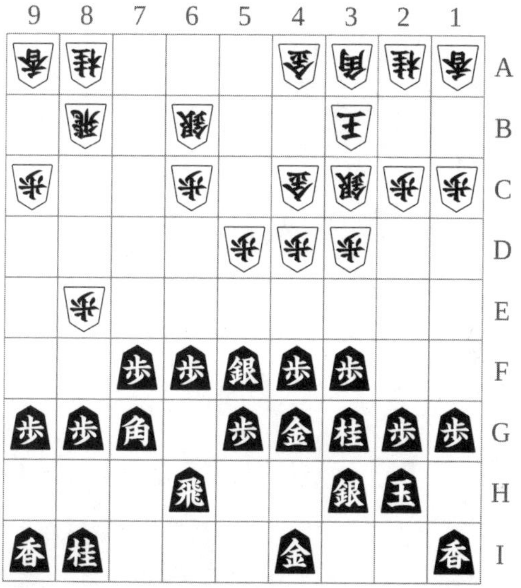

▲AAYUMU:

▲ P-7F	△ P-3D
▲ P-6F	△ P-8D
▲ R-6H	△ P-8E
▲ B-7G	△ S-6B
▲ S-7H	△ K-4B
▲ K-4H	△ K-3B
▲ K-3H	△ P-5d
▲ S-6G	△ G6A-5B
▲ K-2H	△ S-4B
▲ S-3H	△ S-3C
▲ G6I-5H	△ P-4D
▲ P-4F	△ G-4C
▲ G-4G	△ B-3A
▲ S-5F	△ P-7D
▲ P-3F	△ P-7E
▲ P×7E	△ B×7E
▲ P×7F	△ B-3A
▲ N-3G	

FALL

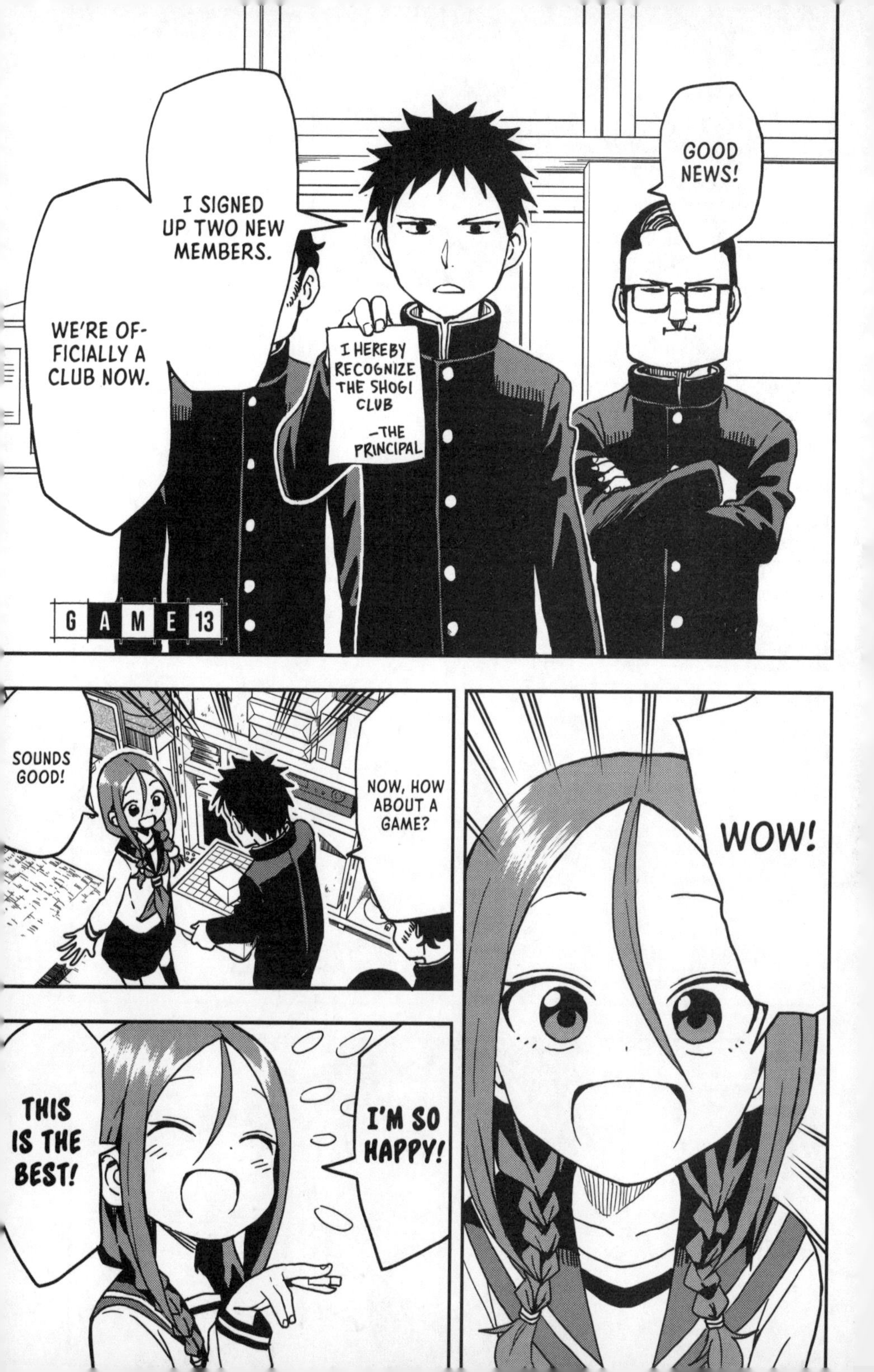
GOOD NEWS!
I SIGNED UP TWO NEW MEMBERS.
WE'RE OF-FICIALLY A CLUB NOW.
I HEREBY RECOGNIZE THE SHOGI CLUB —THE PRINCIPAL
GAME 13
WOW!
NOW, HOW ABOUT A GAME?
SOUNDS GOOD!
I'M SO HAPPY!
THIS IS THE BEST!

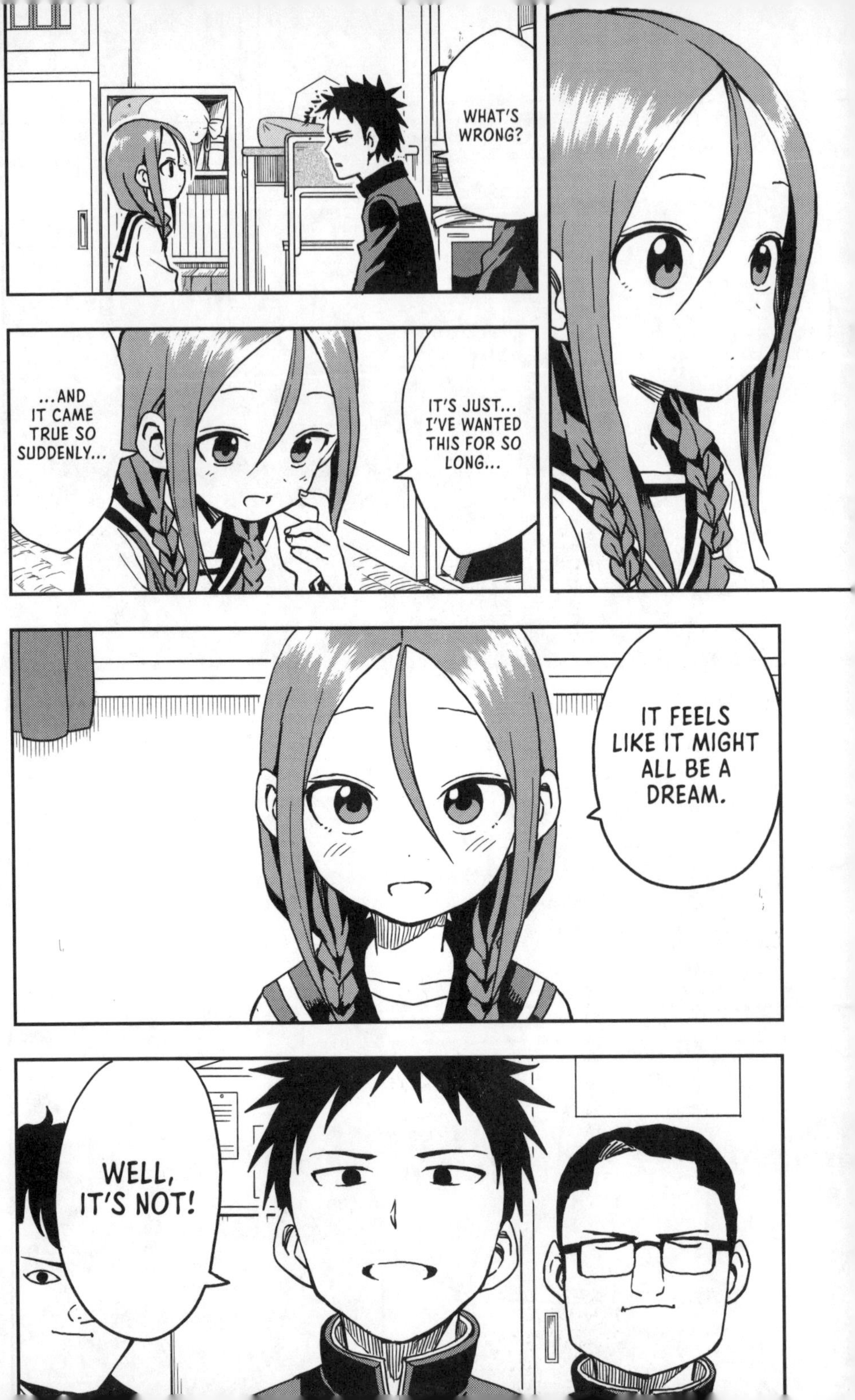
WHAT'S WRONG?
IT'S JUST... I'VE WANTED THIS FOR SO LONG...
...AND IT CAME TRUE SO SUDDENLY...
IT FEELS LIKE IT MIGHT ALL BE A DREAM.
WELL, IT'S NOT!

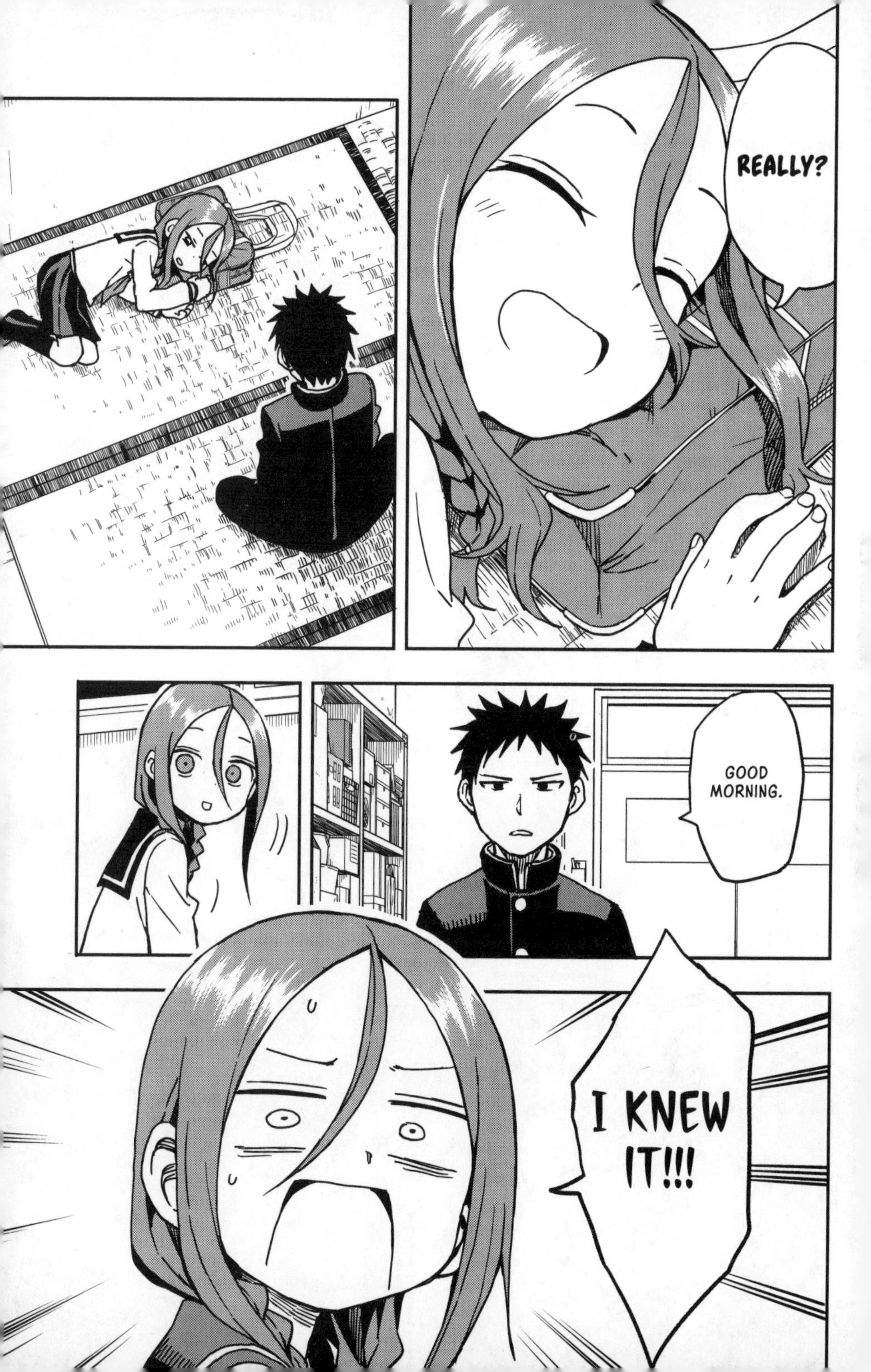
REALLY?
GOOD MORNING.
I KNEW IT!!!

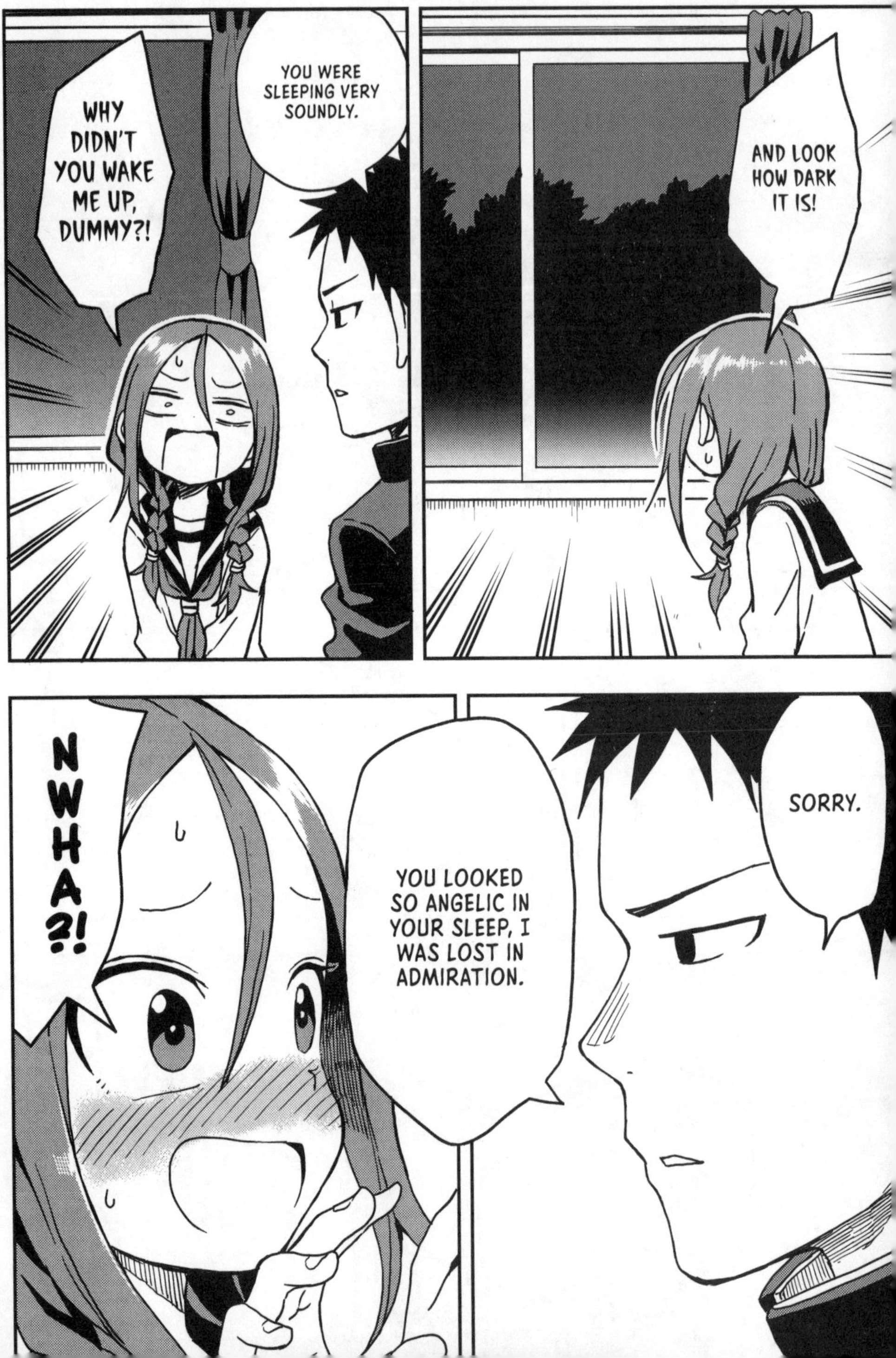
AND LOOK HOW DARK IT IS!
WHY DIDN'T YOU WAKE ME UP, DUMMY?!
YOU WERE SLEEPING VERY SOUNDLY.
SORRY.
YOU LOOKED SO ANGELIC IN YOUR SLEEP, I WAS LOST IN ADMIRATION.
NWHA?!

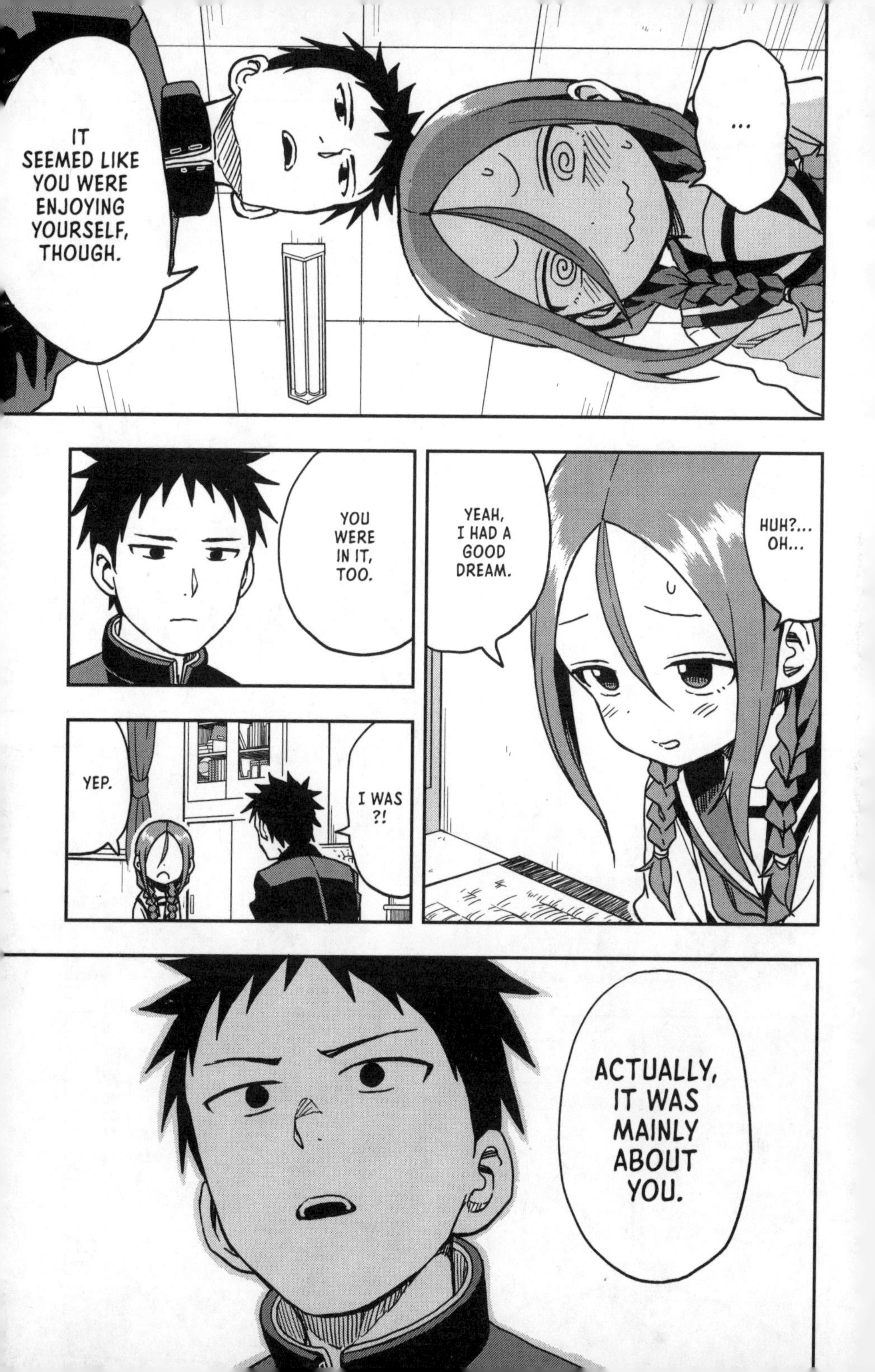
...
IT SEEMED LIKE YOU WERE ENJOYING YOURSELF, THOUGH.
HUH?... OH...
YEAH, I HAD A GOOD DREAM.
YOU WERE IN IT, TOO.
I WAS ?!
YEP.
ACTUALLY, IT WAS MAINLY ABOUT YOU.

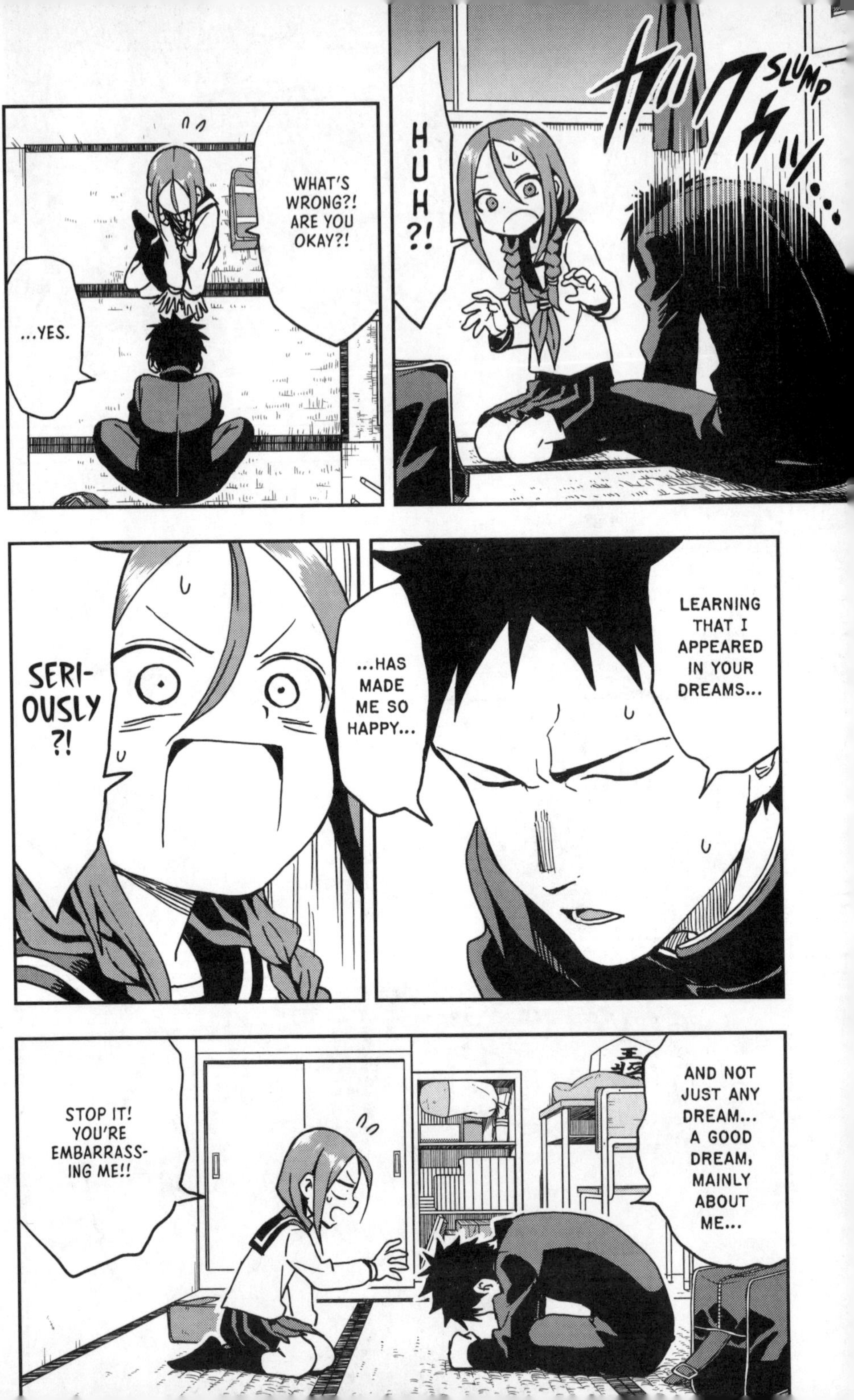
SLUMP
HUH?!
WHAT'S WRONG?! ARE YOU OKAY?!
...YES.
LEARNING THAT I APPEARED IN YOUR DREAMS...
...HAS MADE ME SO HAPPY...
SERI-OUSLY?!
AND NOT JUST ANY DREAM... A GOOD DREAM, MAINLY ABOUT ME...
STOP IT! YOU'RE EMBARRASS-ING ME!!

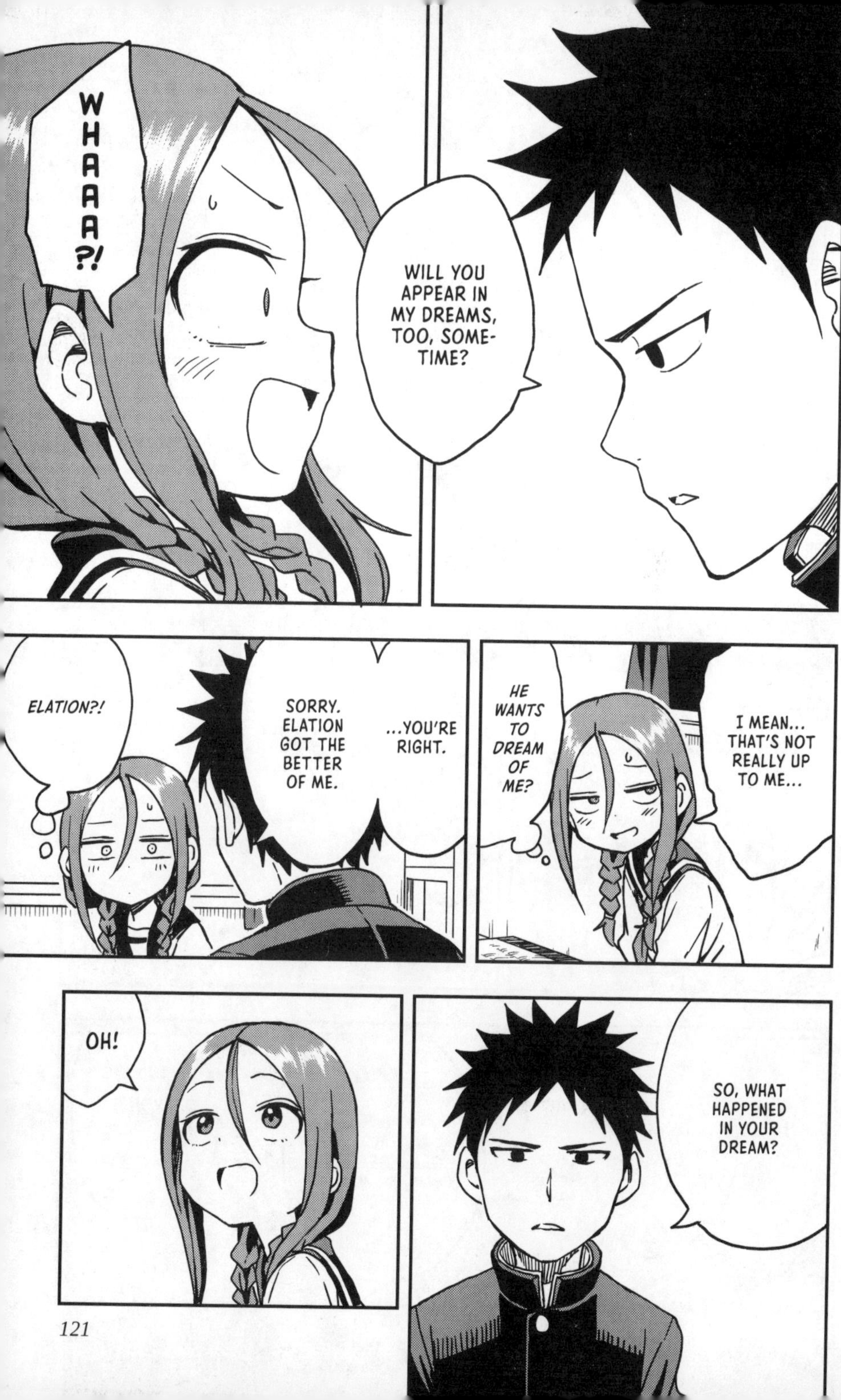
WILL YOU APPEAR IN MY DREAMS, TOO, SOME-TIME?
WHAAAA?!
I MEAN... THAT'S NOT REALLY UP TO ME...
HE WANTS TO DREAM OF ME?
...YOU'RE RIGHT.
SORRY. ELATION GOT THE BETTER OF ME.
ELATION?!
SO, WHAT HAPPENED IN YOUR DREAM?
OH!

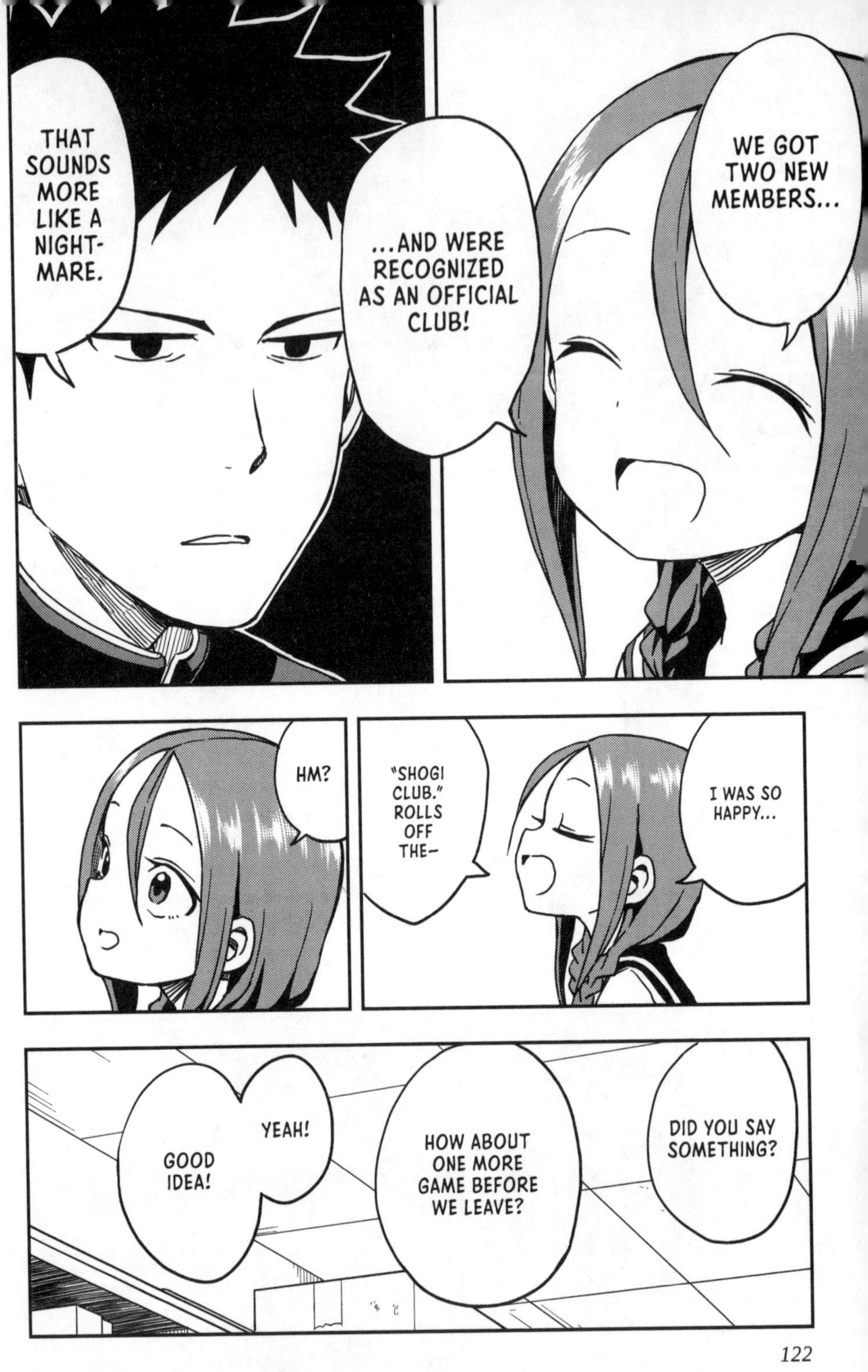
WE GOT TWO NEW MEMBERS...
...AND WERE RECOGNIZED AS AN OFFICIAL CLUB!
THAT SOUNDS MORE LIKE A NIGHT-MARE.
I WAS SO HAPPY...
"SHOGI CLUB." ROLLS OFF THE–
HM?
DID YOU SAY SOMETHING?
HOW ABOUT ONE MORE GAME BEFORE WE LEAVE?
YEAH!
GOOD IDEA!

WHEN WILL
AYUMU
MAKE HIS
MOVE?

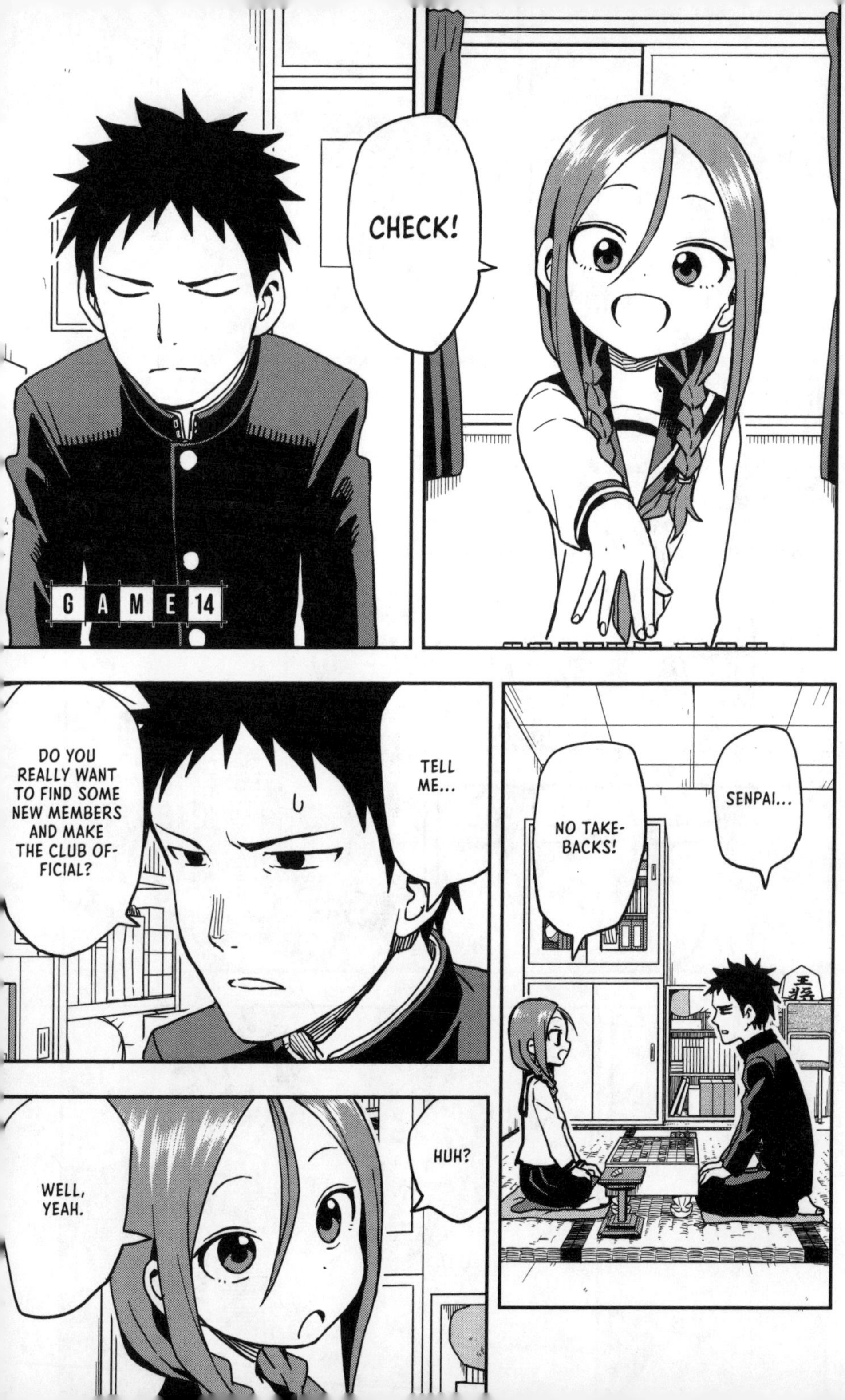
CHECK!
GAME 14
SENPAI...
NO TAKE-BACKS!
TELL ME...
DO YOU REALLY WANT TO FIND SOME NEW MEMBERS AND MAKE THE CLUB OFFICIAL?
HUH?
WELL, YEAH.

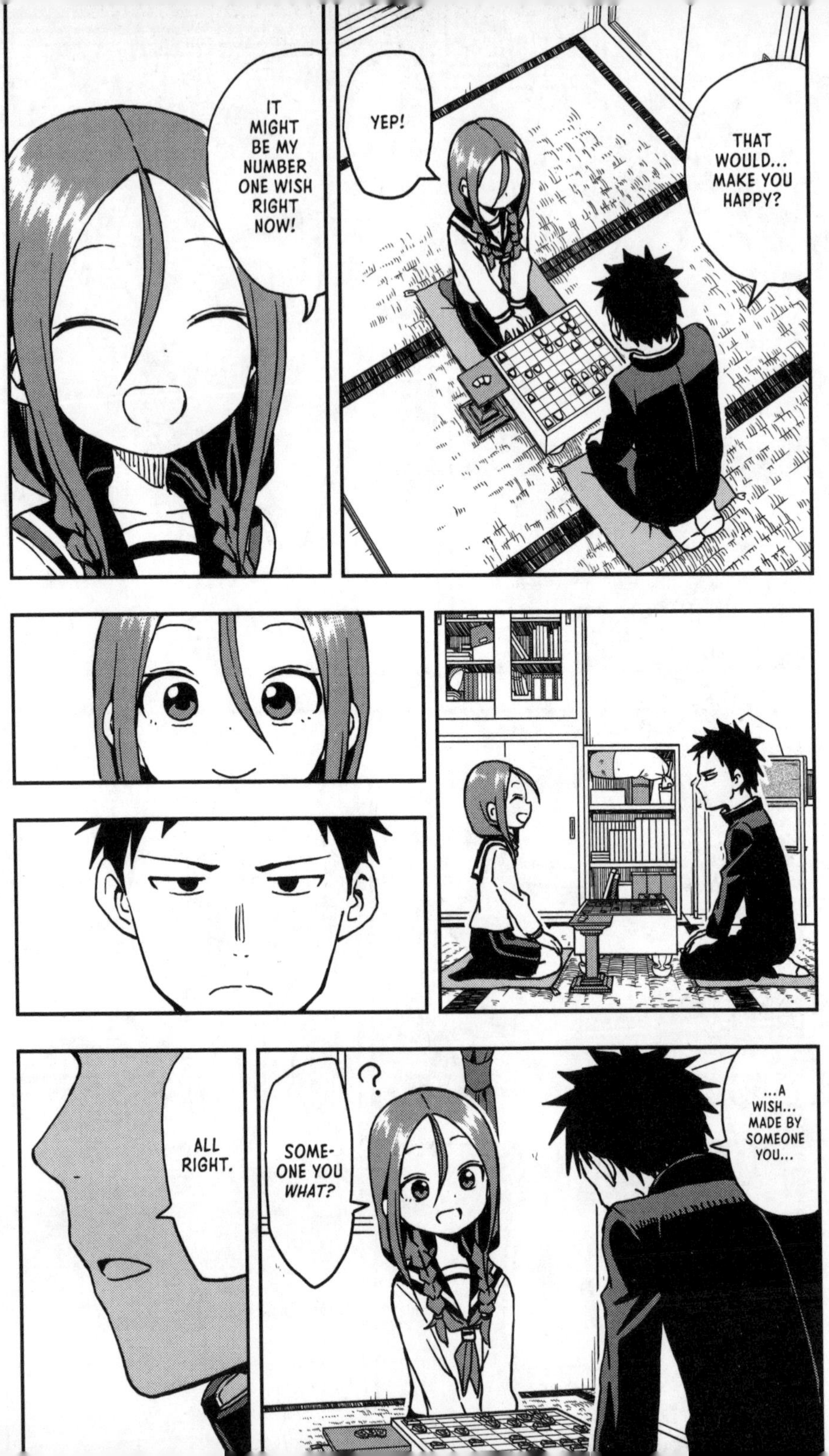
THAT WOULD... MAKE YOU HAPPY?
YEP!
IT MIGHT BE MY NUMBER ONE WISH RIGHT NOW!
...A WISH... MADE BY SOMEONE YOU...
?
SOME-ONE YOU *WHAT?*
ALL RIGHT.

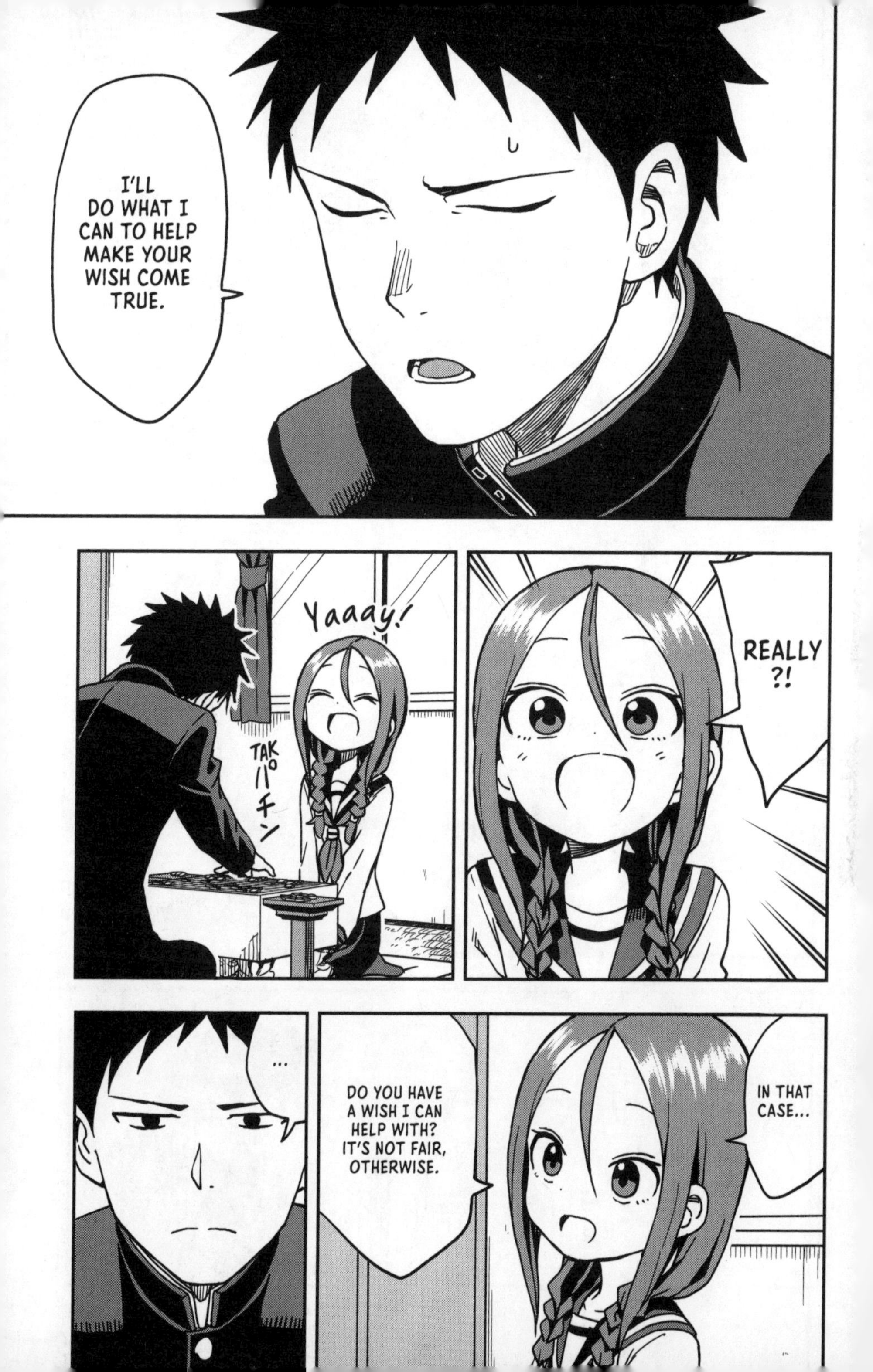
I'LL DO WHAT I CAN TO HELP MAKE YOUR WISH COME TRUE.
REALLY ?!
Yaaay!
TAK
パチン
IN THAT CASE...
DO YOU HAVE A WISH I CAN HELP WITH? IT'S NOT FAIR, OTHERWISE.
...

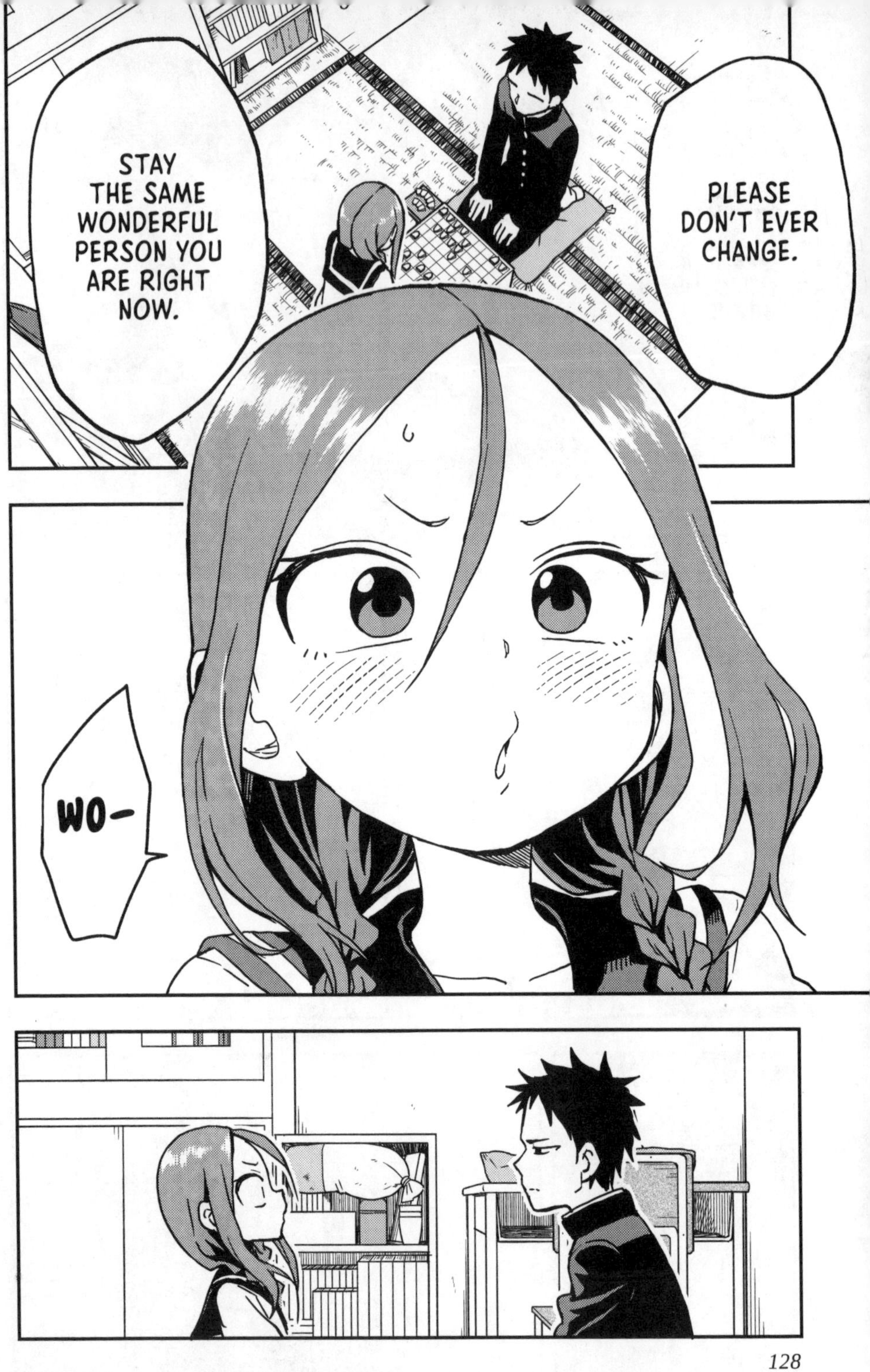
PLEASE DON'T EVER CHANGE.
STAY THE SAME WONDERFUL PERSON YOU ARE RIGHT NOW.
WO-

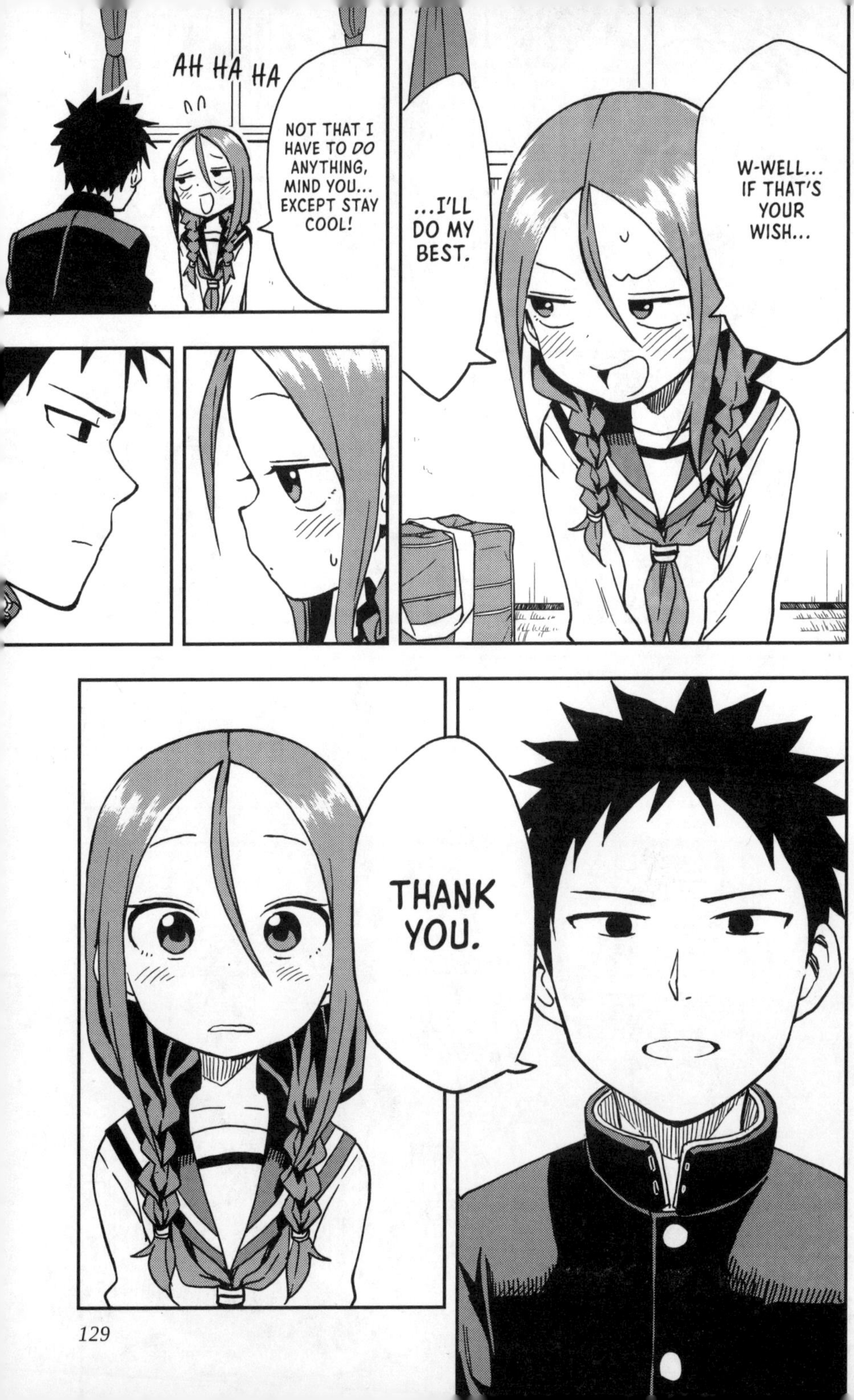
W-WELL... IF THAT'S YOUR WISH...
...I'LL DO MY BEST.
AH HA HA
NOT THAT I HAVE TO *DO* ANYTHING, MIND YOU... EXCEPT STAY COOL!
THANK YOU.

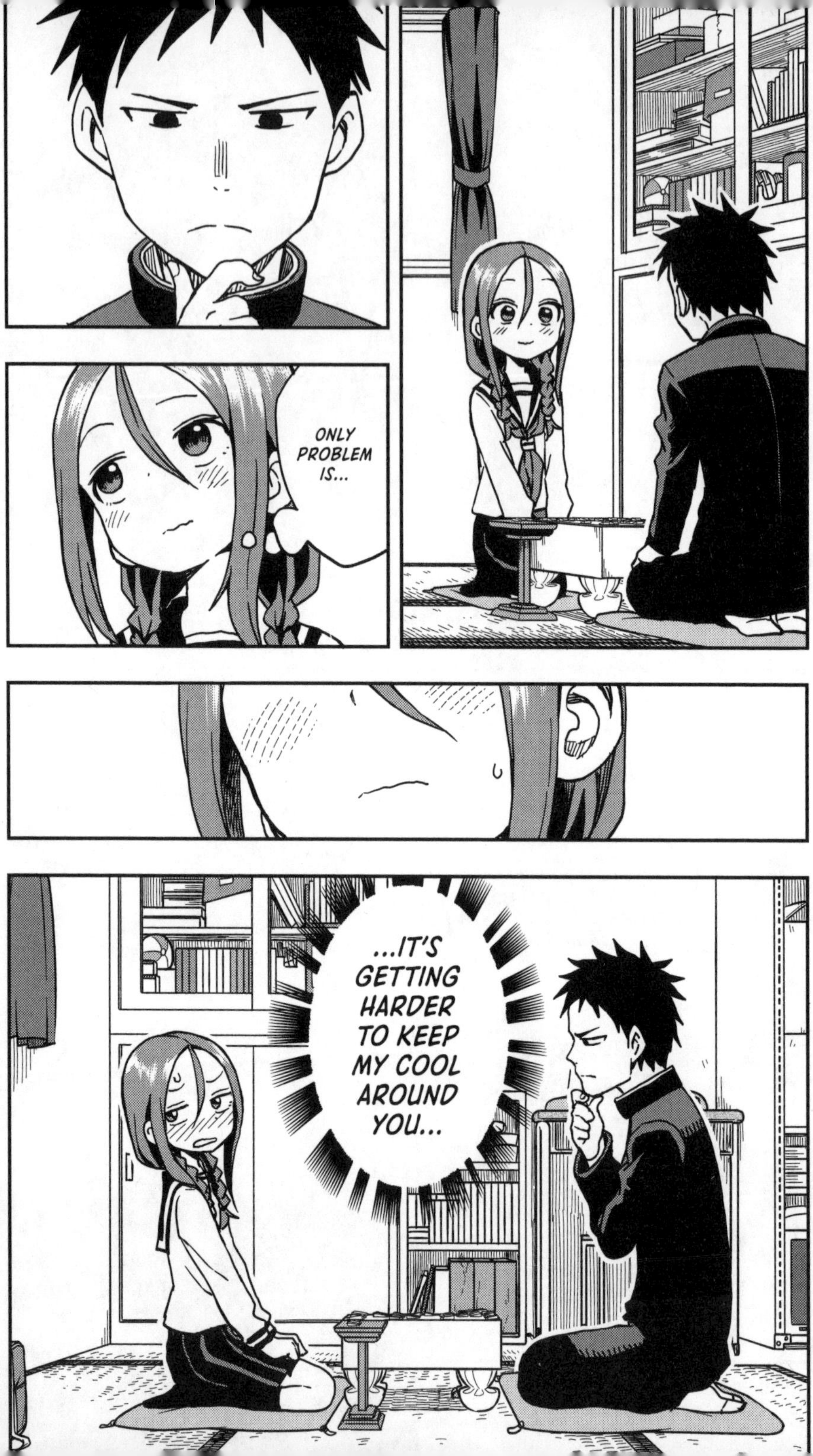
ONLY PROBLEM IS...
...IT'S GETTING HARDER TO KEEP MY COOL AROUND YOU...

GAME 14 RECORD

▲ BLACK (SENTE): AYUMU TANAKA △ WHITE (GOTE): URUSHI YAOTOME

(WHITE WINS ON MOVE 82, △ G×2H)

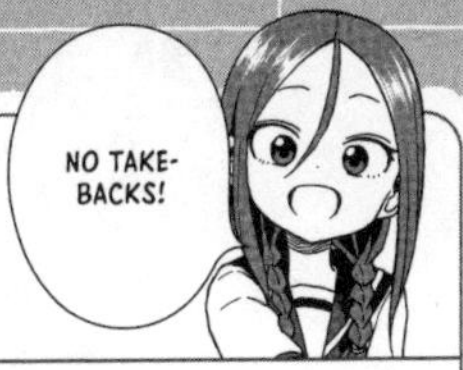
NO TAKE-BACKS!

◁URUSHI: N, P×2

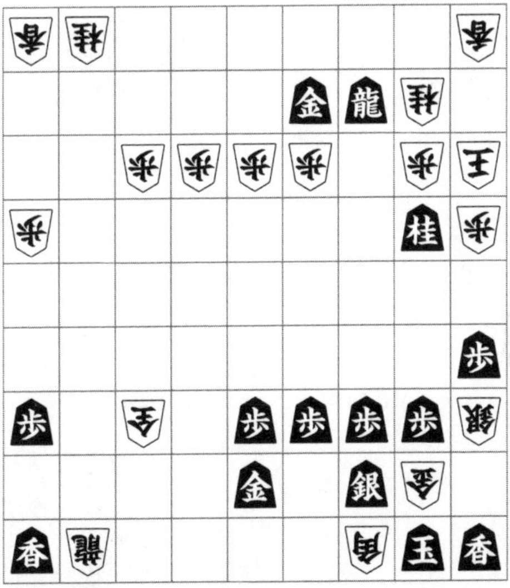

▲AYUMU: B, G, S, P×3

▲ P-7F	△ P-3D
▲ P-6F	△ P-8D
▲ R-6H	△ P-8E
▲ B-7G	△ S-7B
▲ K-4H	△ K-4B
▲ K-3H	△ K-3B
▲ K-2H	△ G6A-5B
▲ S-3H	△ P-1D
▲ P-1F	△ S-8C
▲ S-7H	△ S-8D
▲ G4I-5H	△ P-9D
▲ S-6G	△ S-9E
▲ P-6E	△ P-8F
▲ B×2B+	△ S×2B
▲ P×8F	△ S×8F
▲ S-5F	△ S-8G=
▲ P-6D	△ P×6D
▲ R×6D	△ P×6C
▲ R×3D	△ S-3C
▲ R-3F	△ S×7F=
▲ B×5E	△ R×8I+
▲ B×3C+	△ N×3C
▲ S×3D	△ G5B-4B
▲ S×3C+	△ G×3C
▲ N×2E	△ S×4B
▲ S-4E	△ S-7G+
▲ N×3C+	△ S×3C
▲ N-1G	△ B×7F
▲ N-2E	△ N×2A
▲ N×3C+	△ N×3C
▲ S-3D	△ G-4B
▲ S×2A	△ K×2A
▲ S×3C+	△ S×3A
▲ +S×4B	△ S×4B
▲ G×3B	△ K-1B
▲ G×4B	△ B×5H+
▲ R-3B+	△ N×2B
▲ N×2D	△ K-1C
▲ G×5H	△ B×3I
▲ K-1H	△ S×1G
▲ K-2I	△ G×2H

WHEN WILL AYUMU MAKE HIS MOVE?

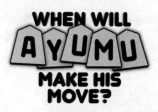

BONUS GAME

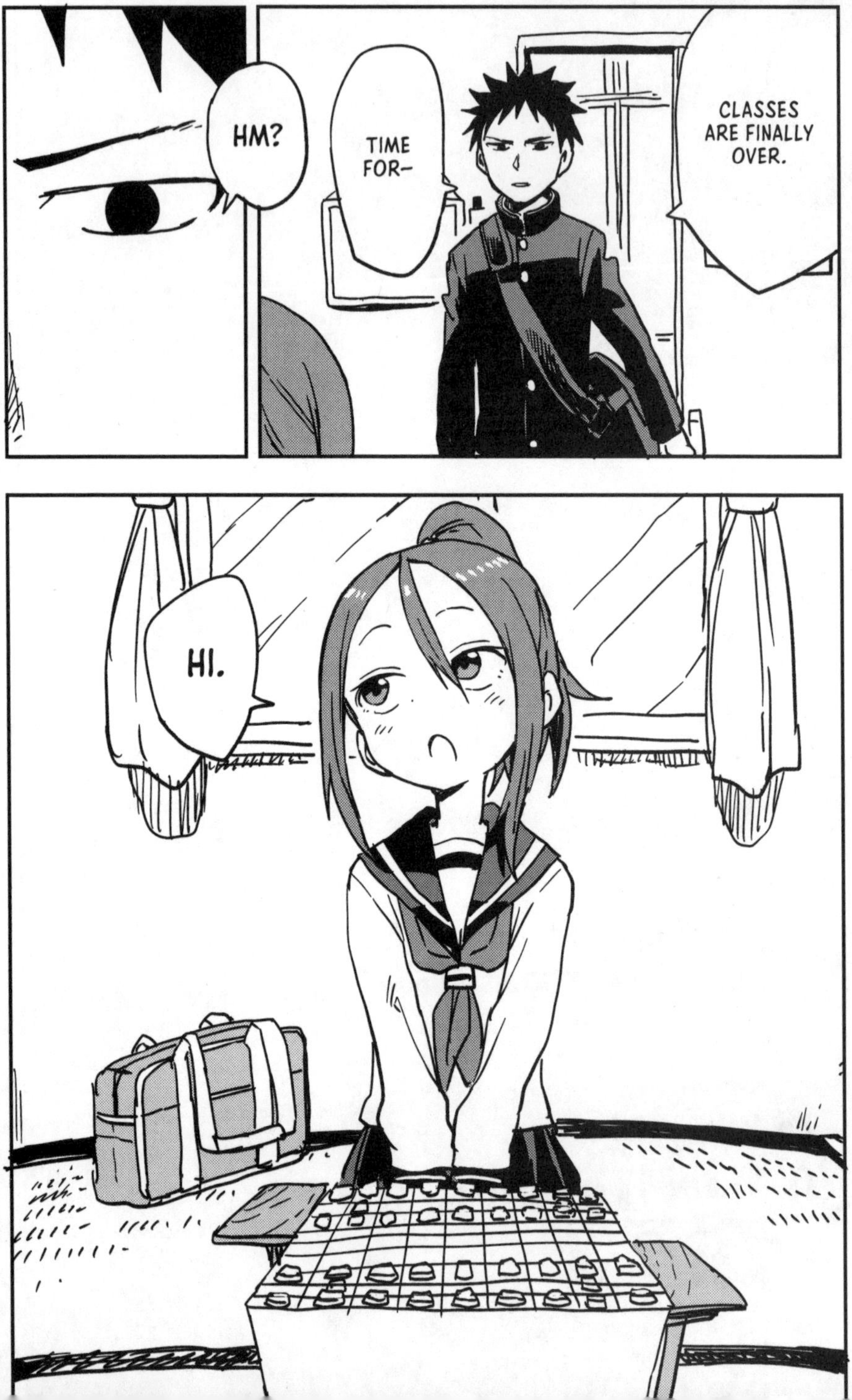
CLASSES ARE FINALLY OVER.
TIME FOR–
HM?
HI.

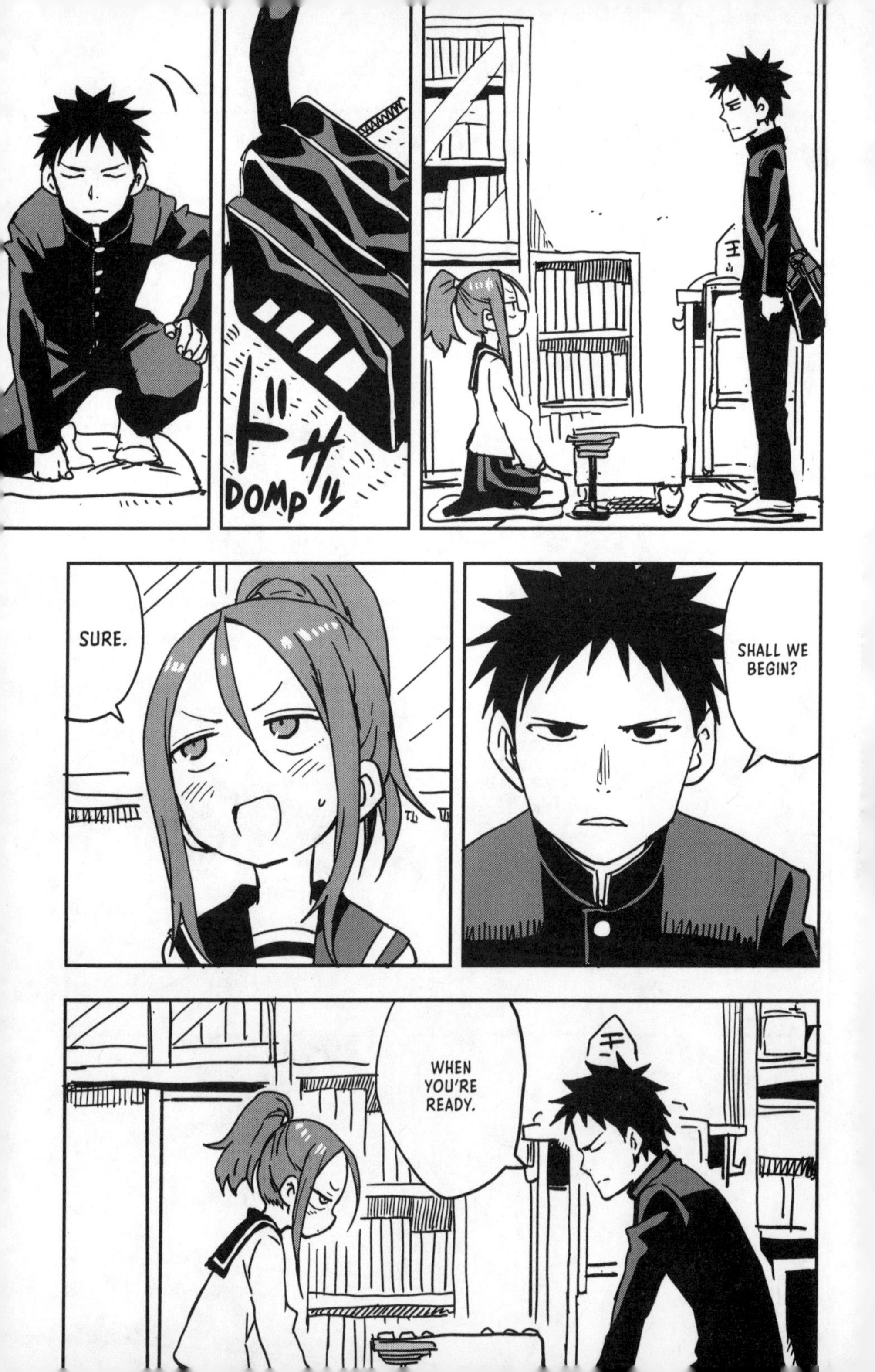
ドサッ
DOMP
SHALL WE BEGIN?
SURE.
WHEN YOU'RE READY.

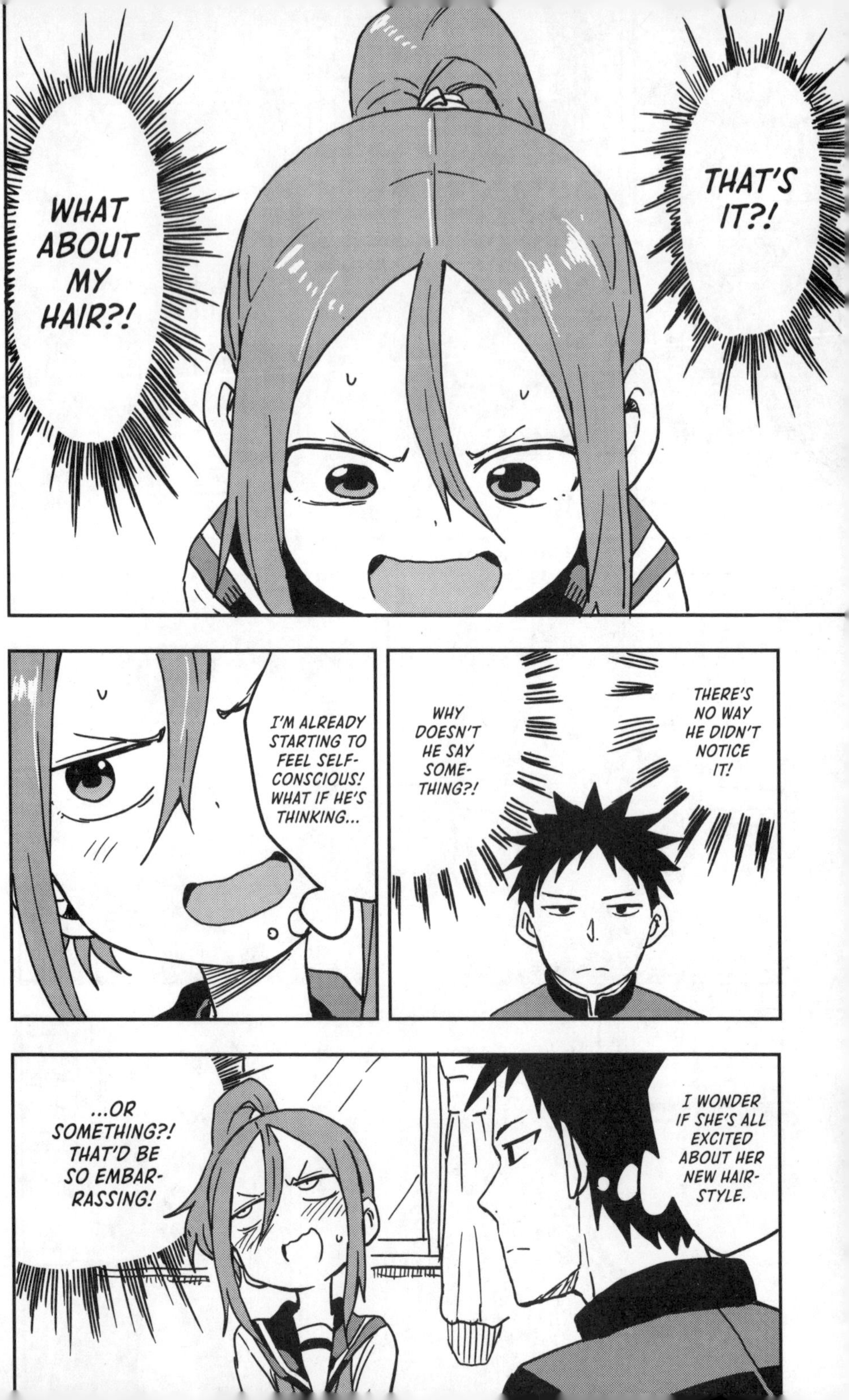
THAT'S IT?!
WHAT ABOUT MY HAIR?!
THERE'S NO WAY HE DIDN'T NOTICE IT!
WHY DOESN'T HE SAY SOME-THING?!
I'M ALREADY STARTING TO FEEL SELF-CONSCIOUS! WHAT IF HE'S THINKING...
I WONDER IF SHE'S ALL EXCITED ABOUT HER NEW HAIR-STYLE.
...OR SOMETHING?! THAT'D BE SO EMBAR-RASSING!

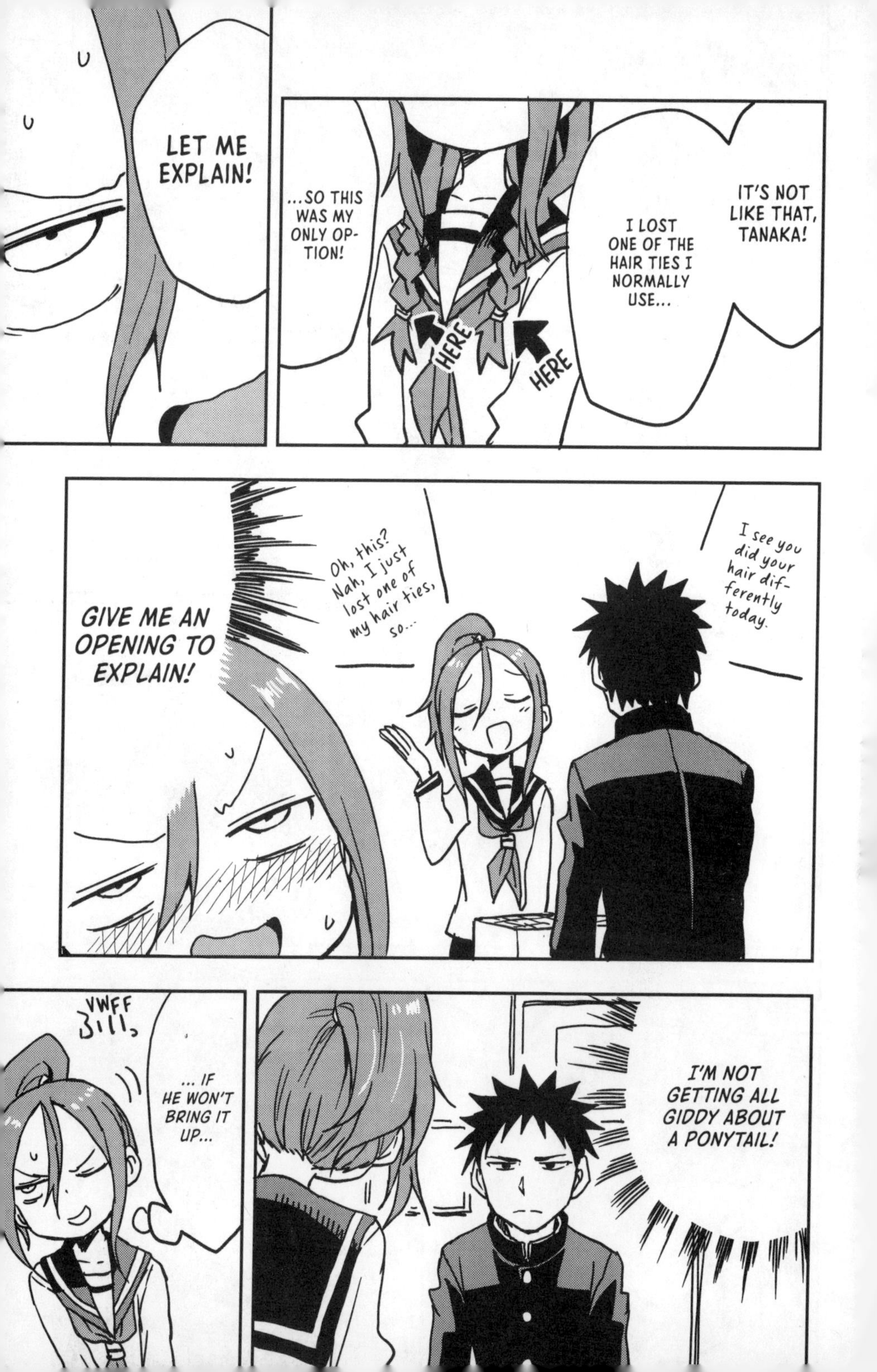
IT'S NOT LIKE THAT, TANAKA!
I LOST ONE OF THE HAIR TIES I NORMALLY USE...
HERE
HERE
...SO THIS WAS MY ONLY OPTION!
LET ME EXPLAIN!
I see you did your hair differently today.
Oh, this? Nah, I just lost one of my hair ties, so...
GIVE ME AN OPENING TO EXPLAIN!
I'M NOT GETTING ALL GIDDY ABOUT A PONYTAIL!
VWFF
... IF HE WON'T BRING IT UP...

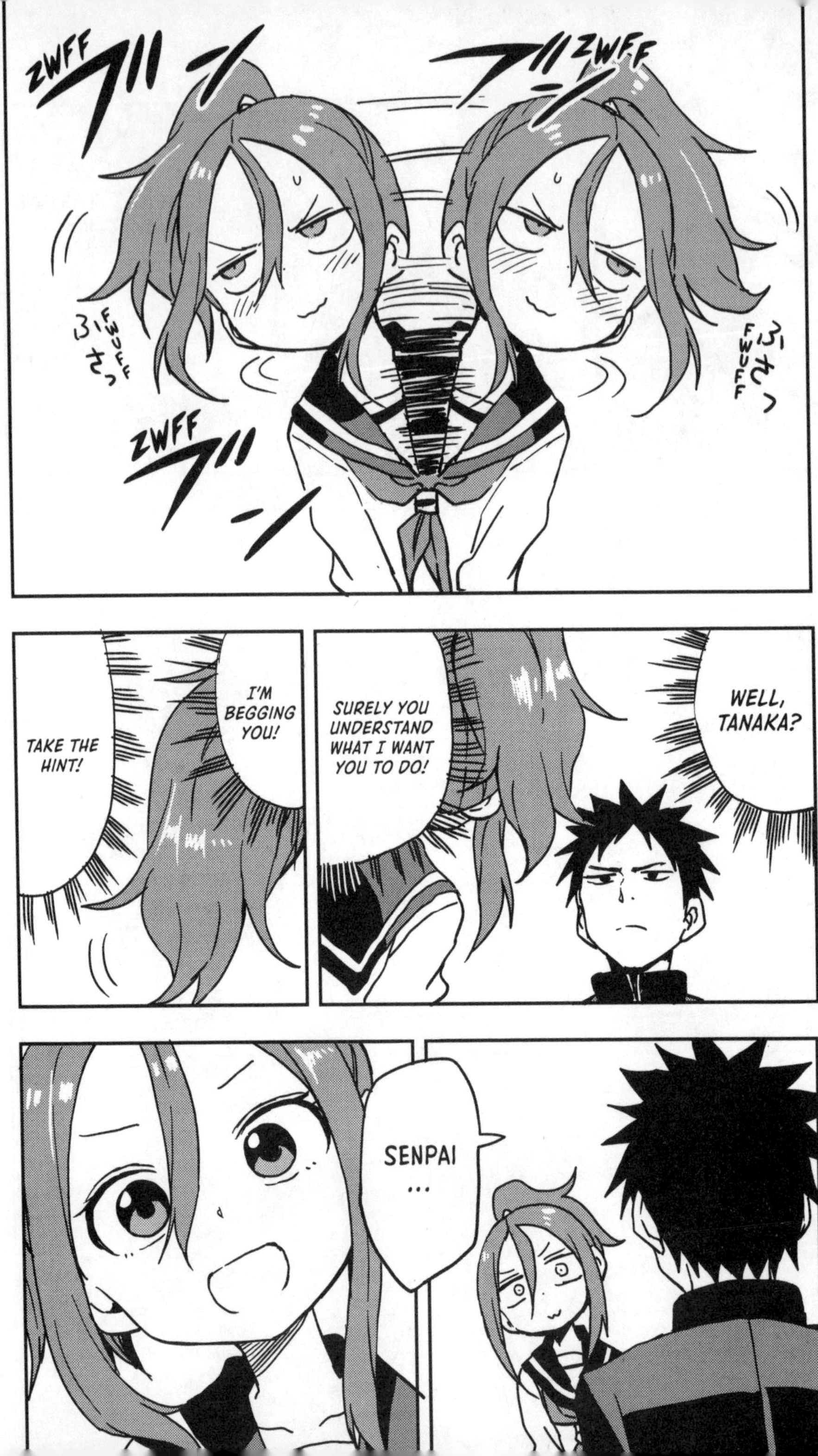
ブッ ZWFF
ブッ ZWFF
ふさっ FWUFF
ふさっ FWUFF
ブッ ZWFF
WELL, TANAKA?
SURELY YOU UNDERSTAND WHAT I WANT YOU TO DO!
I'M BEGGING YOU!
TAKE THE HINT!
SENPAI ...

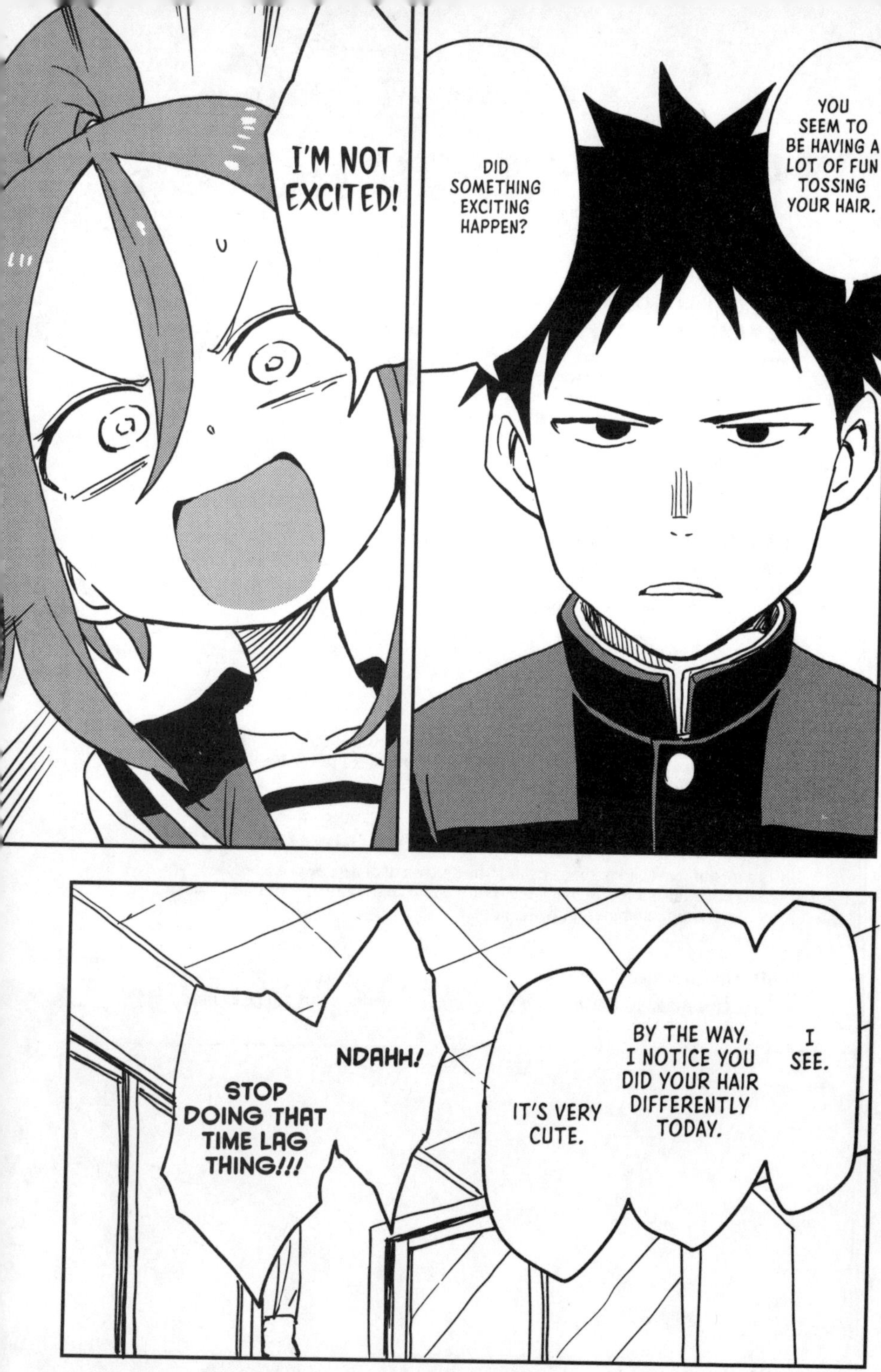
YOU SEEM TO BE HAVING A LOT OF FUN TOSSING YOUR HAIR.
DID SOMETHING EXCITING HAPPEN?
I'M NOT EXCITED!
I SEE.
BY THE WAY, I NOTICE YOU DID YOUR HAIR DIFFERENTLY TODAY.
IT'S VERY CUTE.
NDAHH!
STOP DOING THAT TIME LAG THING!!!

THE END

TRANSLATION NOTES

TANAKA THE IMMOVABLE! UNSHAKEABLE AS THE MOUNTAIN!, PAGE 42

"Tanaka the Immovable" is a reference to the "Immovable Wisdom King" (*Fudo myo-o*), a fearsome but righteous protector in East Asian Buddhism. "Unshakeable as the Mountain" is a reference to *furin kazan* ("Wind, Forest, Fire, Mountain"), a phrase used on the war banner of sixteenth-century daimyo Takeda Shingen. The phrase is an abbreviated version of a passage from Sun Tzu's *The Art of War*: "Swift as the wind, silent as the forest, fierce as the fire, unshakeable as the mountain."

THE KING INSTEAD OF THE JEWEL, PAGE 44

Many shogi sets only have one actual "King" piece. The other player—usually the lower-ranked one—uses a piece with the kanji for "Jewel" instead. The two kanji look the same except for a single dot:

KING

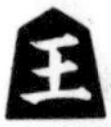
王

JEWEL

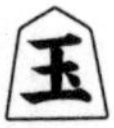
玉

This also makes it easier to tell the two apart in board diagrams that use the kanji to represent pieces, since without the dot it is hard to tell whether an 王 is upside-down or not!

FALL IS IN THE AIR. DOESN'T IT MAKE YOU HUNGRY?, PAGE 105

In Japan, autumn is sometimes called "the season of hearty appetites" *(shokuyoku no aki)* because so many delicious foods come into season as the exhausting, appetite-draining summer heat subsides.

TAIYAKI, PAGE 106

A fried cake shaped like a sea bream *(tai)* with sweet bean paste, custard, or some other filling inside.

WHEN WILL AYUMU MAKE HIS MOVE?

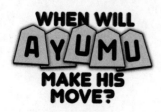

When Will Ayumu Make His Move? 1 is a work of fiction. Names, characters, places, and incidents are the products of the author's imagination or are used fictitiously. Any resemblance to actual events, locales, or persons, living or dead, is entirely coincidental.

A Kodansha Trade Paperback Original

Published in the United States by
Kodansha USA Publishing, LLC, New York.

Publication rights for this English edition arranged through
Kodansha Ltd., Tokyo.

First published in Japan in 2019 by Kodansha Ltd., Tokyo
as *Sore demo Ayumu ha yosetekuru*, volume 1.

ISBN 978-1-64651-349-9

Printed in the United States of America.

1st Printing

Translation: Max Greenway
Lettering: Nicole Roderick
Editing: Nathaniel Gallant
Kodansha USA Publishing edition cover design by Phil Balsman

Publisher: Kiichiro Sugawara

Director of Publishing Services: Ben Applegate
Associate Director of Operations: Stephen Pakula
Publishing Services Managing Editors: Alanna Ruse, Madison Salters
Production Managers: Emi Lotto, Angela Zurlo

KODANSHA.US

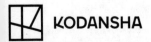

KODANSHA